GW00600589

I Seek a Kind Person

My Father, Seven Children and the Adverts that
Helped Them Escape the Holocaust

JULIAN BORGER

JOHN MURRAY

First published in Great Britain in 2024 by John Murray (Publishers)

This paperback edition published 2024

3

Copyright © Julian Borger 2024

The right Julian Borger to be identified as the
Author of the Work has been asserted by him in accordance
with the Copyright, Designs and Patents Act 1988.

A CIP catalogue record for this title is available from the British Library

Paperback ISBN 978 1 399 80331 1
ebook ISBN 978 1 399 80332 8

Typeset in Bembo MT Pro by Palimpsest Book Production Ltd,
Falkirk, Stirlingshire

Printed and bound in Great Britain by Clays Ltd, Elcograf S.p.A.

John Murray policy is to use papers that are natural, renewable and
recyclable products and made from wood grown in sustainable forests.
The logging and manufacturing processes are expected to conform
to the environmental regulations of the country of origin.

Carmelite House
50 Victoria Embankment
London EC4Y 0DZ

www.johnmurraypress.co.uk

John Murray Press, part of Hodder & Stoughton Limited
An Hachette UK company

The authorised representative in the EEA is Hachette Ireland, 8 Castlecourt
Centre, Dublin 15, D15 XTP3, Ireland (email: info@hbgi.ie)

For our mum, Wyn, who held us together
when everything fell apart.

Contents

Dramatis Personae ix

Introduction 1

1. The Untold Stories of Leo, Erna and
   Bobby Borger 15
2. George and the Unbearable Longing for Vienna 34
3. Gertrude and Eichmann's Pianos 49
4. Means of Escape: Alice and the Westbahnhof 67
5. Bobby and George in Exile 82
6. Siegfried, Paula and Coming to Britain 98
7. Salvation and Captivity: Internment in Britain 116
8. Shanghai 130
9. Fred and the Trail to Auschwitz 151
10. Defiance and Aunt Malci 184
11. George and the Return to Vienna 211
12. Lisbeth and the Will to Live 235

Epilogue 265

Acknowledgements 271
Picture Credits 275
Notes 277
About the author 286

Dramatis Personae

The Borgers

Robert Borger, 'Bobby', the author's father, advertised on 3 August 1938 as 'an intelligent Boy, aged 11, Viennese of good family'.

Leo Borger, Robert's father, owned a shop in Vienna selling radios and musical instruments. A committed Social Democrat, he had fought for the empire in the First World War and hoped that his service would protect his family.

Erna Borger, 'Omi', née Barbak, Robert's mother, who kept the accounts at the shop. Her father's family had come to Vienna from Galicia, now western Ukraine.

Malvine Schickler, 'Malci', née Borger, Robert's aunt, a devoted Communist, who left the Jewish faith and the family business to marry a fellow party member from Galicia and take over the care of his two young children.

Mordechaj Schickler, 'Motti', Malci's stepson, Robert's cousin. He was an infant when his mother was committed to a psychiatric hospital, and his father remarried. Like his parents he became a loyal Communist. In his teens he took his mother's family name, Sorger.

Valerie Borger, 'Vally', née Kohn, Leo's second wife and Robert's stepmother, also a refugee from Vienna, whose mother and first husband had been killed in the Holocaust.

The Children in the Adverts

George Mandler, born Georg, the son of a successful leather merchant in Vienna. Living a little more than a kilometre from Robert Borger, he was advertised on 28 July 1938 as a fourteen-year-old boy 'out of grammar school . . . with knowledge of English'.

Gertrude Batscha, 'Gerti', was fourteen when she was advertised on 29 July 1938 as the only daughter of a Jewish merchant: 'well-mannered, able to help in any household work'. In later life in Israel, she became Yehudith Segal.

Alice Hess, the fourteen-year-old daughter of Josefine and Béla Hess, who ran a printing business in Vienna. The advert for Alice appeared directly below Robert Borger's, and described her as 'well educated, Jewess: very fond of children: good sewing, household help.' Her married name was Schoen.

Siegfried and Paula Neumann's father had already been killed in Dachau when sixteen-year-old Siegfried placed an ad for himself on 10 October 1938, declaring he would be 'so glad to become an Apprentice or Au Pair'. Their story was told by his sister, Paula, in a handwritten memoir.

Gertrude Langer was fourteen when her advert appeared under those of Robert Borger and Alice Hess on 3 August 1938, asking: 'Will a Philanthropist take a much-gifted Girl

. . . as foster-child?' Her father Karl was a Viennese lawyer who hid his neighbours from the Nazis but refused to hide himself.

Fred Schwarz, born Manfred, another lawyer's son who was advertised on 3 September 1938 as a 'healthy, modest Viennese boy' aged fifteen. His elder brother, Frits, was not advertised but it was the boys' close bond that ultimately determined their fate.

Lisbeth Weiss, **'Lis'**, the only child of Wilhelm and Rudolfine, who advertised the eleven-year-old girl on 27 August 1938, as a 'clever child worthy of support', promising to 'join her later' and pay for her education.

Tuition

FERVENT prayer in great distress.—Who would give a Home to a grammar school scholar aged 13: healthy, clever, very musical. F. B. W., 106/29 Wd. Hauptstrasse, Vienna 5.

I Seek a kind person who will educate my intelligent Boy, aged 11, Viennese of good family. Borger, 5/12 Hintzerstrasse, Vienna 3.

I Look for an au pair for my Girl, aged 14, well educated, Jewess: very fond of children: good sewing, household help. Hess, 126 Gudrunstrasse, Vienna 10.

TWO very modest Sisters, aged 14 and 17, Jews, half orphans, well trained, pray to be accepted as foster children in a very good house. Manheim, 77 Obere Donaustrasse, Vienna 2.

Wanted, immed., Conversation with educated French lady: pay or exchange. P 160, " M/c Guardian."

WILL a Philanthropist take a much-gifted Girl, 14 years old, daughter of an Austrian Jewish lawyer, as foster-child ? Kindly write to Dr. Karl Langer, 14 Praterstrasse, Vienna 2.

The original adverts listed in the *Manchester Guardian* seeking 'tuition' for my father and other Viennese children, 3 August 1938.

I feel as though half of me is fighting the other half by trying to forget, rather than remember, and I realise that is probably what I have been doing all my life.

Yehudith Segal (born Gertrude Batscha)

My father, Robert Borger, 1966.

Introduction

On 15 SEPTEMBER 1983, I had a dentist's appointment. My family had been going to the same man to fix our teeth since childhood and he believed, for reasons I can no longer remember, that anaesthetic should be avoided whenever possible.

Random moments from that Thursday morning have stayed with me: the walk home along our local high road, the dappled light of early autumn, feeling hopeful about life and realising I need never go back to the same dentist. And then I arrived home and opened the front door for the last time that things were just about okay.

My mum was sitting at the kitchen table, looking at me as if she was horrified I had come home. 'He doesn't know yet,' she said, and it took a moment to realise she wasn't talking to me. She was talking about me. I was the one who didn't know. In the same instant, I noticed the shadow of a policeman's uniform in the background.

The policeman was very young, and seemed at a loss over how to behave in front of a distraught woman. Coming to our house must have been one of his first jobs, my mum said, recalling the agony of the occasion years later. It seemed unfair to everyone. He was not nearly old enough for his task: to tell this woman that Robert Borger, her husband and father of her four children, had been found dead that day.

Our dad had taken his life with whisky and painkillers in a lonely room away from home. I only recently found out the mundane details. He had stolen the pills from my grandma's bedroom. Annie McCulloch, a tiny woman who loved butter-scotch sweets, ginger wine and the Queen, had lived with us almost all my life and had died just three months earlier from respiratory complications caused by her modest smoking habit and reliance on coal fires. He must have gone into her room after her body had been removed and taken her prescription tablets. They were called Distalgesic, a brand name for a com-bination drug which featured in so many suicides it was withdrawn from the UK market twenty years after our dad made such effective use of it.

He had been missing for about a week before his body was found. Our mum, Wyn, had told him she could no longer put up with his behaviour: his moodiness, starting each day with a groan, and the inescapable fact that he had maintained a relationship with another woman despite repeated promises to stop. Mum had said she had had enough. He asked if that was her final word. She said it was and he walked out of the house.

Some hours later she gathered me, my elder sister Charlotte and two younger brothers Hugo and Bias (our abbreviation of Tobias) in the kitchen to try to imagine where he might be.

We probably did not treat the task with its proper urgency, but then we did not know what she knew: he had gone missing ten years earlier, calling home on an icy Christmas morning to tell her he had taken an overdose and was in a telephone box near Uxbridge. She called 999, but there was some diffi-culty getting an ambulance sent, as it was the height of the turmoil of Ted Heath's government and the hospital ancillary workers were striking.

Wyn left us at home with grandma and went off looking for him, eventually following his trail to a hospital ward. She got him home, put Christmas dinner on the table and the next day took us out for a walk in the park with friends. Nothing more was ever said about the episode.

This time, there had been no call from a phone box, and she had to try to restrain her growing panic in front of us. My sister Charlotte and I were assigned people to call to enquire whether they had by any chance seen our father. We sat around the kitchen table and tried to think up new possibilities, and none of us came up with the right answer, despite the trail he had laid for us.

Some months earlier, he informed us that he had joined the National Liberal Club in Whitehall, an announcement we had greeted with astonishment and derision. He took our mum to see it and all she could think of was how dreary and stuffy it was. It seemed an absurdly grand and unnecessary thing to do. Members were allowed to stay in its rooms for a reasonable price, but he lived in London, so what was the point?

It had cost money up front that we could hardly afford. I found it funny and irritating without properly considering how sad it was. In retrospect, it was probably part of the staging for his suicide, and no doubt he felt it had a ring to it – 'he died at his club'. He was trying to depart the world as 'a man of substance' at a time when he felt at his most insubstantial.

After more than two decades lecturing in psychology at Brunel University, he had seemed likely to inherit the chair and finally become a professor, a position that must have seemed preordained in his teenage years when he shocked everyone with his precocious academic achievements. At the last moment, however, he was passed over and Brunel chose a younger psychologist from another university who had written popularly accessible books and frequently appeared on television.

My father had told me he blamed himself for mentioning this man's name to someone in the university administration, and wondered whether, if he had kept his mouth shut, they might have forgotten to ask this outsider to apply. He sank into gloom.

I was twenty-two at that time. I had left university and was working at an adventure playground in Fulham for the summer. One sunny day he turned up unannounced and sat at a picnic table watching the kids on the climbing frames. I did not know what to make of it, as I had never known this methodical man to spring surprises. Most evenings, I would go to his study, and he would set aside his work and we would play chess on a makeshift desk he had fashioned from a sheet of plywood and a single metal leg on a hinge that balanced on the armrests of his chair. He was far from emotionally expressive, and to the extent that we had a bond, it was forged in these games: the careful placing of chess pieces and occasional comments on the wisdom or otherwise of the move.

Turning up in Fulham that day, he seemed to have shrunk. We sat and talked for a while at a picnic table but about nothing of consequence. All the questions I had for him would only come to me much later.

In his suicide note he left for us four children, he said he could not see another 'tolerable way out', and that he was sure it would be better for us in the long run to have a dead father than a 'lonely and depressed old man'.

I kept the note, in his neat, even handwriting, in a file of old documents, where it remained unopened for decades. I had to force myself to read it again, so I could write this chapter.

'To be pathetic is the ultimate sin,' he wrote. It is a line that to this day sets my mind racing to list all the sins that are so very much worse. He wondered if he had loved us in the wrong way and whether he had tried to compensate for his own shortcomings through us, a reference to his ceaseless goading over academic achievement.

'Apart from that, there is no moral,' he said.

There were other envelopes he left behind, including a separate note for our mother, which was pointed and recriminatory. There were bank statements underlining our precarious financial state. There were no savings.

A few envelopes were addressed to him but had remained unopened. Inside, my mum found pictures of a small fair-haired boy. We had a half-brother. His name was Alex and Robert had refused to have anything to do with him, cutting off relations with Alex's mother, the woman with whom he had had an affair for more than a decade, after she had insisted on having the child. It still astonishes me that our mum continued to function at all, but she called us together, and insisted we meet Alex who, she pointed out, bore no blame for the collapse of our world. So not long afterwards, we picked him up from his mother's flat and took him to London Zoo. He was a self-assured four-year-old with very clear views on what he wanted to do and what animals he wished to see. We, his four half-siblings, were willing to be guided by him, wandering around the cages and enclosures staring at the animals, uneasy and overwhelmed by the sheer weight of all the things we had just discovered.

My brothers and sister spent the weeks following our dad's suicide struggling with the impossible task of comforting our mum and thinking up ways to distract her. At one point, Bias rowed her in circles around the Serpentine in Hyde Park.

I was going around town doing the practical things, relieved to be out of the house. The bureaucracy of untimely death kept me moving, filling forms and answering questions.

Besides the suitcase of clothes and formalities at the club, there was a car to be extricated from the police pound, and a body to identify. I volunteered to do all of it.

Westminster Public Mortuary on Horseferry Road is round the corner from the Houses of Parliament. As I remember it, you had to go up some stairs to a sort of gallery where there was a long thin window. I was asked if I was ready and a curtain on the far side was pulled back, and there he was lying on a gurney some three metres away, obviously him but at the same time utterly unrecognisable with all life extinguished.

I was numbed by the experience but later thought I had been luckier than my siblings. It is surely better to see the dead one last time, before they disappear forever.

The next job was to pick up his suitcase from the Liberal Club, where I was met by the housekeeper who had found him. She was a short woman with a Spanish or Portuguese accent. She took me to the room in which he had died and on the way up in the vintage wooden lift, she began to cry. Fumbling for something to say, I could only apologise.

The hardest task was making calls to family and friends to tell them the news. My sister and I had our own lists. I still have a vivid mental image of the piece of paper with scrawled names lying on the blue carpet by the phone. With each call, I was afraid people would ask what had driven my father to abandon us all, but no one did.

The call I left until last was Nancy Bingley, whom we all knew as Nans, the Welsh foster mother who had brought my father along the journey from boy to man, from when he first arrived as a Jewish refugee from Nazi Austria. She had been a kind, calm, grandmotherly presence in our lives.

Nans answered the phone, as people did in those days, by reciting her number, and I delivered my prepared script. On the other end of the line, there was an intake of breath, a pause and then Nans said firmly: 'Robert was the Nazis' last victim. They got to him in the end.'

For the first few moments, the words buzzed in the plastic phone and I had nothing to say. She had delivered them with the resigned conviction of someone stating the obvious, but I had no idea what she was talking about. This was 1983 after all, forty-five years after my dad fled Vienna. We had all assumed he had been dragged down by more immediate concerns, a sense of turmoil, failure and disappointment in his personal life and career. His single-page suicide note to us said nothing of Hitler and the Nazis, but seemed preoccupied with whose account of events we, his children, would believe after his death: his or our mum's. We did not care. We did not even know there were competing accounts to be told and we certainly did not want to hear them.

Nans had a broader view of the life that had just ended. She had met our dad when he was a terrified eleven-year-old refugee newly arrived in Britain, and she had never lost sight of the fearful boy curled up inside the ageing man.

By the time Robert had met our mum in the mid-1950s, when they were both young teachers, that boy had already been tidied away. He did not discuss his childhood, and neither did his parents, Leo and Erna. Wyn learned not to even ask.

To them, he was Bobby, a fact I found somehow shocking. We had never heard him called anything other than Robert, and it would have been unthinkably cheeky to address this serious, melancholic man by such a whimsical nickname. Evidently there was a lot we did not know about our father, and that sense of having lived with a stranger only grew in the months after his death.

I had no way of knowing whether Nans' instinctive response was right. We grew up aware of the bare skeleton of my father's story: he had escaped Vienna when he was eleven, seven months after Hitler carried out his Anschluss (the annexation of Austria); Erna had secured a visa as a maid so was able to accompany him on the train and the ferry but was not allowed to live with him in Britain; Leo had escaped later, in March 1939, and soon after found a job as a factory worker in Shrewsbury. Although his parents had managed to reach safety, they were not allowed by the conditions of their visas to live with him, and so Nans and her husband Reg Bingley took Robert in during the war at their home in Caernarfon, Wales.

Beyond that summary, everything was opaque. It was a handful of details that told us what happened, but not how it happened and how it felt. Neither he nor my grandparents spoke about their Viennese past, save for the occasional passing remark. My fitful attempts to dig deeper were gently rebuffed and another woolly layer of reticence was wrapped around whatever was left unsaid. And then our father had cut off any possibility of further conversation the day he walked out of the house forever.

In time, his suicide fossilised from an emotion into a fact, buried thinly by the passage of time but still hard and jagged. Some six years after his death, I was taken by surprise by my boss at the time, a BBC editor who prided himself on his blunt inquisitiveness, when he questioned me about my parents in front of my colleagues. I was flustered and found myself unable to tell the truth. I should have waved away the question and claimed my right to privacy, but instead I found myself making up a story about a violent death by mugging, adding the anxiety of being unmasked as a liar to the shame and grief over a loss I had locked away without comprehending it.

And alongside all that, I took what Nans had told me, her calm certainty about what our father's death meant, and packed it away without exploring it, like an inherited book put away on a shelf unread.

It would no doubt have remained there forever if it had not been for a chance exchange which set in train a sequence of discoveries, not just about my father and his family, but about scores of other children who had fled Vienna at the same time.

In December 2020, I was writing a story about the blanket deportation of West African asylum seekers, particularly Cameroonians, in the dying months of Donald Trump's turbulent administration. I began corresponding with a retired law professor called Ruth Hargrove, who was trying to stop the deportations of some of the Cameroonians on the grounds that they were quite possibly being sent to their deaths in the midst of a brutal civil conflict.

On 28 December, Ruth wrote to me: 'We keep living the same trauma. My father escaped from Vienna in 1938, just after the Gestapo took over. My mother's family escaped the pogroms of Odessa in 1906 . . . My parents' wounds never healed.'

I wrote back immediately to point out the coincidence of our fathers' backgrounds, and we exchanged notes about it, each email a mix of what we knew about our families' experiences under the Nazis and the latest news about her African clients.

Ruth sent me a short reflective essay about the fate of Jews and Cameroonians, in which she quoted Holocaust scholar Yehuda Bauer, who had suggested the addition of three more commandments to the original ten on Moses' tablet: 'Thou shalt not be a perpetrator, or a victim and thou shalt never, ever, be a bystander.'

At one point in my email exchange with Ruth, a memory shook loose about something my mother had told me long before, about Leo and Erna advertising their son in the classified ads in the *Manchester Guardian*, the forerunner of the *Guardian*, in an attempt to get him out of Nazi-ruled Vienna.

It was something I had meant to look into but had put off, imagining it would mean spending days in the *Guardian* archive or worse still, turn out not to be true. Over the years, I had stopped thinking about it.

'What is it with the *Manchester Guardian*?' Ruth replied when I mentioned it. 'That's how my grandfather got my father out.'

Her grandfather, Oskar Fritsch, had seen an announcement of the engagement of the daughter of a British member of parliament on the society pages, and noticed that this MP was a collector of fire department paraphernalia. So Oskar crossed Vienna, braving Nazi patrols to find some Viennese fireman's gear and sent it off, with a note saying something like: 'Congratulations on your daughter's happy news. Could you possibly save my son?' In reply, I sent a brief version of my family story and its unhappy ending.

'I am so deeply sorry about your father. People think that just because our parents got out, they escaped,' Ruth wrote.

'My father never recovered from whatever he went through. We didn't get the diagnosis until he was in his '80s and was imagining vermin on the kitchen counter, but he was diagnosed with post-traumatic stress disorder (PTSD) at the same time he received the Alzheimer's diagnosis.'

Her eighty-eight-year-old father, born Peter Fritsch, would relive the Anschluss in his confusion, switching back to the German he had not spoken for seventy-four years and begging Ruth 'to save him from the Nazis coming for him'.

Not long after that, he died.

'The PTSD diagnosis finally gave a name to the unpredictable violence of my childhood,' she said. 'Hitler's gift continues.'

I was struck by the echo of Nans' words about my own father two decades earlier, with the same message: violence is often just the beginning. The real story of war is also the years and decades that follow, all the days the wounded and bereaved survivors have to struggle through, only to bequeath the anguish to another generation.

On 29 December, I wrote to the *Guardian*'s archivist, Richard Nelsson, explaining my 'family lore' about the *Manchester Guardian* and Ruth's account, suggesting that together they could make a story. Richard replied the next day to say he had found something in the archives, an advert from August 1938. 'Could this be it?' he asked. His email had an attachment.

I opened it in the car park of a supermarket in northern Virginia. The groceries were in the back and I was about to drive home, but checked my phone first to make sure I was not needed at work. It was a newspaper cutting, a block of six short advertisements under the heading 'Tuition', in the slightly uneven and blotchy pre-war typeface of the era, from the *Manchester Guardian* on 3 August 1938. The middle ad had our name in it.

'I Seek a kind person who will educate my intelligent Boy, aged 11, Viennese of good family. Borger, 5/12 Hintzerstrasse, Vienna 3.'

I recognised my family's last address in Vienna from Leo's documents. There was no doubt the 'intelligent boy' was our dad, and that my grandparents had placed the advertisement. I was taken unawares by the emotional force of these words even after so much time – a father and mother's desperate effort to save their only child by extolling his virtues in a foreign language. I wondered how I would advertise my own son, also an only child. What words would I choose if everything I cared about depended on it? And if I picked the right words and strangers took him in, would I ever see him again?

If I had never been in touch with Ruth, or if she had not mentioned her own father, I would never have thought to mention the advertisement to Richard in the archives. The entire sequence of events was as tenuous as a gust of wind uncovering a long-forgotten artefact.

This was, in a way, our origin story and surely had something to do with the fact that I was here in northern Virginia eighty-three years later, working for the same newspaper. I had after all grown up in a household in which the *Guardian* was a revered daily presence, and no wonder.

One glance at that old newspaper cutting showed that our family story was one of many. On the day my father was advertised there were six children in the 'Tuition' section whose lives needed to be rescued.

'FERVENT prayer in great distress,' the top ad declared. 'Who would give a Home to a grammar school scholar aged 13: healthy, clever, very musical.' The parents placing the ad identified themselves by the initials FBW, with an apartment on Wiedner Hauptstrasse in Vienna's 5th District.

All the ads had the same Germanic practice of capitalising nouns, suggesting that people unfamiliar with English had placed them, using dictionaries for guidance.

The ad below my father's read: 'I Look for an au pair for

my Girl, aged 14, well educated, Jewess: very fond of children: good sewing, household help.' The family name given was Hess, from Gudrunstrasse in the 10th District.

Below that, someone called Manheim in the 2nd District had written: 'Two very modest Sisters, aged 14 and 17, Jews, half orphans, well trained, pray to be accepted as foster children.'

Among these appeals from the Nazi Reich, an 'educated French lady' had placed an ad offering conversation for 'pay or exchange'. Below that, the last ad for a Viennese child, the daughter of a Dr Langer: 'Will a Philanthropist take a much-gifted Girl, 14 years old, daughter of an Austrian Jewish lawyer, as foster-child?'

These were just the advertisements in one section of one day's edition. There were scores of Jewish children from Vienna being advertised through the pages of the *Manchester Guardian*. Scrolling through the archives, moving forward in time from 11 March 1938, the date of the Anschluss, I could see the tide of panic gathering pace in the Tuition and Situations Wanted columns as the awful year rolled on.

The initial references to Vienna concerned only tourism and opera, but on 10 May, a Viennese woman called Erna Ball offered herself as a housekeeper, then, a fortnight later, there was an ad placed by Julie Klein, who described herself as a 'distinguished Viennese lady, Jewish, good appearance, blond, 35'.

On 7 June, the first of the children appeared: Gertrude Mandl, a 'young Viennese Girl . . . not Aryan' who 'seeks position as Cook Housekeeper'. She was the first of a wave of children which peaked in August, September and October before beginning to peter out in November, when Britain launched the *Kindertransport*. These organised mass transports of unaccompanied minors from Vienna, Prague and Berlin brought some ten thousand Jewish children to Britain in the months leading up to the outbreak of war.

Before the *Kindertransport*, however, newspaper ads were one of the very few options available for Jewish parents trying to get their sons and daughters out of Nazi-run Austria. A total of eighty children were advertised in the *Manchester Guardian*, almost all from Vienna, their virtues described in brief to fit the confined space at the cost of a shilling a line. They had grown up on the same streets at the same time as my father. So what happened to them all? Had they managed to survive or had their parents' appeals for help gone unheeded?

I set out to trace them. Having stumbled on their names it seemed unthinkable not to try to find out what had happened to them, and if it was too late to track them down in person, to at least find their children, who would presumably be about my age. At the same time I felt compelled to follow my own father's faded traces, overlooked for so long.

I had no clear preconceptions of where the search would take me, and I would frequently be astonished by the stories that lay behind those three-line ads. The trail led from the hushed Vienna archives to the Shanghai ghetto; to a suspected Bolshevik spy deported from 1920s France only to vanish mysteriously; a secret Austrian cell within the French Resistance and a lapse in judgement that led to its obliteration at the hands of the Gestapo; a US military intelligence unit chasing the remnants of the SS through the German forests and finding a hoard of Nazi cash; a phenomenal Jewish football team which beat the world's best before being burned off the pages of sporting history in the Holocaust; an astounding tale of love and survival that led through Theresienstadt, Auschwitz-Birkenau and the chaos of the war's final days. It finally led to a video call to New York in which I got to ask questions of a living witness, questions I should have put to my dad.

The exploratory journey into my own family's past was like spooling a video ever faster backwards across the generations. Colour turned to black and white, cities gave way to villages, modern roads petered out into rough tracks, leading to younger incarnations of men and women whom I had only known in their last years, and other ancestors I had never met, speaking different languages and leading unrecognisable lives, all blithely unaware of the horrors hurtling towards them.

Hilary Mantel once said that history is 'what's left in the sieve when the centuries have run through it', and that is exactly how it felt researching this book. I spent months sifting through remnants and guessing how they might fit together, what they might tell me about my family, and the ways they shaped me and my generation, the children of survivors, and the way we see the world. They were long dead but not yet departed. Just now and then, they flickered back to life, stepping out of history in their prime, some as heroes, some as victims, all transformed in ways I could not have anticipated.

I

The Untold Stories of Leo, Erna and Bobby Borger

WHEN WE WERE growing up in London, our grandmother Erna would occasionally come to lunch on the weekends, bringing with her all the frustrations of an exile and a taste of our past. To us she was Omi (a Viennese variant of granny), a formidable figure, stolid and thickset in heavy cardigan, wool skirt, thick buff tights and boots whatever the season.

On her visits, Omi would typically arrive late and no matter what meal had been planned or prepared, she would insist on making Viennese food from scratch, unpacking her plastic shopping bags on the already set kitchen table.

There she would beat veal fillets into schnitzel with a jagged steel hammer, making the whole kitchen shake. Later on, she would make a chocolate cake assembled from round wafers that came in blue-and-white paper packets.

Young Erna had been a lively and attractive woman, judging by the old photographs, but in Britain she had divorced our grandfather Leo, put on weight and allowed her sense of humour to give way to resentment. She never quite accepted London as her real home.

Despite her limited grasp of English, Omi had found herself a job as a cashier in Lyons' Corner House on the Strand, a huge West End cafeteria where as children we were taken for an occasional treat, served by 'nippies', waitresses in black uniforms and white aprons, so named for the speed at which they moved between tables.

Omi was an exile there, among the grilled gammon, bacon sandwiches and Battenberg cake, all crudely inferior in her eyes to the cafe culture she had left behind. In their last few years in Vienna, the Borger family had finally attained a reasonably comfortable lifestyle in an apartment in an elegant Art Nouveau building with a grand entrance and wrought-iron balustrades. In London's Swiss Cottage, Omi was consigned to a small boxy flat high up in a modern block on a council estate.

Her visits were a trial for our mum Wyn, and not just because Omi would blatantly ignore her plans for what and when she should eat. She was also well aware that her mother-in-law had made it known to others that our father could have made a better match, to a rich, Jewish girl. Wyn had been born Mabel in a working-class Manchester family, and was stressed enough raising four children while adopting southern vowels and manners to better approximate the sort of wife our father and his mother felt he should have married. Being disrupted and displaced in her own kitchen stretched her to the limits of tolerance.

Our dad Robert would usually absent himself when his mother turned up, withdrawing to his study at the top of the stairs. Omi craved his presence. She was proud of his academic achievements and his respectable university teaching job and clearly found solace chatting to him in German, the sing-song Viennese version of it, an act of intimacy preserved from his youth.

Robert, on the other hand, was irritated by his mother's lack of education or sophistication, her fixation on food, and the constant reminder that before he was Robert, urbane British university lecturer, he was little Bobby Borger, a nervous refugee boy, an outsider. It was a history he had tried to cauterise.

I find myself straining now to scrutinise these memories for all the clues I had missed when he was alive. I had always assumed that he sounded like a typical Englishman, but friends now say they noticed a tinge of a foreign accent, that precise use of a language that has been carefully learned, rather than simply absorbed from birth.

He did not teach us German. I once found a basic textbook and persuaded him to go through the first chapter with me. I was in my early teens and keen to cultivate whatever trait might set me apart from my peers. I once spelled out the words 'Republik Österreich' with stick-on letters on the back of my school tracksuit, which was all the more absurd because I hardly spoke a word of the language. My efforts to enrol him as a teacher quickly petered out. He did not refuse directly but would find other, more pressing, things to do when we were supposed to study, and I did not have the resolve to pursue the issue.

For all our dad's lack of enthusiasm, Austria and Vienna remained a subtle but constant undertone to our childhood, the faint background radiation of a distant star that had imploded long before we were born.

For the benefit of elderly relatives at family gatherings, my sister Charlotte and I were dressed up to the age of six in lederhosen and grey cardigans with dark green piping. They were the sort of traditional clothes Bobby had grown up wearing for special occasions, but which were prohibited for Jews under Nazi rule.

We grew out of the clothes, and mine were later destroyed in a flood at our mum's flat, sparing future generations from their chafing awkwardness. Vienna would not be ignored, however. Leo had two Viennese wives. After divorcing Omi in the late 1950s, mostly over the dilemma of whether to return to Austria or not, he married his landlady in Shrewsbury, Valerie Klinger, a widow whose first husband had been murdered in the Holocaust.

Vally was the longest-lived of that generation and the most forceful personality. Her theatrically Viennese rendition of the

English language worked its way so far into our brains that decades after her death, we cannot help but switch into her accent to pronounce certain phrases and place names, using its lyrical cadence and abrupt consonants. She never mastered the softness of the English 'W'.

Much of my time in Shrewsbury with Leo and Vally was spent in the lean-to shed my grandfather had erected on the side of their bungalow, improvised from glass doors which he had bolted together and corrugated clear plastic for a roof. Inside, we pored over his stamp collection, which told the story of the Austro-Hungarian empire and its conquered provinces. The central character in that philatelic tale was the heavily whiskered Emperor, Franz Joseph, the last giant of the Habsburg line and revered protector of the Jews. His glowering face and mutton-chop sideburns were on every page.

Vienna would also infiltrate its way into our picnics and packed lunches, in the form of *Liptauer*, a blend of cream cheese and herbs or paprika, and the mix of nuts, raisins and chocolate we knew as *Studentenfutter*, Student Fodder.

Leo's sister, Malci, our great-aunt and the last surviving relative in Vienna, would send us *Manner* hazelnut wafer biscuits wrapped in foil and distinctive pink packaging, as well as *Mozartkugeln*, chocolate-covered marzipan balls in gold foil bearing an image of the great composer. She sent extra consignments during the strikes, three-day weeks and Winter of Discontent of 1970s Britain.

If our Viennese past gave a faint but distinct tint to our lives, the Jewish side of our heritage was all but invisible. In the eternal trade-off between cultural identity and assimilation, the Borger family, for generations, had bet on blending in.

Mendl Borger, my great-great-grandfather, came from a small town called Neu Raussnitz, or Rousínov in Moravia, today's Czech Republic, which had been home to a Jewish community since the fifteenth century. I know almost nothing about him, other than that, in the mid-nineteenth century, he married a Jew with a gentile name, Marie Schlesinger, and together in April 1860 they had a son whom they named Johann, the least Jewish moniker imaginable. They clearly saw a future for him far away from the shtetls of the Czech-speaking provinces, in the embrace of the imperial metropolis.

A Jewish-American historian, Harry Zohn, described the story of Vienna and its Jews as 'the most tragically unrequited love in world history', and as unrequited love stories go, it is surely the longest. Jews have lived in Vienna since its origins, though not continually. Over the centuries the community was wiped out three times. The first recorded mention of the town of Wenia was in 881. In 966, less than ninety years later, a town document refers to 'Jews and other legitimate merchants'. In 1194, the local lord, Duke Leopold V, made a Jew called Shlom the master of his mint, though that only lasted a year before Shlom and his whole family were murdered by crusaders on their way east.

That would be the pattern for ever after: a foothold, then achievement and recognition, followed by shockingly violent retribution. It would be the recurring motif of Jewish existence. By the mid-nineteenth century, when my forebears were longing for Vienna, the city's masters had already twice obliterated its Jewish community.

By the fourteenth century, Vienna had the biggest Jewish population in the Germanic world and was a rabbinical centre of learning. This was the first Viennese 'paradise', and it lasted until 1420, when a wealthy Jew was accused of buying up communion wafers so they could be desecrated, one of a long ludicrous catalogue of crimes Jews would be accused of over the centuries. The archduke of Austria at the time, Albrecht V, ordered the arrest of rich Jews, to whom he happened to be personally indebted for the financing of his military campaigns. These wealthy merchants were tortured until they revealed where they hid their money. The rest were told to convert or face death or expulsion. Many were put on rafts without oars and pushed into the currents of the Danube. Jewish children were taken from their parents and forcibly baptised.

Hundreds took their own lives and by the end of a year-long pogrom, a population of 1,600 had been reduced to 212 Jews, 92 men and 120 women who had refused to convert. They were rounded up and burned alive in a mass execution. The obliteration of the community is known as the Wiener Gesera, the Viennese Decree, after the order that began it and the title of a chronicle of the massacre.

The synagogue on Judenplatz, the site of the first ghetto, was dismantled and its stones used in expanding the University of Vienna, but if you walk downstairs at the Jewish Museum that stands there now, you can see the foundations, the deepest of the three buried layers of Jewish life, sediment of the city's trauma, each stratum covered in ash.

Jews were outcasts from Vienna for two centuries after the Wiener Gesera, but eventually the Habsburgs, who had taken over Austria as well as the throne of the Holy Roman Empire, needed money to fund their battles with religious and political rivals in what became known as the Thirty Years War. So wealthy Jews prepared to loan funds to the throne were grudgingly allowed back in. A small ghetto of some five hundred families grew up in the seventeenth century, on an islet in the Danube. It was called Im Werd, old German for island.

In a world of kingdoms, empires and absolute rule, Jewish survival was ultimately the style choice of each individual ruler, who could simply change their mind or just die, ushering in a successor whose views on the matter could be entirely different.

In 1658, Leopold I, a socially cold but religiously fanatical teenager who had been raised for the priesthood by Jesuits, became emperor. He married Margarita Teresa, a Spanish princess who was both his first cousin and his niece. When their first son did not survive infancy, it was blamed on the Jews, who were also held responsible for a fire at the palace not long after.

Leopold banished them from the city. Im Werd was renamed Leopoldstadt in honour of the emperor, and the Great Synagogue at the heart of the community was pulled down and rebuilt as Leopold's Church. There is still a stone plaque above the church entrance, noting in Latin that it had been built on the site of a 'Synagogæ Perversa', although what seems particularly perverse is that a few centuries later, many assimilationist Jewish families would call their children Leopold or, in our own grandpa's case, Leo. Such was the yearning to belong.

After the Leopold pogrom, the cycle of tolerance and annihilation began again. Christians were reluctant to shoulder the city's entire tax burden so wealthy Jews were allowed back in if they paid a special levy. But they remained aliens, governed by different laws. By the middle of the nineteenth century, Austria was the only major Western power to retain medieval restrictions on its Jewish population.

In 1848, the year of European revolutions, the roulette wheel of imperial lineage was spun again, and another teenager inherited the throne, Franz Joseph; but this time Vienna's Jews could count themselves lucky. The new emperor was arguably the first Habsburg ruler not to have been antisemitic to his bones.

Under his reign, a new constitution established that legal rights were not dependent on religion. Jews were allowed to live anywhere and own their homes. The emperor appears to have been genuinely annoyed when Jews were passed over for promotion in the army, and he used his power to try, albeit unsuccessfully, to stop a blatant antisemite, Karl Lueger, becoming mayor of Vienna.

'In this vast empire, everything stood firmly and immovably

in its appointed place, and at its head was the aged emperor,' Stefan Zweig wrote in his paean to Vienna, *The World of Yesterday*, completed shortly before Zweig took his life in Brazilian exile in 1942.

No wonder Franz Joseph was such a hero to my grandparents and their generation, who displayed the emperor's jowly face as an icon in their homes. No wonder his birthday was added to the calendar of festivals in Vienna's synagogues. He presided over a blossoming of Jewish life. The community in Vienna exploded from 6,000 in 1860 to 150,000 at the beginning of the twentieth century. It was a city bursting with talent and possibilities, the dazzling hub of an empire of fifty million people and eleven nationalities. Each member of Franz Joseph's cabinet owned twenty uniforms for the plethora of ceremonies they would be required to attend among the empire's ethnic groups. The emperor himself had two hundred uniforms, as befitted the omnipotent ruler of so many peoples.

It was a place where Jews could get on in society. They represented a tenth of the Viennese population but over sixty per cent of its lawyers, and more than half of its dentists and doctors. Jews owned nearly a quarter of all businesses. The emphasis on learning, thrift and hard work, which had made them rabbis and merchants in the villages and shtetls of east Europe, made them bourgeois in Vienna. This was the city to which our great-grandfather Johann migrated from Rousínov in the last years of the nineteenth century, in the wake of a construction boom. The emperor had ordered the rebuilding of Vienna on a grand scale, befitting the capital of a glittering empire. The medieval walls around the old city were torn down and replaced with a magnificent, curving, tree-lined boulevard, the Ringstrasse.

On arrival, Johann was classified by the tireless Austrian bureaucracy as a *Kaufman*, a merchant, just like his father, Mendl, and once he had set himself up, he married upwards to a woman from a more established Viennese family. Her name was Hermine Dörfler, and the couple were married in the city's Tempelgasse synagogue in 1896.

They were relatively old at the time: he was thirty-six and she was thirty, and the one thing I know for sure about their marriage was that it was filled with grief. Hermine would give birth to five children, all given typical Viennese gentile names, of whom only two survived into adulthood: my grandpa Leo and his sister Malvine, Malci. Another sister, Marianne, died at the age of three, and a second brother, Emil, only survived until the age of eight before succumbing to tuberculous meningitis. It seems likely that tuberculosis killed Marianne too. It was endemic at the time and Austria had the highest rate of infant deaths in Western Europe. A third brother, Eugen, survived to the age of seventeen, dying of tuberculosis in 1921 just as he was starting out as a trainee mechanic. The existence of these three lost children was a complete surprise to me when I came across them in the Austrian archives. As I was discovering, the painful and the perished had been comprehensively edited out of our family story, replaced mostly by silence.

The two surviving children, Leo and Malci, both went to trade school, where it is fair to say that Leo did not shine. A school report dated 14 February 1914 records that he scored 'satisfactory' grades in arithmetic and trade, but only just 'sufficient' in double-entry bookkeeping, geography and civic studies.

Four months later, all of that would be irrelevant, and the only skills you needed would be those that could keep you alive under fire. On 28 June, in the centre of Sarajevo, another student from the Austro-Hungarian empire, nineteen-year-old Bosnian Serb, Gavrilo Princip, shot the heir to the imperial throne, Archduke Franz Ferdinand, and his wife Sophie, and triggered the First World War.

My grandpa Leo went straight from trade school to the army

and was posted to a howitzer battery on the eastern front fighting the Russians in what is now Ukraine. His photographs show a crashed allied biplane, fortifications constructed of huge tree trunks, Leo visiting a comrade in hospital and working a field telephone in a private's uniform and a peaked cap, a slim, youthful version of the man I had known.

The war radicalised young people like my grandfather. The camaraderie of the trenches, the realisation that your chances of survival were directly related to your wealth and status, and the sense among those who emerged alive that they were entitled to something better, sent a wave of revolution across Europe and through the Borger family.

Previous generations had remained formally within the Jewish community, registering the births of their children with the rabbis. My grandpa Leo and his sister Malci dispensed with such lip service to tradition. Malci left the *Israelitische Kultusgemeinde* (IKG), the Jewish Community of Vienna, in 1922, when she was twenty-two. Leo, given the Hebrew name *Shmuel Lev* at circumcision, followed his little sister five years later, opting out of the community just two weeks after my father was born. Robert's birth in 1927 was therefore not recorded by the IKG, and Leo no doubt hoped that anyone who came along later, scouring the records for Jews, would not be able to find his son.

Leo and Malci's departure was not uncommon. Half the Viennese Jews who left the faith converted to Catholicism, and a quarter became Protestants. Malci and Leo declared themselves without religion, *konfessionslos*, and instead identified themselves through their politics. Malci became a committed communist and kept that faith until the end of her life. Leo became a Social Democrat, a more moderate take on Marxist doctrine but one to which he was no less committed. Political beliefs were not held lightly in a time and place where a leftist affiliation could get you imprisoned or killed.

Six years after leaving, however, Leo returned to the Jewish fold, officially converting back to the faith in 1933, just after the Nazis took power in Berlin. Perhaps this seemingly counterintuitive move had a certain logic. Opting out of Judaism would not spare you from persecution. The Nazis did not care what you believed, or whether you had made some solemn renunciation of faith. They had deemed Jews to be a race, not just the followers of a religion, and so there was no escape. It was not anti-Judaism but antisemitism. You cannot convert the blood in your veins.

Returning to Judaism in such circumstances was an act of both resignation and of defiance. It was not an act of faith in God. I do not know if Leo ever visited a synagogue after his arrival in Britain. When he died in 1972, the memorial service was held in a chapel at the crematorium at the end of the road he lived on, because it was the most convenient option. It was performed by an Anglican priest who had only met the deceased a couple of times and whose eulogy made it embarrassingly clear that he knew little of Leo's life story.

Robert shared his father's secular outlook on life and social democratic politics, but in most other ways they were unalike. Leo found peace in the routine of a factory job and walks in the hills on weekends. Robert was an academic *Wunderkind* who never found a way of feeling at ease in his own skin. The refugee's curse is to be from two places and none at the same time. Accepting that paradox is often the key to finding contentment, and I do not think my father ever did.

His roots in Britain were shallow but tenacious, and he had to strain to grip the earth under his feet. When the time came for Robert to name his children, he followed family tradition in following no tradition at all, looking instead to the prevailing establishment for inspiration. We were given names that, by design, could only be English, and which suggested a certain status in society, a down payment on the rank and income we were expected to achieve in later life. My full name is Julian Matthew Sebastian. Some of the middle names bestowed on my siblings were Rupert, Makepeace, Augustine and Josephine.

They were a constant source of irritation and ridicule in my youth but now at least I can look on them as part of a broader pattern, the continuation of the eager but ultimately abortive efforts of assimilationist Viennese Jews like the Borgers to burrow deep into Austrian society over generations. The posh names were a learned reflex, meant as armour and camouflage in a new host nation. They made an ill-fitting inherited suit, fleetingly fashionable in their day but already fey and pretentious by the time I was in my teens.

There were costs to choosing assimilation over identity. I grew up feeling that I did not entirely belong even in the neighbourhood where I spent the first eighteen years of my life. Part of me always felt that we were somehow pretending, and that underlying unease drove me abroad at the earliest opportunity. It was as if we had painted layer after layer of tasteful off-white over the top of something garish, more visceral and unsettling, and I was unsure what to do about it other than to leave.

'The past is never dead. It is not even past,' says Gavin Stevens, the Mississippi lawyer in William Faulkner's *Requiem for a Nun*. He is talking about a crime but also about the history of the American South, which seethes relentlessly under the surface of daily life, like Europe's past. The fictional Stevens would have known that, having studied at Heidelberg University.

Another Mississippi author, Greg Iles, writing nearly half a century later, elaborated on Faulkner's theme.

'All of us labour in webs spun long before we were born, webs of heredity and environment, of desire and consequence, of history and eternity,' Iles wrote in *The Quiet Game*. 'The quotidian demands of life distract from this resonance of images and events, but some of us feel it always.'

I felt I was one of those people. Like an over-sensitivity to light or smell, the sense of an unspoken history would impinge on my daily peace of mind, and sometimes the past would come roaring to the surface of its own accord, churned up by sickness and death.

When Omi suffered a stroke in 1975, she was taken to the Jewish Home and Hospital in Tottenham, a red-brick Edwardian establishment founded in the late nineteenth century as the Home and Hospital for Jewish Incurables, a title which was shortened in the 1960s to make it sound less terminally dispiriting. It was a gloomy and cavernous place, with long linoleum corridors smelling of disinfectant. We would visit on weekends and sit alongside Omi for an hour or so, though it felt much longer. The stroke had stripped away her grasp of English, and she would only murmur to our dad in German.

She had been born Erna Barbak in 1901, the daughter of Markus Barbak, a merchant from the small Galician town of Mykulyntsi, now in western Ukraine, and his Czech-born wife, Regina Dubsky. Her parents had met in Vienna, where Markus had set up as a general trader, and they had three other children: Nelly who only lived six months, Marianne who was born in 1918, and Fritz, the only son and pride of the family.

Fritz played football professionally for Hakoah Vienna, a Jewish team that took on the world in the 1920s and beat it. The team's name was Hebrew for 'The Strength', a purposeful attempt to embody the spirit of *Muskeljudentum*, 'muscular Judaism', that was popular for a while in Zionist circles. The club won the Austrian championship in 1925, an achievement all the more remarkable in light of the constant antisemitic attacks and abuse the players suffered. They had to be accompanied by a team of bodyguards, led by Jewish boxers.

Hakoah went on to beat the best teams in Europe, including

the leading Czech champions, Slavia Prague, Poland's Polonia Warsaw, and the top Hungarian team, Ferencváros. In 1923, Hakoah thrashed West Ham United 5–1 in the season the London team reached the FA Cup final. A Munich-based sports paper, *Fussball*, declared in 1924: 'Hakoah has helped to do away with the fairy tale about the physical inferiority of Jews.' The club achieved these results by approaching the game professionally. It paid its players above the going rate, and it brought in gentile as well as Jewish coaches. Some were imported from England, where the most advanced tactics were practised at the time.

Admittedly, Great Uncle Fritz joined the team on the downside of this glittering trajectory, after a US tour of the 'Invincible Jews' during which some of the leading players were feted in the White House by President Calvin Coolidge, and poached

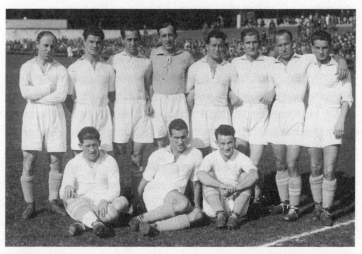

The celebrated Hakoah Wien football team, 1928. My great-uncle, Fritz Barbak, is standing third from the left. Team captain, Max Scheuer, standing second from the right, was later killed in Auschwitz. Ignaz Feldmann, sitting on the left, survived Auschwitz and helped to save the lives of other inmates.

by soccer teams in New York, one of the many false starts football would have in America. The departure of some of the top players provided an opportunity for Fritz, but the team did not recover. The club never won the Austrian championship again and spent the remainder of its existence struggling with relegation, not always successfully. Fritz was given mixed reviews in the Viennese press. One commentator suggested he had been a fast and effective winger for Slovan and had suffered by being made to play in too many different positions by Hakoah. Others suggested he was better suited to assisting goals rather than scoring them himself.

Fritz died in 1935 of a heart attack brought on by pneumonia. The eulogy in the Vienna *Sporttagblatt* journal praised him as a veteran who had shown 'loyalty in the trenches' of the first division. My grandparents would certainly have been at the funeral; my eight-year-old father too, gathered alongside officials from Hakoah and the players' union. But in later life, he never mentioned Fritz's exploits. I grew up playing and watching football never knowing there was a star player in my family. Perhaps he was embarrassed that Fritz had played for an all-Jewish team. The whole subject of Judaism itself made my father uneasy, a tic that took tangible form at the Jewish Home and Hospital in Tottenham, where Omi spent her last years, where he would mutter under his breath contemptuously at the sight of the black-coated Hasidic men who ran the institution.

Our great-aunt Malci died in 1994, as old as the twentieth century itself, leaving behind the distinctly Austrian legacy of gold Franz Joseph ducats in a Viennese safe deposit box. The instructions for recovering the cache, in Malci's spidery handwriting, brought us back to Vienna and seemed as elaborate and intriguing as any treasure map.

Four years later, our step-grandmother, Vally, the last survivor of the Vienna generation, finally passed away in a Shrewsbury hospice. Alone in the family, she had observed the Jewish high holidays, and kept a prayer book, which she had annotated with the date of her father's death in the Jewish calendar, 27 Nisan.

At her funeral, we said Kaddish and played a recording of Leonard Bernstein's *Chichester Psalms*. I was supposed to make a speech based on notes I had made about her life from our conversations, about her rushed escape from Vienna leaving her mother and first husband behind, but to my astonishment, I found I could hardly finish my short eulogy in the crematorium. Some hand reached out from the remote past and squeezed my throat, and I had to force my way to the end before sitting down in embarrassment.

We may want to let go of history, but that doesn't necessarily mean history is finished with us. I was not witness to the events I was trying to describe. On the contrary, I had led a secure and comfortable life in leafy west London. I just intended to state the facts of Vally's life and let them speak for themselves, so my physical response to my own words astounded me. In the past few years, evidence has emerged for epigenetics, the route by which our environment and experience, particularly trauma, can work its way into our DNA, changing the way genes are expressed. One study observed that the children of Holocaust survivors produced less cortisol and were therefore more prone to PTSD.

So maybe man hands on misery to man after all, though the reality is not entirely bleak, or we would all be wrecks. Trauma does not change our genes, but alters their expression, and that can be reversed. Being able to talk about the past, and reimagine it, seems like a worthwhile first step.

The day after Vally's funeral, I picked up a cardboard box of Leo's things that she had kept for me. Among the stamp albums and old banknotes, there were tiny black-and-white photographs of Leo in the trenches on the eastern front in the First World War, along with a medal that looked like an iron cross. 'Grati, Princeps et Patria, Carolos Imp et Rex' (Thanks,

Sovereign and Fatherland, Karl, Emperor and King), it said on the front, and 'Vitam et Sanguinem' (with Life and Blood), the year 1916, and the two crowns of Austria and Hungary. You got one of these medals if you were with a combat unit for over twelve weeks and had been in at least one battle. About 651,000 were manufactured. They were hardly a mark of distinction, but Leo had held on to his nonetheless. For Jewish veterans they were like a covenant in life and blood with their homeland and their rulers. Across the whole sprawling empire, more than 300,000 Jewish men fought for the empire and one in ten of them died, a disproportionately high sacrifice.

Twenty years later, when the Nazis took over Vienna, this was something almost all the children from the *Manchester Guardian* classified ads had in common: their fathers had believed these zinc crosses would protect them.

There was another manila envelope in Leo's box containing a clutch of documents, some in the gossamer formal script of imperial Vienna, some from cruder times, signed 'Heil Hitler!' Among them was a note asking for the family shop to be spared from vandalism because of Leo's service record, and a legal document recording the transfer of the family business, a radio and musical instrument shop in Vienna, to an approved Aryan businessman in 1938.

Stuck in a corner of the box was a small, enamelled metal badge showing a red carnation on a black background, the old motif of Austria's Social Democratic Workers Party, which ran Vienna between the First World War and Austria's brief civil war in 1934. The city became known as Red Vienna, providing free health care, education for workers and social housing, which gave Leo and his young family shelter when he was unemployed in the late 1920s. The party also provided that elusive thing, a sense of belonging. Members greeted each other with the word *Freundschaft!* (Friendship).

For many Viennese Jews, it was the ideal vehicle for assimilation. It provided a framework of political, social, cultural and
sporting activities in which there was no distinction between
Jews and non-Jews. Leo remained a fee-paying member long
after he fled Austria, into the mid-1950s, and in the trove he
bequeathed me was a little red booklet, recording the receipt
of his regular payments with neat rows of coloured stamps.
Alongside that were two green-grey passports, made of thin
card, which secured Leo and Omi's passage out of Vienna,
imprinted on the front with an eagle clutching a swastika, and
inside a big red 'J' for *Jude*, together with stamps recording
every bureaucratic requirement for leaving the Reich, crossing
Europe and entering Britain.

Bound to the passports with a rubber band was a slightly
smaller booklet, this one dove grey and printed in English:
Leo's enemy alien certificate which he was obliged to carry
with him at all times in wartime Britain. It recorded the official assurance that he would not be interned and, a few pages
later, it noted the fact that that promise had been broken, and
he was incarcerated as an enemy alien on the Isle of Man in
1941. An entry on the next page marked the point the following
year, after his release, when he was sufficiently trusted by His
Majesty's Government to be allowed possession of a bicycle.

The significance of this and Leo's other relics has become
clearer to me over time, but when I first picked up that cardboard box, they were simply curiosities. I had little context in
which to place them, so I had no grasp of the story they told.
They were dots I was incapable of joining, so I kept them in
their box, and took them with me as talismans as I moved
from one foreign correspondent's posting to another, from
Bosnia to Jerusalem to Washington, back to Britain and then
Washington again.

That is how my relationship with my familial past remained,
an unpacked box among my luggage, until that day in a Virginia

car park when I received the email about my father's advertisement, which led me to take another look at the traces of our family's past, and the stories of other Viennese Jews; those who fled and survived, and those who remained and perished.

Their ads in the *Manchester Guardian* were like telegrams from another age: urgent and compressed, with no room for detail. They were abbreviations of other lives, which started off running parallel to our father's before spinning off in different directions. Coming across the adverts sent me back to Leo's box and all the other fragments of the Viennese past, and I began to reassemble them into a story that made sense of what happened to my family.

2

George and the Unbearable
Longing for Vienna

THE ADVERTISEMENTS FOR Viennese Jewish children in the
Manchester Guardian in 1938 sat alongside listings for the
day's radio programmes, the crossword, appeals from the Royal
Air Force for prospective pilots and all sorts of competing sales
pitches for houses, stamps, musical instruments and financial
services.

The children's adverts looked like all the others, but came
from another world. They were appeals from frantic parents
trying to save their sons and daughters, all within the space of
an epigram. It was impossible to read them without needing
to know how these stories unfolded. What happened next and
were these children saved?

My first attempts to track down the children were flailing.
I put out appeals on Twitter and in the journal of the Association
of Jewish Refugees. They elicited kind responses and other
family tales of flight from the Nazis, but no stories connected
to the *Manchester Guardian* ads.

Clearly, if I were to find out what happened to these children, it would be on the basis of the clues in the ads themselves,
which in most cases were frustratingly incomplete: usually just
the age and gender of the child, a surname or merely initials,
and a street address in Vienna of a home that would have been
abandoned soon after the advert was placed.

There were a few exceptions in which both a first and
second name were provided, and in a small handful of cases,

the name given was of the child rather than the parent. In just one instance, that child was easy to find, and by happy co-incidence, his life had been comprehensively recorded. It was an early breakthrough and helped to fill many of the gaps in my knowledge of my dad's formative years.

George Mandler was advertised six days before Robert Borger, on 28 July 1938. He was on the second page of the paper, under a heading that read: 'Tutors, Governesses &c' and then a sub-head 'Situations Wanted'. The ad was the only one in the section. In uncertain English, it asked: 'Will an English family be kind enough to take au pair my son, aged 14? (out of grammar school) with knowledge of English and to procure him employment? best references. Georg Mandler, 2, Lowengasse, Vienna 3.'

The first Google search result for that name brought up the Wikipedia entry for an Austrian-born American psychologist, George Mandler, a distinguished professor, born on 11 June 1924. It was clearly the boy in the ad with just an added 'e' to anglicise his first name. Like my father, he had become a university psychologist, albeit a more celebrated one.

The second Google result was 'George Mandler – In Memoriam' on the website of the psychology department of the University of California in San Diego. He had worked there for nearly thirty years, but at the time of his death, in May 2016, he had been living in Hampstead, London.

'Mandler, who left his native Austria after its annexation by Nazi Germany, made signature contributions to the psychology of memory, consciousness and emotion,' the obituary read. 'His decisive influence is felt to this day.'

There was an accompanying portrait of him in pleasant contemplation looking off to the side, with his hands loosely clasped. He had a white goatee, tinted square glasses and grey hair voluminous enough to flop over to one side.

His colleagues, friends and former students had brought

out a book in his honour in 1991 called *Memories, Thoughts and Emotions*. In 2009, the University of Vienna awarded him an honorary doctorate. My immediate thought was that this man, who had emerged from Vienna at the same time and in the same way as my father, had the career that my dad had dreamed of.

The obituary said he had left behind a wife, Jean, an equally distinguished psychologist who had been George's professional partner for much of his career, and two sons, Peter and Michael.

Both had become senior academics. Peter was a professor of history at Cambridge; Michael was an economics professor at the University of London. I emailed Peter at 11 p.m. on 16 February 2021, explaining what I was trying to do, and attaching the Mandler ad. Might this be his father? His reply came a minute after nine o'clock in the morning in Britain.

'It is indeed my father,' he wrote, expressing some astonishment that he, as a historian who spent much of his time searching through newspaper databases, had not come across it before. Peter explained that, in his father's case, the ad had not ultimately provided the means of escape. George Mandler was sponsored instead by a boarding school and then by a Jewish family in London, but in order to get there, he went through a 'hair-raising' trip alone through Germany.

George had written a memoir about it all, first published in 2001, suitably called *Interesting Times*. Peter sent me a copy, which arrived a week or so later. It was a wonderful read, full of wit and acute introspection. Most importantly from my point of view, it was a detailed telling of a parallel story to my father's.

George Mandler had spent his childhood about a kilometre from Robert Borger, on the other side of Vienna's 3rd District, near the Danube Canal. He grew up playing *Doppelspitzer* (two-touch football) in the local park, where you could buy a classic Viennese pudding on the street, a cone of chestnut puree, *Kastanienreis*, topped with whipped cream. It was something I recognised as being a taste of my own youth: we would have it at home on special occasions.

The young George Mandler would cheer on the Austrian skaters at international competitions at the city's ice ring, and in the summer he played in the meadows of the Prater, site of the giant Ferris wheel made famous in *The Third Man*, my favourite film, set against the backdrop of ravaged, post-war Vienna.

George's father, Richard, was originally from Slovakia, and had served the empire in the First World War in a signals unit on the Italian front. Once he arrived in Vienna, he worked his way up in the leather trade, until he became a partner with a wholesale leather company that did business all around Europe. The woman he married, Hedwig, was from a prosperous Viennese family of industrialists, and young George grew up in a comfortable milieu. The family employed a maid and a governess, and even a chauffeur when the firm acquired its first car. Summer holidays were spent at Laurana on the Italian Adriatic, now Lovran in Croatia.

There was a certain religious tension at home. Richard was an observant Jew, putting on tefillin for morning prayers and attending synagogue regularly. Hedwig was raised as an agnostic Zionist. Whenever George fell ill, Hedwig would smuggle ham sandwiches into the house for him, as a forbidden treat to raise his morale.

Hedwig's secular world view ultimately triumphed. Facing a lung operation in 1940, George swore he would get through it without divine intervention, and when he did indeed survive unscathed, he took it as a sign he did not need God.

George may have left God behind, but not Vienna. In later life, he went back to visit the streets of his district, the familiar buildings and places, taking trains through the countryside. He liked the sing-song sound of Viennese German and would go out of his way to seek out Viennese food, *echtes Wienerschnitzel* (authentic Viennese schnitzel), *Leberknödelsuppe* (liver dumpling soup), *Mohnstrudel* (poppy seed 'strudel') and *Indianerkrapfen* (a chocolate, whipped-cream confection).

That hankering after all things Viennese reminded me of our Omi. The last words of the Passover Seder are 'next year in Jerusalem', but for Omi and many others, Vienna was Jerusalem, the source of eternal longing, but at the same time the scene of heartbreak and unfathomable tragedy.

Central Vienna in the 1930s.

George Mandler grew up in Vienna without feeling any particular sense of threat. Antisemitism was a fact of life in pre-Anschluss Vienna, a background buzz. George recalled the 'Viennese experience of the occasional spitting of the label *Jude* as an epithet', but apart from that, he said he could remember 'no major anti-Semitic disturbance' in the four years between 1934 and 1938.

There were four Jewish boys in his class at school, who did not know each other particularly well before the Anschluss, and felt no need to stick together. Everyone knew who the Nazis were among the pupils and staff, but the party was officially banned. Its members kept their heads down and their activities secret, making it easier to forget they were there. They wore their small round swastika badges on the inside of their lapels, out of sight.

George recalled ruefully: 'We lived relatively unharried, happy lives, considered ourselves good Austrians, and, for most of the time, were quite unprepared for what was to come.'

I knew next to nothing about my dad's early years in Vienna, but George Mandler provided the recollections of a boy of similar age, growing up in the same district and going to the same school. His memoir did not just fill factual gaps. I had no idea how my father felt about what happened to him. George reflected at length on his feelings at the time and how the experience shaped him. Who knows if their reactions were the same, but they grew up to be similar in some ways, both psychologists with leftist politics. It seemed reasonable to see some of my dad in George.

Most of all, it gave me something to hang my imagination on. I could picture Bobby in the line behind George for chestnuts and cream near the Danube Canal, and going to school amid the invisible but growing menace of the Austrian Nazis.

Like Richard Mandler, George's father, our grandfather Leo had fought for the Austro-Hungarian empire in the First World War, though he was on the eastern front, in what is now western Ukraine, where he was the radio operator for an artillery regiment.

After the war, Leo had found himself a job as an accounts clerk in the Allgemeine Depositenbank, a financial establishment with a grand headquarters in Vienna's 1st District and branches around the empire. But he chose a bad time to be a bank worker. The new Austrian republic was trying to run an imperial-sized civil service with a severely shrunken tax base and bridged the gap by printing money. The result was hyper-inflation and a worthless currency, the short-lived krone, that at the peak of 1922 and 1923 was carted around Vienna in wheelbarrows. One of the oddities among Leo's relics was an envelope stuffed with krone, and the peculiar improvised currencies, *Notgeld*, issued by provincial banks and even small firms to keep the local economy running when the state financial system imploded.

The Allgemeine Depositenbank stumbled on for a couple of years but collapsed in 1925 after an unsuccessful attempt to speculate against the French franc. Forty thousand depositors forfeited their savings and one and a half thousand employees lost their jobs, including Leo. The bank wrote him a general recommendation letter acknowledging that he had been 'a very hard-working, diligent, and valuable clerk, who distinguished himself by his great sense of duty and his proficiency'.

Two years after marrying Erna, Leo was unemployed, and the couple depended on social housing provided by socialist-run Red Vienna. My father's first home was in one of these brand new 'workers' palaces', a solid complex of brick and concrete on St Nikolaus Platz in the 3rd District, which declared in proud Art Deco font that it was 'built by the Vienna municipality with funds from the housing tax'. The words, half a metre high, are still there, and despite the tarnish of the intervening decades and the odd bit of graffiti, they still exude the optimism of the age, that a modern state would be built in which everyone would have the same rudimentary dignity: a home, basic healthcare and an eight-hour working day.

It was Leo's mother, Hermine, who saved the family from penury after Leo lost his job and the country sank into economic crisis in 1931. Both she and Johann ran separate junk shops in the 3rd District that survived the financial crash. But it was Hermine who diversified into selling radios, just as they were becoming affordable.

She handed the shop over to Leo in 1930 when she retired, and he named it Radio Borger. Within five years, Leo and Erna were able to move from social housing into their own private apartment on Hintzerstrasse, around the corner from the shop. It was a proper Viennese flat, quite small, but in an opulent setting. There was a grand hall with red and yellow floor tiles, white marble panels, and a high ceiling, which led through a magnificent wood and glass door to a courtyard garden. Turning right from the hall up some stone steps led to a landing, with a black glass panel in which doorbells were set, with the apartment number inscribed above in gold. You would then climb up a curved stone staircase with a wrought-iron balustrade depicting intertwined plants.

The contrast to the utilitarian box of the municipal flat on St Nikolaus Platz could not have been more complete, and it

Radio Borger, the family shop selling radios and musical instruments on Vienna's Landstrasse Haupstrasse, 1933.

must have seemed like the Schönbrunn Palace itself to my father, who was eight at the time. There was a park around the corner and the primary school was within walking distance. After school he would have gone to Radio Borger and sat behind the counter, or visited his grandparents at the second-hand shop just around the corner.

You can tell from the photographs of the time that this was a short-lived but wondrous period. There are many shots of Leo standing in the doorway of the shop, first identified by a banner proclaiming it to be Radio Borger, and then a proper sign, with the letters standing proud over the street. They must have thought it was the start of a family business that would stand for generations.

The family bought a summer cabin in the woods at Kaltenleutgeben, twenty kilometres south-west of Vienna. A photograph shows my father, beaming, looking over his parents' shoulders on a sunny day in the countryside. Others show weekends at the spa town of Baden, larking about in swimsuits, and one of a crowd rolling a giant ball. All these old photographs are tinged with doom, the knowledge that these commonplace joys were about to be obliterated.

Austrian democracy died in 1933, five years before the Nazis rolled into Vienna, collapsing in the manner of a comic operetta. A Socialist deputy had to go to the toilet during a critical vote and asked a fellow Socialist to vote on his behalf. The government was defeated by that one vote, and a row blew up about the right of the absent Socialist to cast his vote by proxy. It led to the resignation of the President of the Parliament, and then his deputies. The session was adjourned and the Christian Social leader, Chancellor Engelbert Dollfuss, seized the opportunity to shut down parliament.

Politics was increasingly fought out on the streets between a right-wing militia, the *Heimwehr*, and the armed wing of the Social Democrats, the *Schutzbund*. In February 1934, the street conflict escalated into a full civil war, in which Dollfuss deployed the army in support of the *Heimwehr*, pointing their cannon at the socialist stronghold, the Karl-Marx-Hof public housing estate. The *Schutzbund* was crushed.

I grew up familiar with Dollfuss's face from Leo's stamp collection: round and cherubic with hopeful eyes and a Hitler-style truncated square moustache. He wanted to project strongman bravura like Hitler and Benito Mussolini but he was too soft-spoken and tiny, less than five feet tall. The prohibition of jokes about his height under the dictatorship did not stop him being called the 'pocket chancellor', or wags in cafes on the Ring ordering a 'Dollfuss' when they only wanted a demi-tasse of coffee.

The Socialists had offered to find common cause with him and join forces against the Nazis, but he crushed them instead, and in so doing he ensured his own demise and the death of his nation by misadventure.

Dollfuss thought that Austro-fascism, run by his Fatherland Front, and under the protection of Mussolini to the south, could exist independently of the Nazi regime to the north. In making that mistake, he was supported by the Catholic hier-archy and big business, who were so disoriented by their terror of Social Democracy and its egalitarian message that they believed the Nazis to be the lesser evil, one that could be controlled.

Five months after the civil war, Dollfuss was murdered by a group of Austrian Nazis who called themselves *SS Standarte 89* and took direct orders from Hitler. They broke into the chan-cellery in an attempted *coup d'état*, and shot Dollfuss twice. As he lay bleeding to death he begged for a priest to attend him, but his killers just watched him die.

It was Hitler's first attempt to take over another country and the putsch fell short. Power passed to a minister in Dollfuss's Fatherland Front government, Kurt Schuschnigg, and Austro-fascism lived on for another few years, while Hitler bided his time. Leo's party, the Social Democrats, was banned, but the family business prospered. Vienna's Jews were not targeted by the state. They thought they could weather the storm, and that the Nazis would be held at bay. There were just fewer than 200,000 Jews in Austria in 1934, ninety per cent of them in Vienna. Despite Hitler's rise to power in Germany and his clear, frequently stated intention to absorb the country of his birth into a greater Germany, very few took the opportunity to leave. In fact, the community grew. Only 1,739 Jews emigrated in the years leading up to the Anschluss, but three times as many Jewish immigrants arrived in the city.

Viennese Jews felt protected, convinced that their presumed covenant with the long-gone emperor Franz Joseph, consummated by their service in the First World War, would extend into the indefinite future. It was a mass delusion, a collective act of denial.

Throughout the winter of 1937, Hitler tightened the garrote around the neck of the Schuschnigg government. By the end of the year, Nazi mobs were on the streets, ignoring the ban on the party and showing their numbers, confident their time was about to come.

On 12 February 1938, the Austrian chancellor visited Hitler in his mountain retreat outside Berchtesgaden in the Bavarian Alps. He thought he had been invited to a one-on-one meeting, but he arrived to find the Führer flanked by his top generals, threatening Austria with imminent invasion if Schuschnigg did not bow to German demands to legalise the Austrian Nazi Party and hand the interior ministry to its leader, Arthur Seyss-Inquart.

My dad told me next to nothing about his memories of those days with a single exception that I can remember. I had chosen Austria in 1938 as a history project at school, no doubt hoping he would be able to help. He made little contribution but for a memory that amused him. Among his friends, Seyss-Inquart was known as 'Scheisse-im-Quadrat' (Shit-Squared). It had been funny until March 1938, and then it was no longer a joke.

The Schuschnigg government publicly hailed the Berchtesgaden accord as a victory in which Hitler had guaranteed Austrian independence. Very few ordinary Austrians believed that.

Among the relics of his former life our grandfather Leo kept in his Shrewsbury bungalow was a small stack of 78 rpm records, heavy and brittle shellac discs in mustard-coloured sleeves. There was orchestral music by Beethoven and Mozart and Johann Strauss, but mixed in with them were recordings of political speeches. I was surprised to find one by Josef Goebbels among them, and put it on his turntable for the chilling experience of hearing his rasping voice, expounding some racial theory with blithe certainty.

Leo had also preserved Schuschnigg's final address to the nation, delivered after the chancellor's hasty surrender, the cancellation of his plebiscite and his order to the Austrian army to stand down as the Germans marched in. This was the Chancellor's formal capitulation on 11 March 1938, crackly and despairing, just as it must have sounded on the wireless sets at Radio Borger on Landstrasse Haupstrasse the day it was delivered.

'We decided to order the troops to offer no serious – to offer no resistance,' he said, correcting himself mid-sentence for the sake of honesty.

'And so, in this hour, I take leave of the Austrian people with a word of farewell uttered from the bottom of my heart: God protect Austria!' *Gott schütze Österreich!*

Within seconds, Austrian Nazis were piling into the Vienna streets, waving swastika flags and assaulting any Jews they could find, a coiled spring of hatred unleashed on the city.

'*Ein Volk! Ein Reich! Ein Führer!*' was the chant – one people, one realm, one leader. From then on, there would be no further need for variety, choice or doubt. The Anschluss was signed into Austrian law by Shit-Squared.

In the early hours of 12 March, German troops crossed the border and were greeted by ecstatic Austrians as the sun came up. Hitler arrived at his birthplace, Braunau am Inn, and made his way from there, through Linz, to Vienna. He was feted all the way.

One of the questions I wished I had asked my dad was what it was like to be a boy in Vienna when the Nazis marched in, and in his memoir George Mandler gives his own account. On 13 March 1938, he was thirteen years old and bedridden with pneumonia and pleurisy. Looking up from his bedroom window, he could see German planes swarming over the city. From that moment on, his every thought and action would be 'under a cloud of anxiety and foreboding'.

By the time George returned to his school, everything had changed. The Nazis who had skulked in secret for the previous four years were now swaggering along the corridors, swastika badges on their outer lapels, with nothing to hide any more. They were the new masters.

The shock of having his classmates turn on him would haunt George Mandler for decades. The Anschluss, he realised, had 'legitimised latent beliefs' which they had quietly held all along. Whenever he returned to Vienna in adult life, the sense of dread, of having to look over his shoulder, would invariably return. My father's solution was to go back as little as possible, but I believe that fear, of being spurned and disowned overnight by those he counted as friends just the day before, never left him. He would never again feel totally secure.

At George's school, the four Jews in the class were initially allowed to come to lessons, albeit consigned to the very back of the class. A few weeks later, they were moved to a different school, in the same district but in a rougher area further from home, by the canal. My dad would have been sent there too. Jews from all over the area were sent to the same place. He never talked about the experience of being kicked out.

At this new school, George remembered handing in an essay on Schiller's play *Wilhelm Tell*, and getting a grade 2 for it (a B). The teacher took him aside and told him it was excellent, but it was no longer permitted to give Jewish students top grades for German literature.

Walking the streets as a Jew immediately became dangerous. Bands of Hitler Youth and *Sturmabteilung* (SA Brownshirts) were looking for Jews to beat up. My dad was identified as a Jew by his former classmates and chased through the streets. When the Brownshirts caught the ten-year-old boy they took him to the nearest synagogue at Untere Viaduktgasse and barricaded him in for several hours, while his distraught parents searched the streets for him.

A few months later he watched as his grandmother Hermine's apartment on Hörlgasse in the 9th District was ransacked and her piano was thrown out of a window to shatter on the street below.

Adult Jews were told to report to the police or were just picked up on the street and forced to scrub pavements and walls to remove the pro-Schuschnigg graffiti that proliferated in the run-up to the Anschluss. It was by design a near-impossible task. The ousted chancellor's supporters had written their slogans and painted his symbol, the *Kruckenkreuz*, a cross with crossbars at the four ends, in heavy white oil paint, and the city's Jews were given tools for the job as small as toothbrushes and had buckets of lye deliberately emptied over them, searing their skin.

The SA came to Hintzerstrasse to take Leo Borger to the Landstrasse police station, where he was put to work on the pavement with other Jews, surrounded by his jeering neighbours, who had greeted him politely in the street or in the shop just a few days before. When the Jews were down on their knees they were often assaulted by those who might not have had the courage to confront them when they were standing up. The hatred that had festered for so many years broke out across Vienna like a rash under the weak spring sunshine.

In the months following the Anschluss, more and more Viennese Jewish men disappeared from Vienna, arrested and deported to Dachau, the Nazis' first concentration camp. Dachau was established in Bavaria soon after the Nazis took power in Germany, and it was initially intended for political opponents, but after the Anschluss it evolved into a jail for Austrian dissidents and Jews.

Among those rounded up in Vienna, the question of who was sent home and who was sent to Dachau seemed to be determined at random. In one police station, Jewish detainees were assigned numbers from one to three. If you were assigned a one, you were sent home, the twos would be made to do forced labour in Vienna, cleaning floors and toilets. If you were a three, you went to Dachau and might never return. For some families, the first sign of a father or brother or son being incarcerated was a telegram inviting them to come to Dachau to pick up their ashes.

Concerned he would be next, our grandpa Leo took the whole family into hiding. They spent five days and nights in the cellar of a friend's house. Ultimately, however, Leo had to risk returning to the surface and the prospect of being sent to Dachau if he was to find any way out of Vienna for his family. They could not hide forever.

3

Gertrude and Eichmann's Pianos

T HE ANSCHLUSS WAS the original catastrophe in the lives of the children in the *Manchester Guardian* advertisements, destroying everything they had known until that point. It was a torrent that separated them from their families, and carried them off into the unknown, where they would have to find their way alone.

Sending sons and daughters away to strangers in a foreign country was a last resort. A parent's instinct in times of danger is to hold their children close. But by June 1938, when the first adverts appeared, the realisation was starting to spread that Nazi rule would only get worse. Parents would ultimately be powerless to protect their families.

The idea of putting ads in the *Manchester Guardian* was promoted by Vienna's Jewish Community organisation (IKG), which had set up an office dedicated to giving the city's Jews all the tools they needed to leave. It was the condition on which the organisation was allowed to continue functioning after its initial closure at the Anschluss. It could provide leadership for its people as long as it led them out of the Reich, and in that way, the IKG was forced to be an accomplice in the community's own erasure. Its leaders felt they had no choice. To refuse would have meant that Vienna's Jews would not have been able to influence when and where they went, and many more would have gone to Dachau and the other camps.

One of the options suggested by the IKG was a Viennese

company, Oesterreichische Anzeigen-Gesellschaft, which arranged the placement of ads in foreign papers for a fee. The IKG would also have steered emigrants towards the *Manchester Guardian*. Similar ads were placed in *The Times* and *Telegraph*, but the *Manchester Guardian* was seen as more sympathetic. The city was home to the biggest UK Jewish community outside London, with ties to Vienna through the textile trade, whilst the *Guardian* had focused more than the rest of the British press on the plight of Jews under Nazi rule, and their hardships in the UK. The relationship explains why almost all the children's ads in the *Manchester Guardian* were from Vienna.

The IKG also trusted the paper's correspondent, who was a fellow Central European Jew. Marcel 'Mike' Fodor was a Hungarian who had learnt his English working as an engineer for an iron and steel company in Scunthorpe. He returned to Budapest as a correspondent for the *Manchester Guardian* in 1919, and four years later the paper's editor, C. P. Scott, appointed him correspondent for Austria and the Balkans.

I did more or less the same job some seventy-five years later, though I was never based in the old imperial capital. I covered Eastern Europe from Warsaw, and then at the beginning of 1995 moved to Zagreb and Sarajevo, entirely oblivious to the fact that I was treading the path of such an interesting and illustrious predecessor.

By the 1930s, Fodor was the unquestioned doyen of the foreign press in Vienna. American and British journalists would gather in the Café Louvre and take notes as he briefed them on the events of the day. Among those sitting around the table at one time or another were Dorothy Thompson of the *New York Herald Tribune*, the first American journalist to have been expelled from Nazi Germany; her husband, the Nobel Prize-winning author, Sinclair Lewis; and an array of other greats of inter-war journalism: CBS's William Shirer, just hired by Edward Murrow, John Gunther and the future

US senator J. William Fulbright, who had travelled around the region with Fodor in the late 1920s and concluded that he 'seemed to know more than all of the other correspondents put together'.

Mike Fodor and his circle would typically gather in the late morning for a second breakfast and coffee, and skim through the world's press, delivered to the Louvre daily. Fodor would return to his apartment in the old city at lunchtime to finish his article, if he was writing that day, dictating it to Manchester by phone at 4 p.m.

He carefully charted the spread of the Nazis' underground movement in the run-up to the Anschluss, and followed Chancellor Schuschnigg around the country in his last days in office as he sought to appease the Nazis and fend off Hitler's invasion. When that inevitably failed and the German Wehrmacht rolled over the border, Fodor saw Austria offer itself up willingly. Two hundred thousand people came out on Heldenplatz, Vienna's Heroes' Square, to hear the Führer rejoice in the conquest of his homeland.

'The crowd is fickle, and if yesterday it was cheering others, today people cheered themselves hoarse when they witnessed Hitler's triumphal entry,' Fodor wrote.

On 1 April, he described the brutal humiliation of Viennese Jews, forced down on their knees to scrub streets and public toilets. He observed how wealthier members of the community performed the work 'in top-hats and morning coats with all their decorations on' as a final defiant stab at dignity.

Fodor was forced to flee soon after the Anschluss. Not only was he Jewish, he was also on a Gestapo wanted list ever since he had written about Hitler's rustic roots and humble Austrian relatives after the Nazis' rise to power in Germany.

The *Guardian*'s editor, William Crozier, urged Fodor not to delay his escape, telling his correspondent after he had reached safety: 'You might have been all right but if not we might have been able, with the best will in the world, to do very little for you.'

Fodor wrote back when he reached Prague, informing Crozier that the US chargé d'affaires, a personal friend, had sent his military attaché to escort him as far as the Czechoslovak border.

'I had to leave all my furniture, carpets, pictures and silver in Vienna,' he wrote. 'I hope that I will be able to get them out one day.' He would not return before the end of the war.

In a valedictory article, Fodor wrote: 'Though the writer has seen repeated Terrors in his two decades covering Central Europe, the five days that shook Vienna will remain among the most remarkable of his experiences in dangerous times.'

After Bobby Borger was chased through the streets by the Brownshirts, Leo was prepared to try anything to get him out of Vienna. His *Manchester Guardian* appeal seeking a kind person to 'educate my intelligent Boy, aged 11, Viennese of good family' was placed on 3 August 1938, at the start of a wave of such pleas over the following few months. Moving promptly probably made all the difference as it caught the eye of those Britons, like Nans and Reg Bingley in Caernarfon, who were already looking for ways to help Nazi victims. The Bingleys had taken in a German Jewish teacher for the summer holidays, and were eager to do more.

The two families began corresponding. Nans sent postcards showing off the Welsh coastline and mountains, and Omi responded with a picture of her and Bobby, taken in woodland. They are both smiling at the camera, she in a jaunty and fashionable hat, woollen jacket and leather gloves; he in a V-neck jumper and a dark coat draped over his shoulders. The photograph was a year old by the time Omi sent it and she apologised on the back in pencilled German for its crumpled appearance.

Nans and Reg quickly went to work on the formalities

necessary to get Bobby a visa, taking the train to London and sitting on the steps of the Home Office to put pressure on the bureaucracy and cut out postal delays. Leo meanwhile had stashed away the means to buy train and ferry tickets for his son, concealing some gems in the heel of his shoes after the Anschluss, anticipating rightly that the Nazis would confiscate all the Jewish property they could find.

In George Mandler's case, tutors were hired to teach him English and electrical installation, with the intention that when he reached safety in the US or Britain, he would have the wherewithal to earn a living. He was sent out at four o'clock in the morning to join the swelling queues outside embassies and consulate buildings for the required registration forms.

At the same time, the family tried to find sponsors in America and Britain. George copied out the names and addresses of all the Mandlers in the New York telephone directory, about a dozen of them, and looked through trade registers.

There were also a series of lines to join outside government offices, to get the forms to fill in for financial statements and certificates of good conduct from the police. On his way to these errands, Mandler would stick Communist Party leaflets under doors. He became an activist out of a sense of 'something had to be done', that one could not just look on as the Nazis took over the country.

An American sponsor called David Eisenrath did eventually come forward, but because of the quota system, a US visa did not come through until 1940.

So the family put the advert in the *Manchester Guardian*, looking for an English family to be kind enough to take George and 'procure him employment', while at the same time his father Richard contacted business associates in Amsterdam, to find a private school willing to accept him and write a letter of sponsorship.

The Dutch contacts came through with a result before any

suitable reply came from the *Guardian* ad. A school on the English south coast, St Mary's Lodge, offered George a place. His mother, Hedwig, promptly went shopping in Vienna to buy all the items on the school's long list of clothing requirements, including cricket whites.

Identifying George and finding his book owed a lot to luck, opening a window on the circumstances of our own father's escape from Vienna, and it gave me misplaced confidence in how easy it would be to find the other children.

But George turned out to be an anomaly. Most of the other names in the *Manchester Guardian* ads were fairly common, making it much harder to find an individual in the multitude of refugees who fled Nazi Vienna in 1938 and 1939.

While casting around online for clues, I came across the website JewishGen.org, a free genealogy organisation run by a thousand volunteers. It warned sternly on its home page: 'We can't live in the past, and we can't reclaim it.' However, the website added, on a more positive note: 'we can allow the memories of the past to shape us, to shape our sense of identity, and to shape what we will be transmitting to future generations.' It sounded about right, as a description of at least some of my own motives in pursuing the project – motives I had not fully articulated even to myself.

JewishGen had uploaded the basic facts of Jewish life in pre-Anschluss Vienna as recorded by the IKG: birth, marriage, deportation and death. Looking up births under a certain name from the right year, and then cross-referencing to the age of the child I was looking for, would normally produce a handful of possibilities. The more unusual the family name, the better the chances of finding the child.

I had hopes of tracing a Jewish merchant whose name appeared to be Mr A. Batacha. His *Guardian* advert on 29 July 'begs Jewish family in Great Britain, to receive his only daughter, aged 14, into their house'. This daughter was 'well mannered, able to help in any household work, speaks German, French and a little English', the ad said, noting that she also played the piano.

However, there was no such name in the Vienna Jewish community records, or anywhere else in the region for that matter. I took another look at the ad as it appeared in the online archive, hoping it would offer a solution. All the 'a's in the family name were reproduced as inky splodges, all pretty much the same shape. But if one squinted it was possible to read the second one as really an 's'.

When I fed the name Batscha back into JewishGen, there were several results, and one of them was an Adolf Batscha, whose wife was Vally Östreicher. They had a daughter born in 1924. Her name was Gertrude Edith. It had to be her. The riddle unlocked to reveal a fourteen-year-old girl with a name and date of birth that I could take to other genealogy sites.

On Findmypast, there was a single record. Gertrude E. Batscha was listed in Britain's 1948 electoral register as living just south of London in Reigate, Surrey. In other words, she had survived and the elation at that survival reached me as a distant echo through the decades.

There were no other details, however, and certainly no sign of what Gertrude had done next. I tried a few other sites to which I had subscribed. Only after that did I remember to do the simple thing. I googled Gertrude Batscha, and was taken to a page called the Ghetto Fighters House Archives and the collection of 'Yehudith – Gertrude Segal (née Batscha), born in Wien (Vienna), 1924', complete with pictures of letters, a child's exercise book and drawings.

Her children Danny Segal and Ruthie Elkana had donated the collection. An Israeli colleague helped me find Ruthie's phone number in a northern rural community, Moshav Nahalal, famous for being where Moshe Dayan grew up. On 1 March 2021, I called her.

I was nervous and spoke too fast about how Ruthie and I were connected through our parents, Vienna and the *Guardian*. She confirmed that she was indeed Gertrude Batscha's daughter and Danny Segal Gertrude's son, and suggested I write it all down in an email.

I sent a note off right away and within a couple of hours heard back from Danny, a professor of molecular microbiology and biotechnology. He thanked me for the 'exciting message'.

'As with many families with Holocaust heritage, our parents hardly told us, when we were kids, about their past,' he wrote. A few days later, we were talking on Zoom and Ruthie and Danny's faces appeared in separate little boxes. They had already known about the ad, as Danny's daughter had found it in 2014.

'It was really so exciting to find it. It's heartbreaking,' Ruthie said.

After Danny married in 1979, Gertrude, who had become Yehudith, had broken her silence about the past on the prompting of her new daughter-in-law, and wrote a memoir for the family, pointedly entitled 'Because You Wanted To Know'. The family had it made into a booklet in 2002, the year before Yehudith died of cancer. They sent it to me by email. It was a rougher production than George Mandler's, as it was never made for public consumption. She had sat down at her kitchen table each morning for almost a year to put down everything she could remember.

'I feel as though half of me is fighting the other half by trying to forget, rather than remember, and I realise that is probably what I have been doing all my life,' she said. She dedicated it to her 'parents' grandchildren who never had the chance to know each other'. What followed was an intimate account of the destruction of a family. The Batschas had lived in Vienna's 5th District, Margareten, near the Belvedere Palace, on the entire second floor of an apartment building of brick and ornate mouldings. Her father Adolf ran a wholesale grocery business. Her mother Walburga (Vally) had been forced by her parents to break off her engagement to the love of her life, an opera singer, to marry this stocky man, eleven years her senior, with a glass eye which was a different size from his real one.

Adolf worshipped Vally, and Vally learned to accept Adolf. They both adored Gerti, their only child. Every winter Sunday she would go ice-skating with her father, and then listen to the waltzes being played in the bandstand. On spring and summer weekends, the extended family would take a tram up to the Vienna Woods for a walk and a picnic.

Adolf, Gertrude and Vally Batscha, 1939.

In her memoir, Yehudith marvelled at this halcyon childhood, and recounted how it all came to an end. In late January 1938, she was taken to the top of their apartment building to see the aurora borealis, great arches of crimson and green. A mighty magnetic storm swept across the world on 25 January, putting on luminous displays as far south as Sicily and southern California. Catholics called it the Fatima storm, claiming that it fulfilled the prophecy of an apparition of the Virgin Mary to three young Portuguese shepherds. For much of Vienna it was seen as a good omen and crowds gathered in the city to celebrate. Gerti's family and friends stood and watched from their apartment block roof and shook their heads, seeing the sign in the sky as a harbinger of tragedy. They did not have to wait long to be proved right.

Less than two months later, on the eve of the Nazi takeover, Gerti's mother came to collect her from her shorthand class and walked her home, 'hugging the walls of the houses', and there she sat her daughter down to explain what was happening. Gerti asked whether it was a good or bad thing, and her mother told her it was a very bad thing indeed for the Jews.

That evening the family listened to Schuschnigg's address on the family radio, and as he bade his final farewell, their world changed in an instant. A wave of noise pummelled its way through the streets.

'The roar became nearer and louder; a certain rhythm could be perceived and very soon we could clearly hear the dreadful Nazi slogan: "Sieg Heil",' Gerti wrote.

'The rhythm of this slogan is so penetrating to one's senses, that it carries with it its believers and excites them to hysterical enthusiasm, drugging them with the rhythmic chant. On the other hand, it has remained as an antibody in the blood of those who suffered from it, never to be eradicated.'

In later life Yehudith Segal would experience an involuntary reaction in crowds whenever they began chanting, no matter what the message. With the hypnotic rhythm of people giving up their individual will to the throng, she wrote, 'the heart pumps faster, the skin becomes prickly, a weight settles on the chest'.

On the night of the Anschluss, the chanting went on through the early hours, and Gerti could not block it out even with all the windows shut, curtains drawn and bedclothes over her ears. Within a few days, she had to move to a school that was all Jewish, apart from some gentile anti-Nazi teachers, who were later victimised for their work. When the term ended in June, she left and did not return. For the time being, at the age of thirteen, her education was at an end.

That summer, she and her best friend Evi wandered the streets, and at one point witnessed a column of troops marching in front of the opera house, led by field marshal Hermann Göring, standing up in his car in a white uniform, extravagantly adorned with medals, the embodiment of buffoonery and oppression.

Life for the Batschas changed every day, each time for the worse. Their live-in maid had to make an abrupt departure, in line with the Nuremberg laws forbidding any Aryan from living in a Jewish household. Adolf Batscha brought another family into the apartment in an effort to pre-empt expulsion or forced sharing of their living space. These were family friends from Poland, the Katzes, who were focused on escape. Being *Ostjuden*, eastern Jews, they 'knew what persecution meant, and also destitution', fearing the former more than the latter.

'Their skins first,' Yehudith wrote. 'Their money, they reckoned, could be earned again.'

Her father lacked that clarity. Adolf Batscha had built up his wholesale grocery business into a significant concern, employing twenty people. He saw it as his life, and so held on to it too long. Adolf had known poverty, had no desire to revisit it, and at the age of fifty, he believed he did not have it in him to amass another fortune. His wife Vally, by contrast, had never been in need or discomfort as a child, and was more willing to start again somewhere else, as long as it was in Europe and therefore close to her family in Czechoslovakia.

The word of the day among Viennese Jewish families was *Umschulung*, retraining. Most adults and the elder teens scrambled to learn skills that could be marketable abroad in anticipation of the day they would have to take flight. Our grandpa Leo learned the rudiments of hairdressing, buying scissors and a set of clippers, which he would one day, decades later, use to cut my hair. Our grandmother Omi took a cookery course like many other Viennese women, preparing for a life 'below stairs' in a British home. In the Batschas' spacious apartment, one of the Katz girls set up a workshop for making leather gloves.

Gerti's mother was ready to learn the skills necessary to be a maid. She could speak English and knew how to keep house. Adolf, however, was resistant. He had no grasp of the language and had long forgotten how to do basic household chores for himself, let alone for others. He had finally resigned himself to losing control of his business, under the Aryanisation laws, but he clung to the hope that he could somehow save his fortune. So he put off thinking about his own departure.

The grocery company had supplied Adolf with a daily sense of purpose which he had never previously had to think about. Without it, he buckled and fell into despair. Gerti came across him one day kneeling in front of a large oil painting of his late adored mother, weeping uncontrollably and begging her for help. The sight of her would-be protector crushed by the weight of their imploding world terrified the fourteen-year-old girl.

After Adolf's breakdown, Vally Batscha started taking the tap head for the apartment's gas pipe and putting it in her handbag whenever she left the flat, depriving her distraught husband of at least one route to ending his own life.

Vienna had long been the suicide capital of Europe. After the Anschluss, it became an epidemic. Five hundred suicides were reported in the Jewish community in the first two months alone, and those were just the official figures. The true toll was in the thousands. Suicide came to be seen as 'a perfectly normal and natural incident by every Jewish household', *The*

Times's Central Europe Correspondent, George Gedye, recalled. 'It is quite impossible to convey to anyone outside Austria how matter-of-fact a way the Jews of Austria today refer to this way out of their agony,' he wrote in his memoir of the era, *Fallen Bastions*. His Jewish friends talked about their plans to end their lives 'with no more emotion than they had formerly talked of making an hour's journey by train'.

Leo however was preoccupied with survival. On 22 March, he went to the war veterans' association for protection, hoping his military service for the old Austria would have some residual value in the strange, ruthless German province it had become.

He came away with a handwritten note on a small piece of exercise book paper saying: 'According to the presented confirmation of release from military service, Leo Borger was a front-line soldier and is to be treated as such. Following the directive of the Gauleiter, the sign "Jewish shop" can be removed from the business.'

It was one of the pieces of paper in the box I inherited from Leo. It was a flimsy document, and its minimal protective value was further undermined by the fact that it was scrawled in haste, and lacked an all-important swastika stamp.

Going home with that scrap of paper, feeling its worthlessness between his fingers, Leo must have relinquished the last stubborn hope that the Borgers' decades of assimilation were going to save his family.

One day in April 2021, a large and heavy parcel arrived on my doorstep in the Washington suburbs. The stamp announced it as coming from Vienna, and inside was a two-kilo sheaf of papers from the Austrian State Archive, the result of an email inquiry I had sent a few months earlier, asking for anything in the records connected to Leo Borger.

My first excited thought was that so much paper had to include answers to all sorts of questions I had about the

Borgers' life in Vienna. But an initial flick through the pile of photocopies quickly made clear that they would tell me an awful lot about just one thing: the 'Aryanisation' of Radio Borger.

The forced sale of Jewish property to 'Aryans' at nominal prices set by the state was an act of larceny on a mass scale, representing five per cent of all Nazi state revenues in 1938–9. But the theft was wrapped up in a thick layer of bogus legality and paperwork. The fossilised remains of that dense mass of lies was what landed on my doorstep with such a thump that spring day.

The top document was a form printed in *Fraktur* font also known as Broken Grotesque, with heavy black headlines and exclamation marks underlining the severe penalties of not filling it in correctly. It was a 'List of Jewish assets' as required by a decree of 26 April 1938.

Leo gave his name, his occupation, address and date of birth. The next line began *'Ich bin Jude'* – I am a Jew. He listed the radio shop and second-hand goods business but noted that the administrator overseeing Aryanisation had yet to assign a value to these two concerns.

Accompanying this form were dozens of typewritten letters from a succession of temporary administrators appointed to oversee the confiscation of Radio Borger. Some of them patiently explained to our bewildered grandfather why the shop's assets should be discounted: the loudspeakers were old, or the records were outdated, or the sheet music was by Jewish composers and therefore of zero value.

Another pretext was that the furniture in the second-hand shop had been bought for a song from the poor in foreclosure sales as a result of evictions during the Depression.

'We all know that was a situation exploited by the Jews,' the administrator declared. 'I can't see why Aryan buyers should pay higher prices than the Jews if they are going to benefit in any way from Aryanisation.'

There was a separate correspondence about five pianos belonging to Radio Borger that were to be sold on commission. The proceeds would be transferred to the Nazi state under a system which became known as the 'Vienna Model'. It was streamlined to expel Jews while efficiently fleecing them of their property, and was overseen by a rising SS *Untersturmführer* (second lieutenant) called Adolf Eichmann. They had become Eichmann's pianos.

Eichmann's success in ushering out at least 100,000 Jews from Vienna later won him a job in Berlin, running Jewish 'emigration' and ultimately mass deportation of Jews from the whole Reich to the death camps.

In further correspondence, Leo was simply referred to in the third person as *der Jude*, the Jew. The Aryan who was seeking to take over Radio Borger was a thirty-six-year-old electrician, Karl Krejcik, who repeatedly pointed in his letters to his loyalty to the Party back in the time when it was banned. Even in those dark days, he insisted, most of his customers had been Nazis, and he had supplied the Party's covert headquarters with radios, sold at discounted prices.

Krejcik had lost his electrician's job in 1932 in the economic crash and by 1938 he was leasing a tiny workshop in the 3rd District. 'Although I only have a very small area of ten square metres, with no shop window, I have been able to expand my clientele which is almost exclusively National Socialist,' he wrote in his submission. Since the '*Umbruch*', the upheaval, so Krejcik pointed out, he had supplied radios to the office of Vienna's Nazi-appointed Gauleiter, Joseph Bürckel, and a list of mid-level Party operatives.

His application revealed him to be resentful of his fate and fiercely loyal to the Party, just the sort of person who benefited from Aryanisation.

'As a full Aryan, it is absolutely necessary for me and my employees to move my business to a high street,' Krejcik insisted.

The first temporary administrator, a man called Joachim

Fasching, appears to have made a move to grab the business for himself, triggering a complaint from Krejcik's lawyer, and a threat to have him removed.

Krejcik was ultimately awarded Radio Borger and the second-hand shop for 6,000 Reichsmarks (equivalent to about £30,000 now), plus a 1,000 Reichsmark fee, payable to the state.

Unlike Leo, Adolf Batscha, Gerti's father, found a way around the whole bureaucracy of Aryanisation, making a side deal with a local grocer to buy his company for a steep discount. Management would pass to the grocer's son, whom Adolf Batscha would instruct in the secrets of the trade, and Adolf would in return receive a modest stipend, enough at least to pay the required taxes to the Reich.

In Leo's case, the state Aryanisation machine kept churning for months, and the deal had yet to be finalised when evening fell on 9 November, on a night when the lot of Vienna's Jews, already intolerable, was about to get immeasurably worse.

Two days earlier, a seventeen-year-old Jewish refugee from Hanover, Herschel Grynszpan, had talked his way into the German embassy in Paris, and shot a junior diplomat, Ernst vom Rath, declaring that he had done so in the name of all persecuted Jews. Vom Rath died on 9 November, which happened to be the fifteenth anniversary of the Nazis' failed putsch in Munich, so Hitler was in the Bavarian capital that night to commemorate the occasion with SA Brownshirt veterans when news of the shooting reached him. The Führer had a quiet conversation with his propaganda minister, Joseph Goebbels, after which Goebbels delivered an inflammatory homage to the fallen diplomat. 'Comrades, we cannot allow this attack by World Jewry to go unchallenged,' the propaganda chief told the crowd of senior Nazis, making clear that any reprisals would 'not be hindered'.

'In the afternoon the death of the German diplomat vom Rath is announced. That's good,' Goebbels wrote in his diary that day. 'I brief Hitler on the affair. He decides: allow the demonstrations to go on. Withdraw the police. The Jews should feel the people's fury. That's right. I issue appropriate instructions to the police and Party. Then I give a brief speech on the subject to the Party's leadership. Thunderous applause. Everyone dashed to the telephone. Now the people will act.'

A shockwave of destruction spread around the Reich, and the infamy of those events would be memorialised in one awful word, *Kristallnacht*, the Night of Broken Glass. In Vienna, the Brownshirts and Hitler Youth were rampant and unrestrained. All but one of the city's twenty-two synagogues were burned down and forty-two prayer houses were destroyed. Nearly two thousand Jews were forcibly evicted from their homes, 7,800 men were arrested and over four thousand Jewish-owned businesses were attacked.

Radio Borger, with its shop window on Landstrasse Haupstrasse, was an obvious target. The store was ransacked and looted. As it had not yet been transferred to Krejcik, the price was adjusted to take account of the damage. He only had to pay 5,000 Reichsmarks for the business when the transaction finally went through on 21 November, a seventeen per cent discount.

The Reich's Asset Transfer Office pointed out in a letter on 8 February 1939 that because of that devaluation, Leo's assets had fallen below the threshold for paying the 'atonement tax', imposed on Jews after *Kristallnacht* to pay for the damage done to their own property. The tax began at twenty per cent of all personal assets, and was later raised to twenty-five per cent.

Cruel absurdities were piled on top of absurd cruelties. The office changed its mind five months later, claiming that an accounting mistake had led to Leo's assets being underpriced and he was liable to pay the tax after all, but by then he had already fled and was in no position to 'atone'.

Gerti Batscha was fourteen at the time of *Kristallnacht* and could remember few details, just that 'all anti-Jewish measures were intensified, that everything unpleasant, bad, horrible, became more so, fear loomed larger, the trap became tighter.'

One side of the trap was diminishing means. For Jews, there were very few ways of earning income and much of their savings had been expropriated. On the other side was the tax burden on fleeing families, which increased steadily and sometimes exponentially.

Anyone seeking to leave the Reich had to pay a 'flight tax' amounting to a quarter of their property. The tax had been introduced in 1931 as a measure against capital flight, but the Nazis turned it into a means of profiting from the Jewish exodus. What money Jewish families had left after the tax was deducted had to be transferred to frozen accounts, from which money could only be withdrawn with punitive penalties. In June 1934, that penalty was twenty per cent. By September 1938, it was ninety per cent. Meanwhile, the cost of train and boat tickets was rising. The longer it took a Jew to escape from Vienna, the harder it was to leave.

Leo never even received full payment from Krejcik. On 22 November 1938 he wrote to the Asset Transfer Office, complaining that the anticipated bank deposit had not happened. 'I politely request the final Aryanisation of the business to be treated urgently,' Leo wrote. 'I hope to be able to travel abroad in the foreseeable future, for which purpose a larger amount would be needed.'

By then, my father and grandmother, Robert and Erna, had already fled. Leo was left behind, scrambling for a way out.

4

Means of Escape: Alice and
the Westbahnhof

WHICHEVER CORNER OF Vienna they had come from, and wherever they ended up, my father and all the other children from the *Manchester Guardian* ads passed through the same portal, the western railway station, the Westbahnhof.

Setting off from there in 1938 would have served as a reminder that the terminus was once the gateway to a great power. The Westbahnhof was a mid-nineteenth-century palace of modernity with a high gable roof of iron and glass stretching vertiginously above its five platforms, flanked by two towers. It had been where Western visitors were welcomed to an imperial capital, but in the wake of the Anschluss it was reduced to the gullet from which the wounded, subjugated rump of empire spat out its unwanted citizens.

The grand terminal is long gone, bombed beyond repair in 1945, and in its place is a concrete and glass box fronted by gleaming chrome signage. I walked up the steps to the main concourse to get an idea of the view, which would have been the last of Vienna for my father and the other refugee children.

The platforms these days have individual concrete shelters and the railway tracks are open to the sky. It feels more like a suburban station. With the late morning commuters weaving around me on a summer's day, I stood there for a while and looked west along the rails that opened a vista through the city to a green slice of the *Wienerwald*, the Vienna Woods, the beginning of the Alps.

Off the main hall downstairs, there is a bronze statue of a Jewish refugee boy sitting on his suitcase, a memorial to those forced to leave their families, by a Venezuelan artist, Flor Kent. The boy has a round, anxious face and a straight fringe, a loose jacket, shorts and one sock up, one down. He looks about eight, so three years younger than my dad was when he passed through here, but I recognised the suitcase immediately. Brown leather with brass clasps and reinforced corners, it was typical of the period. I still have the identical case my grandparents bought for my father on his trip to London.

The inscription on the grey stone plinth under the bronze boy dedicates the statue 'to the British people with deepest gratitude' for saving the lives of ten thousand children, Jews and non-Jews, who fled the Nazis in 1938 and 1939. At the bottom is a line that the Talmud and Koran have in common: 'Whoever saves a single human life is as if he had saved all of mankind.'

Westbahnhof station, 1930s Vienna.

I pictured the *Manchester Guardian* children in the old Westbahnhof, hauling their leather suitcases, worried over by parents struggling to keep grief and anxiety in check. Some of the children now had names and faces and scraps of biography while others, whom I had yet to track down, remained featureless.

Many could be followed through the archives as far as Britain, and often on transatlantic voyages to New York, but the trail would often peter out, because the refugees changed their names to something typically Anglo-Saxon, or married someone with such a name and faded into the crowds, or simply died leaving no children behind.

It was particularly frustrating that I could not initially work out what happened to the children advertised on the same day as my dad, siblings by fate you could say, related through this one detail of their lives. I let the ads from 3 August 1938 lie for a month or two and worked on others, and then came back to them in early January 2021 to try again.

The advert directly under my dad's was asking for an 'au pair' for a fourteen-year-old girl, described as 'well educated, Jewess, very fond of children, good sewing, household help'. It was signed simply Hess, with an address in the 10th District.

In my first sweep of the archives, for an article in the *Guardian*, I was discouraged by the sheer number of Hesses in the records and could find none who had a fourteen-year-old daughter in August 1938 when the advert was placed.

When I went back to look a second time, I cast my net a little wider, and realised I had overlooked something. Béla and Josefine Hess had a fifteen-year-old daughter, Alice, but she would still have been fourteen when they dictated the advert.

There was an Alice Hess with the same date of birth who surfaced in the British records. Her female enemy alien card from November 1939 gave an address in Salford and, even more helpfully, had been amended in blue fountain pen five years later with a new name. She married Richard Schon on 5 November 1944. The marriage register confirmed a wedding in Willesden, but then there was no further trace of the Schons. I could find no Schons in post-war British records that looked right, nor did they appear on passenger manifests for transatlantic liners, nor in the US records.

This was often the point at which the delicate chain broke, when refugees blended into the British scenery, but I worried away at the problem like jiggling a worn key in a lock, and finally something clicked. Schon would really have been Schön, which could also have been rendered as Schoen.

That instantly produced a result. Alice Schoen, born 18 July 1923 in Vienna, had died in New Jersey on 23 September 2014. She and Richard appeared under the name Schoen on the passenger list of the SS *Batory*, which sailed from Southampton to New York on 6 June 1948. Richard had been interviewed as a Holocaust survivor by the University of California Shoah Foundation, and had died a year before his wife, almost to the day.

In a US newspaper archive, there was a short obituary. He had worked as a hairdresser in New York for thirty-three years before retiring in 1981, and he had died at ninety-nine in retirement in Pompton Plains, New Jersey. He was survived by Alice and their two sons, Dennis and Ronald. I found emails for men with those names in New Jersey and wrote my customary cold introduction on 11 January 2022, asking if they were by any chance related to the woman I was looking for.

It was Dennis who replied. Ronald had initially assumed my mail was a scam. I sent them both a copy of the advert, an 'eye-opener' Dennis called it, on the family's life in Britain, and we arranged a Zoom discussion between the three of us.

The Schoen brothers had grown up under the Holocaust's oppressive shadow. Both Alice and Richard had been survivors. Richard had lost his parents and his brother, who had been arrested with him on *Kristallnacht* and dragged away and shot the same night for complaining about their treatment. Richard had never talked about it, while Alice discouraged the boys from asking him questions.

Dennis sent me an essay he had written about living with that sort of burden. 'Loss, guilt, fear of aggression and punishment were predominant themes growing up,' he said. He also sent me a short memoir which Alice had written for her sons about what had happened to her.

It had been her father Béla's idea to put ads in the *Manchester Guardian* for both Alice and her mother, Josefine. Alice's sister Gerty, nearly two years her junior, was deemed too young to be entrusted to a stranger in a foreign country.

Béla was a Hungarian who had been a journalist during the First World War. By the 1930s he had built up a printing business with eighteen employees, and when she was fourteen, Alice went to trade school to learn bookkeeping, with the idea that she would work in her father's firm. They lived in the Favoriten district, south of the old city and the Belvedere Palace, in a spacious apartment they had shared with, and then inherited from, Alice's maternal great-grandmother.

Gerty and Alice Hess in Vienna, circa 1931.

Josefine received a dozen replies for the ad placed by Béla, but only one came for Alice, from a family in Manchester. At fifteen, she was too old for free schooling in Britain, which only went up to fourteen, but she was young for a nanny or home help, so Béla offered her as an unpaid domestic servant.

There was a big demand for young women to work as maids. With the expansion of prosperous suburbs and the opening up of other work opportunities for British women, there was a shortage of domestic workers in the UK, creating vacancies for outsiders to do the household chores. In its launch edition in February 1939, *Housewife* magazine ran an article declaring: 'Your opportunity! The Case for the Foreign Maid.'

'Maids have become so difficult to find and keep nowadays,' it noted sympathetically. Around the afternoon tea tables of Britain: 'Sooner or later, someone is bound to say to you "But why don't you get a German refugee? Or an Austrian, or a Czechoslovakian", as the case may be.'

The Anschluss created a supply to meet the demand, and alongside the adverts for unaccompanied children in the *Manchester Guardian* was a growing number of 'Situation Wanted' ads from adult Viennese Jews, particularly women. In total, twenty thousand Jewish women came from Nazi-run territory to work as domestics in Britain in the years immediately preceding the war.

The *Guardian* ran an article in July 1938 entitled 'Refugee Housekeeper' in which an anonymous employer detailed the ups and downs of having a live-in German Jewish maid, ultimately concluding that the only real disadvantage was that 'thenceforward one is inescapably aware of the misfortunes of Europe's persecuted minorities'.

Leo and Erna Borger advertised themselves with improvised English in the *Guardian* on 10 October 1938 as a 'couple of old Vienna citizen's family, versatile willing workers' who were seeking posts as 'Servants, couple or separately'.

The 'old Vienna' part was largely aspirational as Leo was the first Borger to be born in the city. Leo also took some liberties in describing Omi's abilities while filling in the questionnaire at the IKG.

'My wife speaks some French, English and Czech,' he claimed, putting a lot of strain on the word 'some'. Just as hopefully, he added: 'She can type and take shorthand' as well as knowing how to cook and run a household.

'She is currently in the process of perfecting her skills,' he concluded, allowing for a certain margin of error.

On the IKG questionnaire Leo said less about his own skills. Dealing with the forfeiture of Radio Borger under Aryanisation, and the legal burden it imposed on the victim, took up a lot of his time. He had taken the basic hairdressing course and he would bring his pair of hand clippers with him from Vienna, though they did not help him get a job or a visa, and it remained a somewhat controversial hobby for the rest of his life.

It was far easier for a woman to get a job as a maid than for a man to find a post as a butler or chauffeur. Maids were common among the English middle class, whereas one would have to be substantially well off to afford a butler or a chauffeur. Furthermore, dependants could leave without paying the flight tax and other levies. Heads of household could not.

By the time their ad appeared in the *Guardian*, Omi already had a job offer organised through the Central British Fund for German Jewry (CBF), for a post as a domestic in Bayswater. It seems likely that Leo inserted the ad just in case the CBF option did not come off, or in the hope that a household could be found that would take a working couple, so that the whole family could leave together.

Ultimately the family decided that it would be better not to wait on the slim possibility of Leo being offered a job, and that Omi would travel with Robert as soon as her papers came through. So on 15 October Leo took his wife and son to the

Westbahnhof. Nobody in my family ever described that moment to me but it must have been fraught. More and more Jewish men were being picked up and not returning, shipped out to Dachau, where the chances of survival started slipping from the moment of arrival.

My dad did tell me one story about the westerly train trip across Europe. For much of the journey, he and his mother shared their compartment with a pair of Nazi officials who chatted amiably with them along the way. Omi and Bobby managed not to let their fear show and remained polite and correct, right up to the point when the Nazis got off at the last stop before the Dutch border. As they were leaving the compartment they turned at the door and gave the stiff-arm *Heil Hitler* salute, something Jews were forbidden from doing. Even if they had wanted to, my father and grandmother were prohibited from responding in kind. All they could say was *Auf Wiedersehen*.

'Their faces fell. All that time, they had been sharing their compartment with Jews,' my father recalled.

Leo would not escape for another five months, during which he survived *Kristallnacht*, hiding as much as possible in basements and staying off the streets. Wearing the yellow star would not be compulsory for Jews in Austria or Germany until 1941. But there was another way of identifying them. Jews were not allowed to wear the Nazi lapel badge that became ubiquitous in Vienna after the Anschluss, so Jews could be identified by their empty lapels.

With help from the Bingleys, a work permit and visa had been procured for Leo as an agricultural trainee, but he had used his last hidden savings on tickets for his wife and his son, and if he waited for the sale of the shop to yield any money, he risked leaving his escape till too late.

Leo and his lawyer tried to get the new Aryan owner of Radio Borger to pay up the small amount he had ultimately been asked to pay, but the transfer of funds was held up in Eichmann's state machinery as it recalculated Leo's tax liability.

On 8 March 1939, Leo appealed to the IKG to cover the cost of a ticket to Caernarfon, and a registrar took notes on his assets and liabilities, including 'various items that could be pawned'.

The official estimated: 'The proceeds from the various assets by far exceed the travel costs.' As for Leo, the notes observed: 'Statements hesitant; not convincing.'

'The request is to be denied,' the IKG concluded. In the end, Leo scraped the funds together for his rail ticket, either by pawning or borrowing from friends, or both. He finally arrived in Britain on 17 March 1939.

The Hess family faced similar dilemmas to the Borgers. Ideally, they wanted Josefine and Alice to travel together. But whereas Josefine had a dozen job offers from Britain, Alice, seeking a place as a fifteen-year-old home help, had just one proposal from a Manchester family by which she would 'take care of their three-year-old girl plus clean the house, cook, wash clothes by hand etc.'

The Hesses were exchanging letters with this family in November, when *Kristallnacht* struck. That morning, 10 November, Béla Hess left the house following his daily routine. He would walk a block to a garage where his Harley Davidson motorbike was parked and then ride it to work.

But on that day he did not return. It was two weeks before his family even found out that Béla was alive, and in Dachau. He sent a note on a prison postcard insisting he was in good health, asking for money to be sent and hoping Josefine had responded to one of the offers arising from the *Manchester Guardian* advert and found a way out of Vienna, so that she could exert pressure from Britain to get the rest of the family out.

With Béla in prison, it was harder for Josefine to leave with

Alice as that would mean abandoning Gerty. So Josefine went to Britain on a maid's visa in early December 1938, leaving both girls with their grandmother. It was hoped that in Britain she would somehow meet people who would help get Béla a job and find education and British homes for Alice and Gerty. It was a tall order for a woman with partial English working as a maid full time, so it was lucky that the key to Béla's release ultimately came from Vienna. After he was sent to Dachau, a Nazi walked into his printing shop and announced that he was the new owner, but the work should carry on as before. The eighteen employees agreed on one condition: the new boss would get Béla Hess out of Dachau.

So the prospective new owner persuaded Alice and Gerty to accompany him to Gestapo headquarters at the Hotel Metropole to plead in person for her father's release, stressing that he had fought for Austria in the First World War. It worked. Béla was freed on condition that he report to the police every day and leave the country within a month. After six weeks in Dachau he turned up on the doorstep a changed man.

'He rang our bell and when I opened the door, I did not recognise him as his hair was shaved off and he collapsed with frostbite on his feet,' Alice wrote.

Having emerged from Dachau alive, Béla now had just weeks to get out of the country or face the prospect of re-arrest and a return to the concentration camp where he would almost certainly die. From East Molesey, near Hampton Court palace south-west of London, where she was working as a maid, Josefine desperately tried to find someone to give her husband a job and the employment guarantee necessary to get exit papers from Vienna.

The month went by with no offers, so when Béla made his daily visit to the police station in late December, he would have known it was possible he would not return. But the Gestapo extended his grace period by another month, and then once more. His service in the First World War and the backing of the new Aryan owner of his printing press was enough to tilt the balance in Nazi calculations from the instinct to punish towards the desire to be rid of him. Finally, in February 1939, Josefine secured a work visa for him.

By then, the *Kindertransport* had begun, and because Alice already had a family who had responded to the *Manchester Guardian* ad and was willing to house her, she got a place on a transport easily. Her father took her to Westbahnhof and saw her off, promising to follow her a few weeks later.

'I went with so many children to a strange country, strange people and strange language,' Alice wrote.

Gertrude Batscha did not leave Vienna for another four months, as her parents weighed up other options. There were few good choices as no one was readily opening their doors for Jewish refugees. In July 1938, the representatives of thirty-two nations met in the French spa town of Évian to discuss the plight of German and Austrian Jews, but all bar one of those countries declared they would not issue visas to save them. The sole exception was the Dominican Republic.

The Batschas' family friends, the Katzes, were pursuing illegal routes. The two Katz boys had been sent to Dachau, but Adolf Batscha used his connections to get them out, and they left Austria immediately after their release, crossing into Italy over the mountains, and eventually finding their way to Britain by ship. The Katz girls obtained fake visas, which were widespread, but only available for Latin American states. US and UK visas could not, apparently, be faked.

The Batschas had no American family connections who could sponsor a US visa, so it was finally agreed that a UK student visa was the best route to freedom. The departure date, 12 February 1939, caused some anxiety for Gerti's mother Vally as it entailed arriving at her destination on the 13th, an unlucky date that Frau

Batscha believed should be avoided if at all possible. In fact, a lot of the planning fell apart at the last moment. Gertrude had been supposed to travel with a cousin who had a domestic servant visa, but at the last minute the cousin's travel plans changed, and Gerti had to make the journey alone.

Vally bought her a heavy wool coat with a grey opossum fur collar to make a good first impression in Britain, and equipped her daughter with a pigskin suitcase, a holdall and a rucksack filled with food for the journey, so heavy that it bent her almost double.

The train was due to leave at 1 p.m., and the Batschas assembled on the Westbahnhof well in advance. Alongside her mother and father were her aunt Manya, her mother's sister, and Adolf's brother, Albert, who had been trying to teach her some basic English. At the last moment he took her aside and made sure she remembered three essentials of the English language: Please. Thank you. Lavatory.

Seconds before departure, as they were waiting for the whistle, Gertrude's distraught mother pointed to an old woman with white hair and declared, 'That's what I'll look like and how old I'll be before I'll see you again!'

At the time it seemed histrionic, and her husband Adolf assured her that the family would soon be reunited once their domestic worker visas came through. Adolf found Gertrude a window seat in a compartment with other Jewish migrants heading for the Hoek van Holland and the Channel ferry.

The trip across Austria and Germany was uneventful but Gertrude felt the tension grow as the train approached the Dutch border, where the passengers would be exposed to Nazi scrutiny one last time. When the moment came, they showed their new grey passports with swastikas on the front, and their newly assigned names. Gertrude, like all female Jews, now had the additional name Sarah, just as all Jewish men and boys had been dubbed Israel.

After all the uniformed officials had left the train and it picked up speed across the Dutch border, a yell rang out along the length of the carriages full of refugees. Gerti's fellow passengers had stuck their heads out of the window and cried out to celebrate their freedom.

Adolf had taken a serious personal risk in a bid to ensure his daughter had the best start possible in her new life. He had sent one large wooden packing case separately through Cook's travel service. All such freight was searched thoroughly by customs officials to ensure that the Reich was not being deprived of any Jewish family valuables. But Adolf had a plan. A sewing box had been packed among Gerti's clothes, full of pins, buttons and cotton reels. While the box was being searched, Adolf spilled its contents in an act of staged clumsiness, and while apologetically helping to repack it, he slipped in two gold bracelets wrapped in a rag.

The rest of the family's precious possessions had long since been confiscated, but Adolf had kept these pieces hidden, just as our grandpa Leo had concealed gems in the heels of his shoes. In their eyes, these were small but essential victories. The Nazis had ripped up their life's harvest by the roots but they had saved these few seeds to plant in a new home. Their importance was so great it was worth risking their lives for.

Adolf's ruse worked. The trunk arrived safely in Britain, with the gold bracelets inside.

George Mandler left Vienna in October 1938, a few days before my father and grandmother. His father had a gold ring made for him and presented it as a last resort in case of adversity. There were tears on the platform at the station but by that time, George reflected, 'it was what Jewish people did'.

He found himself in a carriage with other emigrants, including a young woman to whom the fourteen-year-old boy gravitated in instant infatuation. They crossed Germany without incident but when the train reached the border town of Aachen, the Jews were ordered off with their luggage and told by a local Gestapo official that there was a new decree requiring the passports of all Jews to be stamped with a large red 'J' on the first page. The order had been issued while they were on the train.

The 'J' stamp was an innovation introduced in early October at the request of the Swiss police chief, Heinrich Rothmund, to make it easier for his men to spot Jews as they arrived at the frontier.

Rothmund sent 2,600 Jews back to the Reich, most likely to their deaths, in the interests of Swiss 'purity'. 'One may not flinch from turning them back. We have to think of our own young people,' he declared.

When Mandler's train arrived at the border town of Aachen, the new policy had reached the border officials but without the actual stamps needed to put it into action. So the Gestapo sent all the Jews from the train back to Cologne, where an emergency stamp was to be made. They were billeted around town overnight, and young George found himself in a hotel where the rooms had no wardrobes or chests of drawers. It was a *Stundenhotel*, renting rooms out by the hour.

'I spent the first night of my emigration in a bordello!' he marvelled.

By next morning the stamp had still not been fabricated, so the ad hoc group killed time looking around Cologne and its famous cathedral until it was ready. Finally, their passports duly imprinted with their racial classification, they crossed into Belgium.

Back on the train, George surrendered himself to the flow of events carrying him towards a future which he lacked the tools even to imagine. Looking back, he could remember nothing from the sea crossing from Ostend or the onward train journey, but for the sense of part of himself being left behind on the tracks.

The only physical item he felt deprived of was his stamp collection; the loss he really felt was of a country, a sense of belonging and his adolescent innocence.

5

Bobby and George in Exile

THE ELEVEN-YEAR-OLD BOBBY Borger who got off the boat-train from Harwich and walked down the platform at Liverpool Street station wore a wool coat over the traditional green and grey Austrian jacket his mother had made him wear for the occasion.

His thick, straight brown hair was brushed up and back from his forehead. He had round cheeks prone to blushing, thick eyebrows and a prominent nose. It was 16 October 1938 and Bobby was walking alongside his mother, who was drained by twenty-four hours of travel on train and ferry and no doubt struggling to keep her fear under control.

The station was one of Victorian Britain's cathedrals to the steam age, its vaulted steel and glass roof covered in years of grime from thousands of locomotives ferrying harried commuters in and out from Essex and East Anglia.

This was the dirty, noisy gateway into Britain for my father and the other children from the *Manchester Guardian* ads. Britain was not the first choice destination for many of the new arrivals, but it provided immediate safety, sustenance and a haven that was to prove remarkably resilient. Later in life, all those who reached the United Kingdom were mindful of their debt to their first country of asylum, though many ultimately found homes elsewhere, and some who stayed found their hosts inscrutable or eccentric or even cold. It was a sanctuary, but sometimes a bitter one.

When they arrived at Liverpool Street, Omi and Bobby knew they would be separated for a considerable time, though neither of them could have known then that they would never really live together again. Omi, who had been mistress in her own home and helped run the family shop, was about to start work as a servant in the house of a stranger, whose language she could not speak. The visa stamped in her passport made clear the limits on her existence: 'The holder is not permitted to enter any employment other than as a resident in service in a private household.' Her conditions of service did not permit her to live with her child.

Adding to the stress and uncertainty, Omi had reason to fear for Leo's safety. Her husband was in hiding in a city where Jewish men were routinely being rounded up and sent to Dachau, some returning only as a box of ashes. And now she was about to let go of their son, relinquishing the joys and labour of motherhood to another woman, whom she knew only from the pencilled messages on a few postcards.

Nans Bingley and Erna Borger only had a few minutes together in the middle of the crowd at Liverpool Street station because the representative from the CBF aid committee was waiting to take Erna to the house of her employer, a Mrs Samek in Bayswater.

Nans meanwhile had to take Bobby across London to catch the train back to Wales, taking the London Underground from Liverpool Street to Euston in the sleek new red tube carriages that had been brought into service that year; then on a steam train through the soft rolling countryside of the Home Counties, the smog-ridden heart of the Midlands – Birmingham, Coventry and Crewe – and finally along the North Wales coast looking out over sand flats to the Irish Sea past the seaside towns of Prestatyn, Rhyl and Llandudno.

In their first days together, Nans was struck most of all by Robert's fear. At the Bingleys' home on Y Glyn (The Glen) road in Caernarfon, the new foster parents took the whistle off their kettle because it would make him panic, bringing back memories of the SA Brownshirts and Hitler Youth who had chased him through the Vienna streets and who routinely went through neighbourhoods blowing their whistles, arresting Jews and looting their homes.

When the Bingleys told Robert he would have to go to register with the police, the boy fainted. In his experience, Jews went into the police station and most often did not return. The Bingleys' friend and fellow schoolteacher, Powell Davies, suggested to Bobby that they go for a walk up Bethel Road, towards the school. He went along, pale and trembling, and years later confided in Nans and Reg that he was sure Davies intended to kill him.

In a Welsh-language memoir of the time called *Un O'r Teulu* (One of the Family), a schoolfriend of Robert's, Glennys Roberts, recalled an account he gave of the family's experiences in Vienna.

'In a conversation with me, he spoke of the events of *Kristallnacht* when the family shop was attacked and ransacked,' she wrote. 'He broke down and wept bitterly before he was able to continue and tell how he and his parents hid in a dark cellar for five long days. Fortunately his father was able to hide some gems in his shoes and these were sold and paid for his wife and Robert to flee.'

We, Robert's family, had known none of these details until 2021. They had lain hidden like a coded message in a Welsh memoir we had never heard of. Seeing it translated into English for the first time was yet another reminder of all the things we did not know about him long after his death.

I came to Caernarfon in time for Wales's hottest day on record, 18 July 2022, after following the same coastal train route as my father's first journey. The train ran slower than usual, as there was a fear the rails would buckle under the unprecedented temperatures. In the bus from Bangor, the passengers fanned themselves with newspapers, supermarket coupons or whatever else came to hand. A couple of teenage boys sat at the back, red and sweating as we followed the Menai Strait, the channel separating the mainland from Anglesey, from where the ferry leaves for Dublin. We drove past yellowing pastures, stone cottages glowing with roses in coastal villages with their war memorials pointing skyward.

Everyone else on the bus was speaking Welsh, which made me wonder what my father would have made of it. He had crammed a few English lessons in the months before departure, only to arrive among people who spoke the language that had been driven out of England a millennium earlier. Welsh, and Caernarfon's own version of it, Cofi, represent a triumph of survival. They have outlived the Romans, the Anglo-Saxons, the Vikings, the Normans, a complete ban under Henry VIII and then industrialisation and globalisation.

By the time my bus stopped outside the Iceland frozen food shop in the town centre, most cafes and restaurants had closed to spare their staff the heat, but there was a place open serving cod and chips with a view of the castle walls. Caernarfon's juxtaposition of the modern and the medieval would have been strange for my father. Franz Joseph had removed almost every trace of the old city walls to build the grand Ring and his designer city. Caernarfon is still defined by the huge ramparts Edward I built in the thirteenth century to keep the Welsh down.

I walked up the hill from the castle to trace my dad's progress across town, from his first British address, the little semi-detached house on the corner of Y Glyn and Bethel Road. The pebbledash had been painted blue with small windows looking out onto the Irish Sea in one direction and the mountains behind, the beginnings of Snowdonia.

Within a year of Robert's arrival, the Bingleys had moved, renting rooms in a bigger building in the same neighbourhood, a three-storey yellow brick house called Bryn Dewi (David's Hill) on Lôn Ddewi (David's Lane). But in 1940 they moved back up the hill to a recently built semi called Porth Kerry on a street called Pen-Y-Garth, which would be the house in which my father would spend most of his teenage years. The landlord was Powell Davies, the family friend who had scared Robert soon after his arrival by offering to take him for a walk. He was on the staff at the local school but had been given a job by the London-based National Union of Teachers, and so offered his house to the Bingleys.

Nans had a strong friendship with the woman living across the road from Porth Kerry, Josephine Davies, an Irishwoman who shared her firm socialist beliefs. 'How could you have lived through the twenties and not be a socialist?' Josephine would say. Together they would take their children on educational Sunday outings and bus trips up to the cathedral in Bangor, or to the lakeside village of Llanberis, high up in Snowdonia.

Josephine's daughter, Norah Davies, met me in Caernarfon's Castle Square, to show me the way to her house on Segontium Terrace, after the Roman name for Caernarfon, a row of stately Victorian buildings overlooking the old harbour on the Menai Strait, where generations of Norah's family loaded slate onto schooners bound for the rest of Britain and beyond.

Norah was eleven years younger than Robert but has a memory of a tall boy with thick brown hair standing in the doorway across the road, and her mother telling her how he had survived the Nazis.

Growing up in the orbit of the Bingleys was one of the formative experiences of Norah Davies's life.

'They were interested in everybody, they gathered people together,' she said. 'They'd open their doors to people and they were not wealthy people by any means, but they opened their home and everybody was welcomed there.'

Nancy Maud Griffith and Reginald Kirkby Bingley were both born in July 1905. Nans was Reg's senior by nineteen days. She was from Pontypridd, South Wales, in the heart of coal-mining country. Reg was from Lincoln in the East Midlands, and they met at Cardiff University, where they found each other in a circle of left-wing students. Reg was a devoted admirer of Trotsky. They married in November 1932 and moved up to Caernarfon so they could both get jobs. The education authorities in South Wales were operating marriage bars to maximise employment for men. It meant that when a woman teacher married she had to resign from her job.

Nans was fiercely opposed to the rule, on principle, but also because Reg was in increasingly poor health and it was clear that the couple would be more and more dependent on her income.

They both found positions at Caernarfon County School, a great, gabled red-brick hulk on the top of the hill overlooking the town. Within a year, however, Reg was forced to retire because of a debilitating curvature of the spine, catastrophically worsened by its misdiagnosis as tuberculosis at a sanatorium in the village of Llangwyfan, which had been set up to address endemic TB across North Wales. Reg was prescribed bed rest for a year, and when he tried to get up again, his spine was past saving.

He was persuaded to return to school after the war to teach maths, but by that time he was bent over almost at ninety degrees. Norah, who was one of his pupils at that time, recalls him having to prop his legs up on his desk in order to raise his head so that he could see the children he was teaching.

Nans wore her hair short – it was called an Eton crop – and dressed for class in a masculine dark jacket, white shirt and tie. With her long face and aquiline nose, she resembled both

Virginia Woolf and George Orwell. She had a Master's degree in English and revelled in the poetry of the language.

Her pupils remembered her as a disciplinarian, but a reasonable and kindly one so that the discipline always appeared well founded. She always kept an eye out for children who were struggling as well as the precocious scholars. When the school celebrated its centenary in 1994, there was a long queue of former pupils who waited to shake her hand and thank her for the start she had given them in life.

In his *Manchester Guardian* advert, Leo had said he was seeking a kind person. He found two. The Bingleys were an open tap of kindness that was never turned off. Their kitchen in the house on Pen-Y-Garth was a warm retreat in winter. It was where Norah Davies saw a coffee percolator and smelt coffee for the first time. Reg's mother lived in the front room, which was decorated with a framed oval print of Anthony van Dyck's portrait of King James II as a baby. In the back room was an upright piano, which a neighbour would come to play for Reg when he was confined to his bed. The back garden had a small pond and a morello cherry tree that produced fruit that was too bitter to eat.

Despite Reg's worsening infirmity and their very modest living on a teacher's salary – they were never able to buy their own house – they were always ready to stretch their resources to the limit to make space for a child who needed shelter.

A few years before my father's advert in the newspaper, the Bingleys had offered to host a child during the summer holidays from the New Herrlingen School at Bunce Court, set up in Kent by a German exile for German Jewish children after the Nazis took power in 1933. All the children had been found summer homes by the time the Bingleys enquired, but the school suggested taking one of the teachers, Hilde Tod, a German refugee in her early twenties. They hosted Hilde for a summer, and then when her refugee parents were expelled from Kent along with other 'enemy aliens' as part of invasion security measures in 1940, the Bingleys cleared out and furnished a storeroom for them in their Pen-Y-Garth house.

To reassure Omi, Nans sent her a series of black-and-white picture postcards depicting Snowdon and Caernarfon castle in an effort to show that Bobby's new home would be no less beautiful than Austria.

By the time Robert was preparing to leave for university in 1943, the Bingleys adopted a six-year-old boy, Jimmy, and some six years later, a four-year-old girl, Christine, from a Welsh children's home, where she had been sent after her young mother could no longer care for her. She clung to Nans' skirt, refusing to let her out of her sight, for the first few months after her arrival, and in the years that followed she absorbed the warmth and erudition of an extraordinary home.

'She loved words and often had a quote for any occasion,' Christine wrote to me from her home in New Zealand, when I asked her to describe Nans. Love for the spoken word in poetry and plays was married to a reverence for the written word. She would tell Christine 'never to put in writing that which you wouldn't wish to see again'.

At the end of the war, the Bingleys and Davieses invited German prisoners of war from a small camp at Bontnewydd on the outskirts of Caernarfon to spend Sundays with them during their long wait for release. Some were not repatriated until 1948. It was part of a scheme organised by a nearby Methodist chapel, which set up a library and occasional dinners for the prisoners and found families willing to play host at weekends.

The two prisoners who came regularly to Pen-Y-Garth were Hans Joachim Schweitzer and Konrad Beck, who mostly went to the Bingleys as his English was poor and Reg spoke excellent German. They would continue to write letters to the family with fond memories and news of post-war life for years after returning to Germany.

The final member of the Bingley household was a fourth child whom the couple fostered informally, Megan Griffith. Megan was one of Nans' pupils at the county school and lived in an orphanage in Bontnewydd, not far from the prisoner of war camp. Nans had spotted her potential and nurtured it, encouraging Megan to treat the Bingleys' house as a second home while she was at the orphanage. In the school holidays Megan would have had to go back to the orphanage because she had nowhere else to stay, so Nans suggested she might like to come and help look after Christine, so as not to make the offer of a room look like charity.

'She took a shine to Megan who was very bright. It seems like Nancy had a radar for people in need,' Megan's daughter, Sian, said. 'To get to university from that orphanage was completely unthinkable.'

Under Nans' care and encouragement, Megan became top pupil at Caernarfon school and then went on to the University of Wales at Bangor, becoming part of the Bingley family along the way.

Megan Griffith knew Bobby as well as anyone. Fellow wards in the Bingley house and top pupils at school, they were friends but also rivals. She recognised the ambition and hunger in him and all the forms it took, academic and romantic.

Many years later, when she was Megan Stumbles by marriage, she told me: 'He constantly had crushes on slightly older, more unusual girls, including some assistant librarians.'

Another old classmate of Robert's from the county school called Meurig Hainge got in touch with me in May 2021, after my article in the *Guardian* about the children in the classified ads and my dad's time in Caernarfon. By then, Meurig was seriously ill but insisted that his son Mark contact me to set up a call. The article was the first he had heard of Robert's suicide and, eighty years after the two boys met in a school playground, it still upset him deeply.

'It seems to me that circumstances somehow conspired to kill him. They left him nowhere to go but out,' he said.

The Hainges' house overlooked the Bingleys' back garden on Y Glyn, and Meurig remembered peering across in 1938 and seeing the new arrival.

'I was aware of this little lad turning up. He had a wooden board and throwing knives and he was playing with those. I was tempted to go and introduce myself but teachers were seen as being different beings in those days,' he said. His reverence for Nans' and Reg's status stopped him introducing himself. 'I wish I had. It might have made some difference.'

'In school, I can never remember Robert smiling. He was a quiet boy,' Meurig said in our phone conversation as he struggled for breath, determined to say his piece. Casting his mind back eight decades, he wondered whether, through some butterfly effect, some small difference in 1940s Caernarfon might have somehow changed Robert's destiny.

'We were, to a certain extent, incurious. My parents were not gregarious. They were people who had suffered the Great Depression and had lost a lot,' he said. 'This boy turned up, and looking back, I thought the staff could have introduced him. They could have told us something about his background. I wonder if they purposely avoided that so he could be just another boy among boys.'

'It would have been better if the school staff had instructed us about the fate of these children and what it must have been like to be sent away by your parents. What happened to Robert tells it all really. The lad was damaged from the word go.'

'People didn't really dwell much on his background or talk much about what he must have suffered. We couldn't have imagined what circumstances were like in Vienna after the Anschluss,' Meurig said. These were experiences that were far removed from Welsh life. There were a few Jews in town, like an old man who would string violins and mend other musical instruments, but no record of antisemitism. When a new family moved into the neighbourhood, Meurig's mother would ask, 'What are they', but that meant what chapel did they attend: Methodist or Baptist?

The distinction that mattered to Caernarfon schoolchildren was whether your mother tongue was Welsh. Welsh speakers were bilingual while English speakers tended to have only a smattering of Welsh, but it was the monoglots who had the higher status. 'They were regarded as being rather superior,' Meurig said.

There was no shortage of manual labour in Caernarfon and the surrounding area, so if you had come to live there from somewhere in the English-speaking outside world, the assumption was that you would do more skilled, non-manual, work. And Robert, from Meurig's recollection, sounded just like an English boy when he spoke the language.

'It must have been a strange environment for Robert. It was as thoroughly a Welsh town as a French town might be thoroughly French,' he told me.

My dad had learned some Welsh but was far from fluent. There was a misunderstanding early on with Meurig's group of friends, when one of them asked, '*Sais, ydy e?*' ('English, is he?') in Robert's earshot. *Sais*, which means 'English' in Welsh, sounds a lot like *Scheisse*, shit in German. Robert, primed to hear abuse from Vienna, was visibly upset until the linguistic confusion was resolved.

Gareth Williams, another classmate of my father's, told me that when he got to the county school, my dad 'was naturally accepted by all pupils even though, I believe, he was not that interested in sport!'

Rugby and football were the boys' obsession then. My dad was more interested in girls.

One day, Gareth was out kayaking with friends on the Menai

Strait, which is Caernarfon's northern boundary, and they spotted Robert 'sitting in warm companionship on the beach with a fellow female pupil who happened to be the daughter of the local minister'.

Robert had arrived in Caernarfon at a time when Reg Bingley, a German-speaking polyglot and gifted mathematician, was locked away at home by infirmity and desperate to teach. So in the little end-of-terrace house on Y Glyn, Reg poured all he knew into the refugee kid, and when Robert first stepped into the school, he outshone everyone else, even Megan Griffith.

In 1943, when he was just sixteen and had been in the country for five years, he won the top scholarship for a place at Bangor, the closest university to Caernarfon, at the other end of the Menai Strait, and then, a week later, a scholarship to the University of Aberystwyth. The biggest prize however would be a place at Cardiff University, the leading seat of higher education in Wales, where the Bingleys had met.

Nans wrote to the German Jewish Aid Committee in Bloomsbury House, who provided support to the Borgers, saying that Robert was a child of 'outstanding brilliance' who hoped to win a scholarship to cover part of his costs at Cardiff University, where he wanted to study science. Although both the Bingleys and Leo, who was then earning £4 a week in a lingerie company, would be able to contribute something, she said, the boy would need further financial support. A few days later Omi followed up the enquiry, asking if there was a fund available for gifted children like her son.

As it turned out, Bloomsbury House's help was unnecessary. Nans wrote to the Committee in November, informing it that Robert had won the top county prize of £60 a year for three years, as well as the top entrance scholarship to Cardiff University of £50 a year for three years. 'No further help needed!' an official at Bloomsbury House wrote at the bottom of the correspondence.

But it was all far too much, too early for Robert. He was two or three years younger than the other students. He had been separated from his parents at eleven and now from his foster parents at sixteen. He was good at school, but not so good at independent living. He failed his first year at Cardiff – 'a crisis of confidence', Megan told me – and Nans had to intervene to rescue him. He spent some time back at the Bingleys on Pen-Y-Garth, and it was decided he would go to Bangor instead, as it was closer to home and involved less pressure. He went on to get a first-class degree there.

His achievements stoked his ambition, and his ambition fed his discontent. He complained to Megan that other refugee children 'had been adopted by rich families and had been to Oxford and Cambridge'. My father had been dead for nearly

The Bingleys' house on Pen-Y-Garth in Caernarfon, circa 1950. Nans and Reg Bingley (*top left* and *right*), Erna Borger (*centre left*), Megan Griffith (*centre*), Reg's mother Mary Bingley (*centre right*), Jimmy Bingley (*bottom left*) and Robert Borger (*bottom right*).

forty years when Megan Stumbles told me that, proving he still had the power to make me want to curl up with shame and anger.

Not only was it a profoundly ungrateful and selfish thing to say, it was simply not true. I found no refugee child who had been luckier in their foster parents. Many of the families who took in the Viennese children advertised in the *Manchester Guardian* were looking to combine the appearance of philanthropy with the exploitation of cheap and compliant labour.

George Mandler was met at Liverpool Street station by a woman from a Jewish relief agency, a Mrs Shearer, who accompanied him across London to catch another train to Bournemouth on the south coast. George was amazed at London traffic, which he described as a 'unique event'.

'Bus after bus in distances of three metres, everyone is running and terrible noise,' he wrote to his parents in his first letter home, on 10 October 1938. Immediately on arrival, he sent them a telegram with the two English words: 'Good arrived', a direct translation from the German '*gut angekommen*'. He did not want to use German in a British post office.

He arrived in Bournemouth on a dark October evening and was met by the headmaster of St Mary's Lodge school, Donald Langdon, and a pupil of about his age to keep him company. He went straight to sleep and in the morning had his first ill-fated encounter with English tea-drinking. Someone brought him a teapot but had forgotten to add the hot water, so when George lifted the lid, all he could see was a yellow-brown mix of tea leaves and sugar at the bottom.

'Everybody is very nice and I am surprised how much English I know, I can communicate excellently,' he wrote. However, he added: 'The food is terrible, lunch is passable but otherwise: morning, afternoon and evening hot tea with milk, without sugar, without lemon or rum.'

Like many small private boarding schools dotted around Britain, St Mary's Lodge, occupying a private house two blocks from the seafront, was a weird place. Donald Langdon was a defrocked Jesuit priest and a member of Oswald Mosley's British Union of Fascists, yet, most likely for pecuniary motives, he had agreed to accept a few Jewish refugee children like Mandler, who perceived no obvious signs of antisemitism.

The quality of teaching was mixed at best. One of the teachers, Paddy Minogue, Mandler described as 'the French master, though not really a master of French'. Nevertheless, St Mary's Lodge saw him through his Oxford School Certificate in English language and literature, geography, French, German and mathematics just eight months after his arrival in the UK.

George's favourite teacher in his first weeks was called William Eade, but it quickly turned out that there was an agenda behind Eade's initial attentiveness, leaving sweets and encouraging notes under George's pillow. Eade never made an overt pass at him, but clearly had expectations that George would be seduced by the teacher's attentions. When this did not happen after about a year, Eade sent George a poisonous note, denouncing him as reprehensible and unreliable, and declaring that all Jews were scum.

Somewhat to George's surprise, there was little schoolboy bullying of the newly arrived foreigners from the rest of the boys. It was the sheer awfulness of the food that was the recurring theme of his schoolboy diary.

The deepest and most enduring connection which George Mandler forged in Britain was not with anyone at St Mary's Lodge, but with a family called the Isaacs, assigned to host him for the holidays by the refugee agency. For George, as with the other refugee children, finding kindness or indifference on arrival in Britain seems to have been a matter of luck. George eventually got lucky.

Gina and Stanley Isaacs and their children Alan and Anne

(Tuffy) were to become his second family. Alan, who was close to George in age, took him on ambitious cycling adventures and the two of them remained friends for the rest of their lives. The Isaacs would go on seaside holidays to Poole, near Bournemouth, and George would spend much of his free time with them there. He was with them when war broke out on 3 September 1939. He could remember everyone huddled around the radio, but the event did not leave a deep impression 'because for me it seemed merely a continuation of the world as it was.

'My war had started earlier and this was an expected and logical consequence,' he wrote.

All this time, as he made new friends, learned a new language and sat exams in a new school, George also had the responsibility for getting his parents and sister out of Vienna, trying to secure work visas for his mother and father and a place in a local school for Trudi. Among a variety of tasks, it involved writing endless letters seeking sponsorship from the rich and famous, like the car manufacturer and philanthropist, Viscount Nuffield and Stefan Lorant, a Hungarian immigrant who co-founded the *Picture Post* magazine. They ignored him or turned him down.

Salvation came instead from the slow turning wheels of US bureaucracy. Visas finally came through for George's parents and his sister, Trudi in time for them to travel through Italy to catch a ship to New York before the war began, and he was able to drop the pursuit of sponsorship and financial support which had become a full-time job.

'Sometimes I forget that in these reminiscences I am talking about a thirteen- to sixteen-year-old boy. My recall is more of an adult, presumably due to the adult tasks imposed on me,' he wrote. 'I have always felt that the emigration and the events surrounding it robbed my generation of our adolescence.'

6

Siegfried, Paula and Coming to Britain

SIEGFRIED AND PAULA Neumann's father was killed before they even left Vienna. Karl Neumann, a lawyer, had been arrested and sent to Dachau in April, a month after the Nazi occupation, a victim of the entirely random Dachau lottery. A few days later Brownshirts tore apart the family apartment on Favoritenstrasse, one of the longest streets in Vienna, full of shops and restaurants in the 10th District.

Without their father and breadwinner, the children and their mother, Berta, were left to survive as best they could on their own. On 10 October 1938, Siegfried, just sixteen, placed his own ad in the *Manchester Guardian*, saying: 'I would be so glad to become an Apprentice or Au Pair', adding that he had passed six classes in grammar school, before noting he was, in brackets, a Jew.

Their father, meanwhile, was transferred to Buchenwald camp, and in December, the family received a telegram announcing his death and instructing them that if the body was not claimed within twenty-four hours it would be cremated.

'My brother, who had been the first to read this terrible news, went completely white with shock and my mother's anguish and despair were terrible to see,' Paula recalled in a handwritten memoir she wrote for her family much later in life. 'I watched my brother and mother, feeling the world I had known disintegrating before my eyes.'

Berta left immediately to make sure Karl was buried with

Paula Neumann as a young woman, circa 1952.

Jewish rites, in the town of Gotha, the nearest Jewish cemetery she could find to the camp. The family later heard from a fellow inmate that Karl had died in the Buchenwald 'sick bay' from one of the diseases that were rampant in the camp, most likely typhus.

As 1939 began, life in Vienna became more dangerous. Neighbourhood children yelling '*Jude*' pelted Siegfried and Paula with stones. In April, Siegfried was rounded up with a group of other Jewish boys and disappeared for several days. They had been made to do forced labour before they were returned to their homes and their distraught parents.

Following his appeal for an apprenticeship, Siegfried was offered a position as a trainee cabinetmaker in Liverpool, where a family was ready to foster him, and the German Jewish Aid Committee in London secured another visa for his sister. Berta and Paula saw Siegfried off at the Westbahnhof in mid-April and it was Paula's turn on 12 May. That morning, Berta took

99

her into town for last-minute shopping and Paula concentrated
on the details of every street, thinking 'it is for the last time.
Tomorrow I will be far away and maybe I will never see it
all again.'

Her train departed at 6 p.m. Walking into the station filled
her with apprehension – she was barely nine – but also with
the relief of escape. She was travelling with her cousin Erni
and they found their seats together, before Paula went to the
window to wave to her mother on the platform one last time.
They had talked about when and where their reunion might
be, but Berta's children would never see her again.

The first thing Paula noticed on landing in Harwich was a
'blessed change of atmosphere'. She and the other children
were surrounded by British police and officials but they were
there to help them, unlike their Austrian counterparts who
had frisked them for valuables. In Harwich, they were given
small cardboard boxes of food, including a bar of chocolate,
and ushered along on the next stage of the journey, towards
London.

At Liverpool Street station, the mass of children emptied
out onto the platform, each with a number written on a label
around their neck. Among them were a handful of adults with
very small children whom they had been allowed to accompany,
including a woman carrying infant twins in a basket.

They were moved into the station hall, along the route
Bobby Borger and the other *Manchester Guardian* children had
taken before them, where prospective foster parents from across
Britain had gathered, now anxiously searching for a child
bearing the number they had been assigned. Those first encoun-
ters were a dissonant mishmash of emotions and impulses:
kindness and apprehension; longing and almost inevitable disappointment.

Paula Neumann's impression of the woman who came to
meet her at Liverpool Street was 'of a lady not unkind but of

a being entirely and utterly different to what I had known and expected. I felt lonely and frightened and from that time I also felt "different". Not indeed the "different" feeling of a Jewish child under Nazi rule but still a feeling of not belonging to the society which now surrounded me.'

For her part, Paula's foster mother, Ettie Lebovitz, an East European Jew from an earlier wave of immigration, was taken aback at the otherness of the girl she saw before her.

She had come down from Liverpool with her sister, and for both of them it was their first time in London. They had planned to do some sightseeing with their new charge, but seeing how 'peculiarly' Paula was dressed, they decided to return home by the next train.

Liverpool came as a profound shock. Paula's parents may sometimes have struggled financially in Vienna, but she and Siegfried had always been well fed, well dressed and well educated. In their apartment on Favoritenstrasse, the Neumanns lived amid the splendour and elegance of a post-imperial capital. Liverpool was an industrial town that had been devastated by the Depression. Ettie and Isaac Lebovitz's home was on Great Homer Street in the Everton district, a terrace of blackened brick houses mostly with shops on the ground floor. Theirs sold men's suits, new and second-hand.

'There were streets upon streets of these dreary houses and dirt and poverty were everywhere,' Paula wrote. She was shocked to see 'dirty, ragged and barefoot children' playing in the alleys, smelly outside toilets, and the sound of drunken singing and brawling as she tried to get to sleep at night.

Amid the overwhelming sense of alienation, there was at least one comfort. Her foster parents spoke Yiddish, which had enough in common with Paula's Viennese German for them to understand each other.

Siegfried fared better in the foster parent lottery. His were also poor but more sympathetic. He came to see Paula every

Saturday afternoon, and they would go for walks, buy choco-
lates at Woolworth's, and exchange stories of their woes.

'To me he became both father and mother and I clung to
him as the only human being I felt close to at that time for
many years to come,' she wrote.

Siegfried Neumann in British uniform, circa 1945.

That solitary source of comfort was torn away from her in
1940 when Siegfried, although only eighteen, was interned,
and after his release was no longer permitted, as an 'enemy
alien', to live in Liverpool due to its strategic importance as a
port. He moved to Manchester and then joined the army, and
meetings with Paula became fleeting.

Paula went to the King David Jewish School a half-hour
tram ride away from Great Homer Street and within three
months could speak enough English to get by and make friends,
including non-Jewish girls where she lived in Everton who

would take her to the cinema. There would be holiday trips to the beach at New Brighton, in Wallasey across the mouth of the Mersey, where Paula would look out to sea and wish herself far away from Liverpool.

She called Ettie and Isaac Lebovitz 'aunt' and 'uncle' but her relations with them were cold. Kissing and hugging 'hardly existed' in their household and she was constantly reminded, from the first moment at Liverpool Street station, that she was 'strange', for her liking of classical music, her dancing, and her fits of crying from missing her parents.

'I was not the pretty, jolly little girl my foster parents would have liked me to be,' she recalled. If ever there was deemed to be a problem with her behaviour, she would be reminded that a girl in her circumstances should be grateful enough not to cause trouble.

The Lebovitzes had arrived in England from western Russia a generation earlier as children, who had to work from the age of twelve to support their families. Only boys got a single year of Cheder (Jewish religious schooling), so they were unsupportive of Paula's own aspirations to further education, despite pleas on her behalf from Siegfried.

Her foster brother, Sam, was the same age as Siegfried but in no way a substitute. She said he 'hardly bothered about me at all', except to make fun of her for being skinny. 'Lizzy from the boneyard', he would call her.

Paula wrote and received letters from her mother over the summer of 1939, and she clung to the hope that Berta would arrive in Liverpool one day to reclaim her. But the letters stopped with the declaration of war in September. After that, there was just one telegram from Berta in 1941, asking for reassurance that the children were alive and well. It was the last communication Paula ever received from her mother and she never knew if her reply ever reached its destination.

At the height of the Blitz, her school was evacuated to

Chester, so she once more found herself with a label around her neck on a station platform surrounded by weeping frightened children. But her host family in Chester entirely neglected her to the extent that when her foster mother came to visit her after three weeks, she immediately insisted on taking her back to Liverpool despite the constant threat of bombing. The family spent most nights in 1940 in an air-raid shelter, and their neighbourhood, near the docks, was badly damaged. Great Homer Street itself was half destroyed.

All this time, the Neumann children had to contend with a creeping sense of bereavement as their worst fears became real. None of Siegfried and Paula's close relatives survived the Holocaust. Their mother, Berta, was deported from Vienna to Minsk on 28 November 1941 and died there or on the way. Even after receiving confirmation from the Red Cross, Paula nursed a forlorn hope that her mother would miraculously reappear, and it took years for the hope to fade.

Even though Paula spent her first nine years speaking German, and then Hebrew for the great majority of her adult life in Israel, English remained her dominant language. While in Liverpool, she read almost every literary classic she could find and spent a great deal of her earnings at the theatre. Its vocabulary and cadence left a deep imprint on her.

It took hold just as Paula was becoming self-sufficient. By the age of fourteen, she had started to earn a living as a hair-dresser, and when, in her late teens, the boss at her salon died suddenly of a blood clot, Paula was asked to take over.

In 1951, at the age of twenty-one, she decided to break away from her Liverpool home and try to make a living in London. She had no idea how to tell the Lebovitzes, so delayed the announcement until the day before her departure. The news was met with silence, which continued right up to the moment she walked out of the door. She had no regrets.

'I never felt happy in my relationship with them, of twelve years in all,' she said, ascribing it to the Lebovitzes' emotional reticence, her increasingly left-wing views, her drift towards atheism, and her aspirations to be more than a 'common working girl'.

After the war, both Siegfried and Paula joined the Young Communist League, and would attend festivals staged by Moscow in various Eastern bloc countries. Paula also joined the Unity Theatre, the amateur dramatic arm of the British Communist Party. As far as the Lebovitzes were concerned, this was evidence of pure godlessness.

On reflection, the only thing she missed from her time with the family was spending winter nights by the fire listening to her 'uncle' read articles in Yiddish from the New York paper *The Forward*. Apart from that, there was nothing. The Lebovitzes, who had helped saved her, never thought it necessary to do anything more to make her feel welcome.

Some of the *Guardian* children found only exploitation in Britain, thinly dressed as charity. Liese Feiks was an eighteen-year-old girl, advertised on 28 June 1938 as 'the Viennese daughter of managing director of an insurance company' who had just finished school, spoke German, English and French, and was an excellent pianist, proficient in English and German shorthand and typing. A British family took her in, but they also sought to take advantage of her.

'Not only was she taken away from her family, but cast in this role as a maid and made to feel that she was beneath the people that she was working for,' her son, Martin Tompa, a computer science professor at the University of Washington, told me. Liese, forcibly separated from her family, had to take all her meals alone in the kitchen. 'She told me many times they were the most miserable years of her life,' Martin said.

There were no cases of outright brutality among those I

came across but plenty of ambivalence, a desire to help those in need on the part of the foster parents but a seeming inability to show true warmth or empathy for their suffering, and even a resentment of the very children they were meant to be saving, for being insufficiently joyful or just different.

Gertrude Batscha's time in Britain with her first foster family left her both grateful and hurt.

Annie Partington, who met her off the train in Bristol, presented a formidable figure, dressed from head to toe in tweed ('the most unfashionable clothes I had ever been exposed to', Gertrude was to recall decades later), a felt helmet for a hat, and a scarf half-hiding a burn scar that ran from her chin to her cheek.

The Englishwoman subjected Gerti to a penetrating appraisal, looking her up and down before picking up her suitcase and instructing her to 'Come along' as she led the girl to her car for the drive to Keynsham, a small town between Bristol and Bath.

There, she would become part of a very English, very middle-class family. Mrs Partington was a moving spirit in the local Women's Institute, and played lots of golf and tennis. Her husband, Frederick, the head of a nearby technical college, was handsome and humorous, but seemed to spend much of his time at home reading, and said very little to Gerti. They had two freckled, redheaded children, thirteen-year-old Geoffrey, who would make sport of the new Austrian arrival, and seventeen-year-old Denly, a subdued girl living under her mother's thumb who swung between resentment of Gerti and a sort of conspiratorial solidarity.

It quickly became clear that Annie Partington had mixed motives for taking Gerti in. It enhanced her reputation at the Women's Institute as a philanthropist, and more concretely, was a source of free labour when Gerti was put to work cleaning the house.

The refugee child had to be the first one up in the morning, to sweep the entrance hall and the garden path, as well as bring in the milk. After breakfast, she did the washing-up and then set about cleaning the house: bedrooms, stairs, dusting every surface.

Mrs Partington would check her work by running her finger across hidden crevices to make sure they had been cleaned. She imposed the same regime on Denly, who could not hide her relief that Gerti had arrived to share some of the burden. Nothing of the kind was expected from Geoffrey, who was exempted from such chores.

After a few months, Gerti pleaded with Mrs Partington to teach her how to cook, only to be told she had not reached the required level of proficiency in cleaning to move on to this higher art.

In her writings, Gerti stressed her gratitude to this complicated Englishwoman 'for having got me out of the Nazi inferno', but at the same time it is evident from her recollections that Annie Partington had a stunning lack of empathy. She would lose her patience with Gerti if she found her crying from homesickness and anxiety about her parents.

Gerti would worry about losing her mental images of her mother and father. She called it a 'dread of forgetting' and that fear prompted a secret ritual of walks through the Keynsham streets, pretending to be with her mother in Vienna, glancing in shop windows with her, following favourite routes, reciting the names of the stores while humming Viennese opera tunes to herself.

She was terrified that the memory of her parents would evaporate from her mind, as if her act of will in recalling them was helping keep them alive. It was easier before September 1939, as a letter would arrive in the post each day from her mother, but after war broke out and the letters stopped, the fear of forgetting became more urgent.

'I would look at her photograph and at that instant lose her real image in my mind's eye,' she wrote. 'This is an experience bordering on trauma; I believe it is harder to bear than being separated and certainly turns prolonged separation into endless agony.'

Gerti described this gradual loss as a 'slow orphanhood'. She had become an orphan in 1942 without knowing it. The death of her parents was not confirmed for another three years, and each day was a battle to keep them in her mind.

'As the years went by the faces of my family became the faces of their photographs. For a long time I was able to screw up my eyes very tight and so conjure up the "real" look of my father and mother,' she wrote in later life. That singular focus on the memory of her flesh-and-blood parents was strong enough at first to displace what they looked like in their photographs, but eventually the two-dimensional black-and-white image grew stronger than the memory and replaced it, as it had already done with her lost grandparents, uncles and aunts.

Annie Partington was oblivious to Gerti's sense of displacement, finding it hard to understand how the girl could be unfamiliar with English ways. She insisted she come to church with the family on Sunday and refused an offer from the local Jewish refugee committee to take her to Cheder in Bath at weekends.

Worst of all, the Partingtons do not seem to have responded in any serious way to Gerti's entreaties to help save her parents by securing a job offer for them. There was another Jewish refugee from Vienna in Keynsham, Ruth Deutsch, a year younger than Gerti, who lived with a host family who were poorer and a great deal warmer than the Partingtons. By spring, this family had helped organise domestic permits for Ruth's parents, who were able to escape the Nazi Reich and come to Keynsham. It was quite obvious that such an act of salvation was achievable with a bit of effort from this British family, who did not have the connections and education of the Partingtons.

Somehow, in later life, Gerti managed to forgive them. Annie was a 'jolly woman who tried to be kind', she wrote.

'As unhappy as I was under the circumstances and as miserable as Mrs P. and her son often made me, I have always felt nothing but gratitude towards them . . . For motives not quite clear, they, the goyim, made the necessary arrangements and saved a Jewish child,' she wrote later, as Yehudith Segal.

By the summer of 1939, however, Gerti felt her limited welcome had run out, especially after Mrs Partington dropped hints that the family would not be taking her on their summer holidays and that she should make other arrangements.

The fourteen-year-old Viennese girl went further and found herself a new home. She wrote to the Katz family, the *Ostjuden* friends from Vienna who had plotted exit routes with her parents, and who had managed to escape to Leeds. They had assured Gerti's parents that they would help look after her in Britain, pointing out that they were forever in Adolf Batscha's debt because he had helped extricate their sons from Dachau. When Gerti wrote to them, the Katzes responded right away. 'Come at once,' they said. 'Our home is your home.'

She moved to Leeds in early July 1939. Annie Partington drove her to the station and seemed both sad and relieved when she put her on the train.

Life with the Katzes in Leeds was the very opposite of the Partingtons. Gerti described them as warm, welcoming and cheerful but impoverished. They were a large family sharing two rooms above a kosher butcher's shop. They slept in the available beds in shifts, although Gerti was initially afforded 'royal treatment' and given a bed to herself. But with resources and space so tight, it could not be a permanent home.

Gerti went to stay with a woman called Rosie Fisher who lived in a much bigger house but in an unhappier family. She was considerably younger than her husband, and frequently rowed with him. He constantly tried to grope Gerti (the only instance of sexual abuse I came across), and both he and his wife treated her as a maid.

It was a dark and low point, made far more so by events in Europe. She was in the Fishers' house on 1 September 1939 when the Nazis invaded Poland, and on 3 September when they gathered around the radio to hear Neville Chamberlain declare war. From that moment on, there was no chance her parents would be able to make their way to Britain.

Untethered from home and family, the refugee children were dependent on the goodwill of strangers and the quirks of fortune. Gerti's luck eventually improved: a woman called Sophie Cainer, a cousin of the Fishers, got in contact. They had met a few weeks earlier and Cainer was aware of her misery. Her family was on the point of moving to Bradford where her doctor husband planned to establish a practice.

Her proposal was that Gertrude come to live with them and help look after their two children, nine-year-old Vera and David, who was nearly six. Sophie Cainer had hired a maid and so assured Gerti that she would always be treated as part of the family rather than free child labour.

Gerti wanted to know if she would be able to go back to school, having not stepped inside a classroom since the previous June in Vienna. But education was only free in Britain until the age of fourteen and the Cainers could not afford private school. They would pay for evening classes and Sophie pledged to do all she could to help Gertrude master English.

It was in the Cainers' new house in Bradford that Gerti Batscha finally found some peace and happiness in Britain. Sophie Cainer was the first host who did not attempt to exploit her. She taught her to sew, to cook and bake bread, how to choose fresh fish at the market, and how to raise chickens for eggs to augment the family's wartime rations. When the time came, she helped Gerti get some work experience.

Gerti found a job in a nursery looking after children whose mothers had to work while their husbands were away fighting. Her fellow carers and the children's mothers were from the

Bradford working class, and she came to realise that they were the backbone of the war against the Nazis.

'All of them seemed to me to be ever cheerful, courageous, indomitable and deeply contemptuous of "that Hitler" whom they thought of as too much of a joke to really hate even,' she would say later. 'I deeply admired them and became a confirmed Anglophile!'

She wrote in her memoir: 'They were difficult, hard times, with the war to come and the dreadful revelations of what had happened to all my family. England left its indelible mark on me and I believe it to be a beneficial mark. I liked the English people, whether Jews or Gentiles. I adjusted to the English mentality easily and I don't think only because I was young. I think it suited me and grafted on naturally to my Viennese background and upbringing. Most of all, I appreciated the English sense of humour and do to this day!'

'England in general, and the English in general, treated the refugee children very humanely and took care of their deprivation,' she concluded.

Before the war was over, however, Gertrude was making plans to leave. The Cainers and many of their friends in Bradford were Zionists and Gerti was caught up in their enthusiasm for a Jewish homeland. She joined a socialist Zionist youth movement, Habonim, and moved to Manchester to volunteer as a mentor for other Jewish teenagers aspiring to emigrate to Palestine, while also working in a Zionist nursery.

The war only occasionally impinged directly on her in Britain. During all her time in Bradford, the city was the target of only one air raid when incendiary bombs dropped over the city centre one night, most likely a German plane unloading unused ordnance on its way home from targets on the west coast of Lancashire. By the time she moved to Manchester, the Germans were in retreat and the Blitz was all but over.

When the war in Europe finally ended on 8 May 1945, all

of Manchester poured out into the streets to celebrate, but for Jewish refugees the end of hostilities also brought trauma, the confirmation of their worst fears, as allied troops arrived at the gates of the concentration camps.

Members of the British army's Jewish Brigade came to recuperate in Manchester and gave Gertrude's Zionist group an account of what they had seen at Bergen-Belsen.

'What could be pushed from one's mind and consciousness as rumour or suspicion, now became revealed as stark reality, reality more horrific than the worst nightmare,' she wrote.

The faint hope that her parents would be found alive in some camp somewhere seemed impossibly slim, but as long as there were some survivors, there was still a chance. She registered with the International Committee of the Red Cross (ICRC) which was setting up a vast database to help families find each other in the wreckage of war.

At first her hopes were raised by a note from the ICRC that she was being looked for, but it did not say by whom. She spent three months believing it could be her parents, before she was informed it was her mother's cousin Liesel, who had lived through Theresienstadt and was trying to find out who else had survived.

Then a thick envelope arrived, and when she opened it, family photos fell out; but the accompanying letter was not written by her mother or father. It came from gentile friends who had a fruit and honey farm outside Vienna which Adolf and Vally had visited occasionally in the first two years of the war. They had entrusted this couple with their treasures. Not long after that, a thin letter came from the ICRC with a short list of names and places and approximate dates of death of her family.

'I have no recollection at all of opening that letter or of what it looked like or where it disappeared to,' she said. 'All I have is a pencilled copy of this list on a scrap of paper in my handwriting, buried deep among other documents and looked at only once every ten years or so.'

She had been sitting with Jewish volunteers in Manchester when she opened the letter. She blacked out, unable to function, and had to be helped into bed where she stayed weeping for three days.

'I felt as if the string controlling my nerves, emotions and reactions had suddenly escaped my hand and I was no longer in control of myself,' she said.

The Hess family was forced by circumstance to flee Vienna separately, but they all survived. Alice Hess arrived in London on Monday, 13 March 1939, exactly a year after the proclamation of the Anschluss. Her mother took time off from her duties as a maid to meet her at Liverpool Street station, and spent a short time with her before putting her on the Manchester train.

Her father Béla, who had managed to extricate himself from Dachau, arrived at the end of March. Although Josefine had found someone to sign a guarantee for her husband, there was no real job waiting for him. Josefine supported him with her weekly wage. Ten shillings went for his rent, and another ten for his food. Alice said her mother 'was very badly treated as a domestic but couldn't afford to leave, because my father needed the money to survive'.

The last of the immediate Hess family to get out of Vienna was Gerty, the youngest, who had stayed with her grandmother. She arrived at the end of May 1939 and stayed with Josefine and Béla in London, where she got a job as an apprentice hairdresser. Alice stayed with the Manchester family who responded to her newspaper ad, and found work in a dress factory.

She did not see her father until June 1940, when he came to visit her in Manchester days before he was interned on the Isle of Man, joining thousands of other men from Germany and Austria. Five months later, their fate seemed to take yet another turn. News came that their US visas had come through.

That in turn secured Béla's release from internment, and Alice rushed to London to take the required medical exam at the embassy. But it was all too late.

With each passing week, the Atlantic crossing was becoming more perilous. In early July 1940, the SS *Arandora Star*, carrying interned refugees and prisoners of war to Canada, was torpedoed and sunk by a German U-boat off the Irish coast, killing more than 700 people. On 17 September, the ship *City of Benares* was torpedoed while crossing from Britain to Canada, carrying evacuated British children among its passengers. Of the 258 people killed, 77 were minors, and the disaster led Winston Churchill to cancel the scheme to relocate British children in North America. The Atlantic escape route was severed.

The Hesses had no choice but to stay in London through the Blitz, sharing a single bedroom in St John's Wood. Alice worked as a dressmaker, Gerty as a hairdresser and Béla found office work in London.

In 1941, Britain's Labour minister, Ernest Bevin, introduced the Essential Work Order, which directed workers to war industries and made it compulsory for working-age women to register. Alice and Béla both signed up for training in engineering. She learned how to operate a lathe to make screws, and he was taught how to mill steel.

On her first day at the job, Alice found herself standing at her lathe opposite another Austrian Jewish refugee, Richard Schoen, a twenty-eight-year-old from Gross Siegharts, a small town about a hundred kilometres north-west of Vienna.

Richard had survived four months of beatings, forced labour and frost in Dachau, and he was the only member of his family to escape. He saw his elder brother Poldi dragged away by police on *Kristallnacht* from a holding cell in Vienna because he had complained about their treatment. He never saw him again. Richard's parents got him out of Dachau by securing a visa for Shanghai, although his release was delayed a month until his wounds from Dachau had healed. By the time he was reunited with his parents in Vienna, the option of getting a work visa to Britain had opened up through the Jewish community organisation, the IKG, which gave priority to Dachau survivors.

When Richard arrived in Britain, he set to work trying to save his little sister, Irma, whom his father had sent to relatives in Mannheim, Germany, believing somehow that she would be safer there. But it took time. Irma was fifteen: beyond compulsory school age but young to be a domestic worker. When he finally managed to get her a job offer and the papers she needed to exit the Reich, he had run out of time. War broke out and the exit route was blocked.

Richard had no way of knowing it, but in July 1942, just about the time he met Alice Hess across a lathe, his parents were deported from Vienna to Theresienstadt, and from there, some time later, to Treblinka. The following month, on 17 August, nineteen-year-old Irma was put on a train to Maly Trostenets outside Minsk and was killed there four days later.

Alice and Richard married in 1944 and found an apartment in Westbourne Park Road, in London's Notting Hill Gate. She went back to dressmaking and after the war was over, he had a go at hairdressing like his sister-in-law Gerty. In December 1947 Alice found she was pregnant, and halfway through the pregnancy, the couple's new US immigrants' visas came through, posing a dilemma of where to live. They ultimately decided to make the ocean crossing to America where they would raise sons, and share joy, but Richard brought with him an abyss that could never be filled.

Their son, Dennis, wrote that Richard 'never recovered from the guilt he felt, that he should have done more to save his brother and sister'.

'Tormented his whole life, he suffered greatly, knowing and questioning why he alone was the only member of the family to survive.'

7

Salvation and Captivity:
Internment in Britain

MY GRANDPARENTS HAD both found a haven in Britain. Erna, our Omi, worked as a maid in London's Bayswater, two blocks from Hyde Park, for the Samek family, earning twenty-five shillings a week. On top of that the German Jewish Aid Committee at Bloomsbury House, the converted hotel which was the headquarters for several refugee organisations after March 1939, gave her an extra pound a month and donated some clothes. The donations were noted in red pen on the Committee's records: 'Dress, shoes, 1 vest, 1 knickers.'

Leo got a visa as a result of a guarantee by Walter Williamson, a farmer from Edgmond, a small village in Shropshire, who had stepped forward to offer a room, whether through the Committee or the Quakers, my grandfather was never sure. He had appealed to both.

The official grounds of Leo's visa were that he would receive training as an agricultural labourer, but unpaid. The record from his initial interview with the Committee noted: 'He wants some help.' Bloomsbury House gave him a little over £6 to live in London in his first months in England and then provided the rail fare to Shropshire.

Leo worked as a labourer at the Williamson farm at Standford Hall from May to October, and then when there was no more work for him he moved down the road to an old rectory in Chetwynd, home to Shropshire's most notorious ghost. Madam Pigott died in childbirth there some centuries earlier, having been abandoned by the local squire, and appeared from time to time in a white robe clutching her unborn baby.

Leo was taken in by the Reverend Henry Temple Robins, a sixty-eight-year-old cleric known for fiery sermons castigating his parishioners for their easy lives. Robins would also make news for the unusual nature of his death seven years later, when he mistook a bottle of caustic soda for communion wine and drank it, an excruciatingly painful end.

At the beginning of 1940, Leo was considering a move to London to look for work but there was no way Omi could support them both on her twenty-five-shilling weekly wage, not even temporarily during his job search. In February 1940, a post came up with Morris & Co, Shrewsbury's biggest employer running a string of businesses from oil trading to general retail, bakeries and cafes. It brought Leo to the town that would be home for the rest of his life.

Like all foreigners at the time, Leo had to carry an alien registration booklet that recorded his address and his compulsory visits to identify himself at local police stations. On 27 October 1939, his passbook recorded that a tribunal had classed him as Category C, the lowest threat level as a 'Refugee from Nazi Oppression'.

'The holder of this Certificate is to be exempted until further order from internment and from the special restrictions applicable to enemy aliens', a stamp in the passbook said.

Of the 73,000 German and Austrian nationals processed by the enemy alien tribunals, 66,000 were put in Category C, supposedly protected against incarceration and special limitations.

That promise lasted less than a year. In the spring of 1940, a panic about 'fifth columnists', a recently coined term, was spreading in Whitehall. Following the fall of Holland to German invasion, a British special envoy to the Dutch government, Sir Nevile Bland, filed a highly speculative report about the role of Nazi infiltrators who had made their way behind Dutch lines in disguise.

'Every German or Austrian servant, however superficially charming and devoted, is a real and grave menace,' the Bland report said. It reached King George VI who demanded that the government take action, and it was broadcast by the BBC.

At his first cabinet meeting as prime minister on 11 May 1940, Winston Churchill gave the order for male 'enemy aliens' between the ages of sixteen and sixty to be rounded up. Initially the order was limited to the coastal counties, on the grounds that that is where fifth columnists could do the most damage in the event of invasion, but within a few days the order was broadened to the whole country.

Those arrested included Category C aliens, mostly men but including some women. Once Italy declared war on Britain on 10 June, Italians who had lived in the country for less than twenty years were included in the round-up. In all, about 27,000 refugees were locked away.

Hitler greeted the internment order as a propaganda victory, crowing: 'The British have in concentration camps the very people we found it necessary to detain.'

In a speech to Parliament on 4 June, Churchill acknowledged that the orders would affect many who were 'passionate enemies of Nazi Germany'. 'I am very sorry for them,' he added, 'but we cannot . . . draw all the distinctions which we should like to do.'

A flurry of articles in the right-wing press followed, playing up the threat, and even the *Manchester Guardian*, which saw itself as a champion of refugee rights, presented Churchill's order as a necessary evil.

'It is disagreeable both for those who suffer it and for those who have to take it, but the news of what Hitler has accomplished by attacking so many countries from within is extremely serious,' the *Guardian* editorial said.

'The refugees are welcome here because they long for Hitler's downfall. They feel as we feel, and are only anxious to assist us, but it would be folly not to assume that he will have tried hard to provide some helpers for his parachutists and troop-carriers should he send them,' the 13 May article declared, adding: 'No half measures will do.'

Before May 1940, not a single person interviewed by the polling group Mass Observation suspected refugees of espionage, or suggested that they should be interned. But after Churchill's speech, half of those polled declared themselves in favour of the internment of refugees, a striking measure of the sway of press and government on public opinion about immigrants.

My grandfather Leo, who had managed to avoid Dachau, was sent by boat from Liverpool to the Central Internment Camp, a cluster of thirty-four commandeered houses on the sea promenade in Douglas, on the Isle of Man, and he was

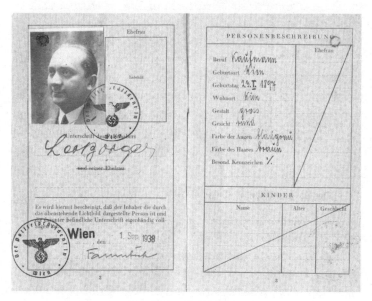

Leo Borger's passport.

held there from the summer of 1940 to 27 January 1941. He never talked about his experience there, perhaps viewing it as a regrettable and temporary lapse on the part of the nation he saw as his saviour.

Siegfried Neumann, who turned eighteen in 1940, was held in another part of Douglas at the Hutchinson Camp, which became known as the artists' colony for the concentration of refugee talent there.

Alice Hess's father, Béla, was also locked up on the Isle of Man but he was released early after he produced proof he and his family had obtained visas for entry to the US.

When she turned sixteen, Gertrude Batscha had to go before a tribunal to decide whether she too should be interned. She was granted Category C status, as Churchill's initial order only applied to men and older boys. She 'passed' but she had to check in at the town hall every so often and was not allowed to live in the strategically sensitive coastal areas of the south and east where an invasion was anticipated.

Internment is a long-forgotten stain on Britain's wartime history. Internees, many of whom had previously suffered imprisonment and persecution at the hands of the Nazis, or lived in the UK for decades, were marched through the streets like prisoners of war. At registration, soldiers or policemen often robbed them of their valuables. While some camps like Hutchinson ran a relaxed and relatively benevolent regime, others were far worse. Two thousand internees were held at Warth Mills, a disused cotton factory on the northern outskirts of Manchester, sharing sixty buckets as toilets, and sleeping on wooden pallets under a leaking roof.

It took a tragedy and a scandal to bring the folly of internment to an end. On 1 July, a converted luxury liner, the SS *Arandora Star* set sail from Liverpool for Canada with over 1,200 internees, who were supposed to be high-risk Nazis and Italian

Fascists. However, to make up numbers and ease pressure on overflowing British internment camps, scores of Jewish refugees and innocent Italians who had lived in Britain for years were forced on board side by side with these extremist political prisoners. On its second day at sea, just after rounding the northern tip of Ireland, the ship was hit by a torpedo fired by a German U-boat. Neither the crew nor the passengers had gone through evacuation drills and there were not enough lifeboats. Seven hundred people – Italians, Germans, Austrians and Britons – were drowned.

The loss of life was not enough in itself to stop the deportation policy, but just over a week later, many of the survivors from the *Arandora Star* were put aboard another ship, HMT *Dunera*, bound for Australia. On board, personal possessions were looted by military and police guards and many of the internees were beaten up, deprived of food and packed together in foul conditions.

The two incidents together swung public sentiment towards sympathy for the refugees. The Home and Foreign Offices issued a joint statement, declaring that they had not been informed of the deportations. As a result, the whole policy of internment was reviewed. By December 1940, eight thousand internees had been released, and another four thousand were freed in the first months of 1941. They tried on the whole to resume their lives, helped by the consistently high demand for labour. Leo returned to Shrewsbury where another guarantee against internment was written into his alien's passbook. Some two years later, the same passbook recorded the fact that he had been made an air-raid warden, and on 30 December 1942, he was: 'Permitted to have in his possession and under his control a push bicycle whilst registered with the Shrewsbury Borough Police.'

After a year at Morris & Co, Leo found a job as a handyman in a new factory in Shrewsbury, called Silhouette. Two German

Jewish families, the Lobbenbergs and the Blumenaus, had brought their underwear business with them when they fled to Britain, where they established themselves initially in London.

The company's best-known product at the time was the 'Radiante' corset, so named because it was impregnated with radium to provide what the company claimed would be the 'stimulating, even rejuvenating influence' of radiation, which would 'cure that feeling of fatigue' and be 'slenderising' at the same time. The firm even had a certificate from the Marie Curie Institute to confirm that it was producing radiation.

It is unclear how many women these corsets may have harmed. When the war began, Radiante production was dropped, and the company was ordered to switch production to parachutes and more utilitarian underwear for servicemen. The company moved to Shrewsbury to escape the Blitz, and Leo joined it on the lowest level, as an odd-job man. He earned £4 a week and rented a worker's cottage in town, but his prospects improved fast. By 1945, he was promoted to the job of 'cutter' in the main factory, the master of his own bench, the job he kept until the end of his working life. One of my earliest memories is going to see Leo on the shop floor and of him, the proud grandfather, lifting me up to sit on the bench's cold metal surface. He seemed an uncomplicated man, content with his lot, who found joy in his grandchildren. He never relinquished the instinctive frugality from his time as a refugee, wearing the same clothes for decades. If he did not have to go out or receive visitors, his trousers were kept up by string.

At the Silhouette factory, he was known as the 'Barber', a reference to his fall-back profession. Hairdressing was the marketable skill that Leo had hastily learned after the Anschluss, and in Britain he seldom went into work without a little brown leather Gladstone bag, containing scissors and hair clippers, in case his skills might be required. Peter Lobbenberg, the son of one of the firm's owners, remembers impromptu crops from Leo, who clearly felt sufficiently secure in his job to trim the boy's hair without asking for parental permission.

He did the same to me when we stopped off at Shrewsbury on our way to Ireland one summer, giving me a crew cut in the garden shed without asking my parents. I loved the feel of it, like animal fur when I rubbed my hand up the back of my neck, but my mum cried most of the way to the Holyhead ferry.

Their visas and living conditions meant that Leo and Omi had to live and labour separately and apart from their son, and they thought he would have better chances in the new country growing up in an English-speaking home. They stayed in touch. Nans had Bobby write postcards to his parents in English to show his progress, and when clothing was hard to come by during the war and after, Leo used to make his son shirts from corset material, dark red and deep green stripes, which Robert would wear with a bow tie.

Leo's cottage was behind Shrewsbury's eighteenth-century prison, and he was eventually joined there by Omi, and then Robert in the university holidays. They became part of a circle of refugees in the town, mostly Viennese Jews, who had come with the Silhouette factory or simply chose it as an escape from the Blitz.

One of the families in the circle were the Graebners, Hans and Lilly, who had fled Vienna because Lilly was Jewish and they were socialists. Their son, Ric, who went on to become a musician and composer, remembered visits to the Borgers' house for Leo's collection of 78 rpm records, antiquated gramophones, and my grandmother's cooking.

'Erna was allegedly a very good cook, but very slow. She invited you for 6 and you were lucky to eat by 9, but it was worth the wait,' Ric wrote to me. He was sixteen years younger than my father, the first baby to be born in Britain to the circle of refugees, but he recalls Robert 'drifting through the house . . .'

'I was theoretically in awe, as a mutual family friend had made it known he was a brilliant mathematician and chess player,' he said.

In the 1950s, the Borger family broke up over Omi's desire to return to Vienna. Their somewhat grim red-brick cottage in Shrewsbury seemed a long way down from the flat on Hintzerstrasse, and labouring in a factory or working as a maid was a similarly steep descent from running a shop.

Leo, who had spent five more months in Vienna under Nazi rule, refused to return, and it severed the marriage. Leo told his son that they were getting divorced when Robert called to break the news that he was getting married. He was teaching psychology at Manchester University and he had met a schoolteacher, Wyn Frost. A mutual friend had brought them together on a group outing to the annual May fair in the town of Knutsford, some twenty miles south-west of Manchester. He turned up in an old Rover convertible with a sleek long bonnet, and she thought he was handsome, dashing and interesting.

Omi later complained to Nans that, after all that university education, her Bobby could have got himself a Jewish girl from a well-to-do family. Mabel Winifred Frost was a gentile from a working-class Manchester background. Her father, William, was a freight clerk for the railway company, who brought home the *Manchester Guardian* every evening and challenged her to find spelling mistakes. Her grandmother ran a corner shop next door, while looking after Wyn's aunt Mabel, who had been struck down by African trypanosomiasis caught from a tsetse fly in a bale of cotton imported by the textile factory where she worked. She sat in a bath chair in a back room shivering, until it killed her at the age of thirty-two.

Wyn had left school at sixteen, but was persuaded to go back and do her A-levels, and was accepted into art college in Corsham, Wiltshire. Art school and the desire to be a sophisticated

Englishwoman for her new boyfriend smoothed out her Mancunian accent and replaced it with the cut glass of 'received pronunciation' in the 1950s, an approximation of how the Royal Family talked.

The couple were married in a Manchester registry office on 16 February 1957, and Wyn's parents, William and Annie, threw them a small party.

Leo, now divorced, left the house behind Shrewsbury prison and took a single room in a shared house to save money. The owner of this substantial home on Shrewsbury's London Road was another Viennese refugee, Vally Klinger, who had arrived at the same time as Leo and started in the clothing trade, but was significantly more ambitious and dynamic. She was, in Ric Graebner's words, 'small, bouncy, glittery and smiling with bright red lipstick'.

While Leo was happy to remain a cutter for the rest of his life, Vally was running her own small factory by the 1950s, making Aertex blouses and other women's clothes.

She had been born Valerie Elisabeth Kohn in the 15th District of Vienna, between the Westbahnhof and the Schönbrunn Palace. Her mother, Anna, worked in a dress shop and her father, Peter, ran a liquor store.

They had a shop assistant who worked in both shops called Rudolf Klinger, who was eight years Vally's senior. They fell in love and married in 1928, when she was twenty-one and he was twenty-nine.

Peter Kohn, the wine merchant, did not live to see the Anschluss. He died in 1931 of appendicitis, which doctors had failed to diagnose in time.

So when the Nazis took over Austria in 1938, Vally, Rudolf and Anna had to face them without the family patriarch, lining up to register as Jews at the local police station, which was now serving the Gestapo.

When it was Vally's turn, she realised that the official taking down her details was one of their neighbours, but he pretended not to know her.

'He didn't look at me once,' she recalled.

The man mumbled something and she was given a bucket and scrubbing brush and ordered to go and wash the pavements outside.

Vally got down on her hands and knees and scrubbed with the other Jews.

It was increasingly risky to be in the streets, but it was impossible to find an escape route without going out, so the Klingers joined the long lines outside the US and British embassies. A family connection had secured an affidavit for Vally, guaranteeing that she would have a job in the US as a maid, which allowed her to secure an American visa.

A second affidavit was supposed to be on the way for Rudolf, and they were so confident that it would arrive that they paid for their bags to be sent to Hamburg for onward shipping to the US.

But the affidavit did not arrive, and the sense of panic swelled. By spring 1939, the family decided that Vally should apply for a domestic servant's visa to Britain, halfway to their goal, and wait for Rudolf there. Her mother Anna, by then a widow in her fifties, seems to have given up hope of ever getting a visa.

So in July, she and Rudolf took Vally to the Westbahnhof to put her on a train heading to Switzerland and then the Dutch coast, all three swearing they would be together again soon, but that was the last time she ever saw them.

In March 1941, Rudolf was transported to a camp in Riga, Latvia and was eventually transferred to Buchenwald, where he died in February 1945, just two months before the camp was liberated by US troops.

Vally had been planning to go to Poland after the war, believing she might find him among the camp survivors there, but the Red Cross letter arrived before she could set out, confirming he was dead.

Vally's mother Anna was deported in 1942, and died most likely in Maly Trostenets where thousands of Viennese Jews were shot in the woods near Minsk.

We children had no clue of the depth of loss that lurked behind our holidays in Shrewsbury, where we sat in the living room eating cake while the adults drank Maxwell House coffee. It was a deep hole under a trapdoor, covered with a bright rug and a jokey catchphrase.

On arrival in Britain, Vally found a job as maid to an elderly, retired woman doctor living on a hedge-lined grove in Hindhead, Surrey.

Clara Fitter had been a pioneer in a profession where women were rare, a kind employer who was drawn to this diminutive, determined refugee, as people so often were.

'In all my life, I never worked so little as when I was a servant,' Vally would tell me.

When the war started and the Blitz began, Hindhead began to feel far too close to the Germans massed on the French coast. By 1940, many people in Britain believed it would be only a matter of months before Hitler launched an invasion.

In the refugee club in London, where Vally would go on her days off in the hope of hearing news of Rudolf or Anna, the looming onslaught hung over every conversation. Those whose US visas had been granted talked about taking ships from Liverpool to New York, but Atlantic crossings were fraught with danger from U-boats. The alternative was to head further north.

Rattled by the anxiety of her fellow refugees, Vally took the train back to Hindhead and handed in her notice. But Dr Fitter, in Vally's telling of the story, would have none of it.

'That's no reason to resign,' she said. 'We'll all go north!' Fitter sold the house in Hindhead and they moved to Shrewsbury, where the elderly doctor had relatives who could accommodate them.

After about a year however, Fitter, now over eighty years old, became ill and moved into a nursing home, leaving Vally to look for work in Shrewsbury. She applied for the post of cutter in a Shrewsbury clothing factory, mentioning her mother's dress shop in the application.

In truth, her mother Anna Kohn had mostly sold factory-made clothes, so Vally knew little about dressmaking, and that became awkwardly apparent when she went to audition for the job. The foreman handed her a huge pair of shears and some cloth and asked her to show him what she could do. When she made a mess of it, he simply looked the other way, having already decided to hire her on the gut feeling that she was smart and desperate enough to learn whatever was required.

She was appointed the firm's chief cutter, sent out by management to jolly the workers along whenever there were grumblings of starting a union, and she eventually became factory manager. She bought the house on London Road, and a worker's cottage on the other side of town to rent out.

When Leo arrived at London Road, looking for a room to rent, Vally had been single for nearly two decades. They were both cut from the same cloth: Viennese, Jewish and lonely. When they wed in 1957, Vally said nonchalantly: 'Well, you know, we have been living under the same roof for a number of years. We may as well get married.'

Their home was a substantial Edwardian building set back from the road with a tiled path and a side gate to a garden where Leo grew raspberries on canes. In summer there was always raspberry fool in the fridge. I cannot think of that house without that taste returning to my mouth.

Like many of Shrewsbury's refugees, they joined the town's bridge club, which had advertised for new players. Its chairman, Ernest Greasley, was a tall insurance salesman who had moved there from Liverpool during the war and stayed. He and his wife Florence would come to the house on London Road to coach Vally and Leo in the subtle arts of the game, while the students would provide brown bread, pickles and sliced sausage (Vally never had much time or inclination for cooking) and the Greasleys' daughter Virginia would watch their television.

Vally and Leo did not own a car until late in life, and Leo never learned to drive, so the Greasleys would take them into the Shropshire countryside, the rounded grass hills at Church Stretton and the Long Mynd, and to the county's highest point, The Wrekin.

These would become our favourite destinations for holiday outings, picnicking on *Liptauer* cheese or salami on brown Germanic bread, and roaming mountain paths and the carpet-like nibbled grass of the hills, peppered everywhere with sheep droppings.

In retirement, Leo and Vally moved to a newly built development a mile further west, around the cricket club, a neat bungalow that was 1970s utilitarian on the outside, early twentieth-century Vienna inside, with wine-red oriental rugs, reproductions of old pictures of landscapes and a lady with a lapdog. Sprinkled around the house were bits of small branches which Leo had found on country walks and fancied them to look like animals or birds, a resemblance he tried to emphasise with a little whittling and the odd coloured drawing pin.

When we would arrive there after three hours on the motorway, my dad would sink into an armchair, switch to Viennese German and, it seemed to me, let down his guard. Soon enough, he would be irritated again by something that was said or something served from the fridge that was far past its best (Vally's culinary skills never improved, and Leo never had any in the first place), but in that hour in between, he was Bobby again, all grown up and nothing to prove, no appearances to keep up.

8

Shanghai

EARLY IN THE morning after *Kristallnacht*, 10 November 1938, visitors started knocking on the door of the Langers' apartment at 14 Praterstrasse. It was at the heart of the 2nd District, the old Jewish quarter of Leopoldstadt, where the synagogues had been burning through the night.

The visitors were Jewish men who had managed to avoid the first wave of round-ups, but now were desperate for somewhere to hide. They had come to Karl Langer, an international lawyer, and his wife, Sofie, because the couple could be relied on to look after their friends and find a place for them to hide in their rambling apartment. It was once a fragment of an old Habsburg-era palace, and it was still riddled with secret passages and hidden rooms. The Langers were ready for the fugitives, having prepared enough food and drink for them all to survive a week.

Karl and Sofie's fourteen-year-old daughter, Gertrude, helped ensure each new arrival was comfortable and provisioned in his assigned cubbyhole. She was also there later in the day when the Gestapo arrived and saw her father open the door to them. Karl Langer had refused to hide, insisting in his lawyerly way that he had broken no laws. Not that laws mattered at all.

'Are you Jewish?' was the first question asked by the policeman at the door, and Karl replied that he was indeed of that faith. Was there anyone else there apart from his wife and daughter? The lawyer insisted there was no one inside and invited the

Gestapo squad to come in and look around, an invitation issued with such confidence that the police did not bother to take him up on it, but simply took him away. Karl was taken to a police station and then quickly put on a train to Dachau.

Kristallnacht destroyed any hope the Langers might have harboured that they could survive in Vienna under the Nazis. As Karl was being taken away, he and Sofie agreed that everything had to be done to get Gertrude out of the country as soon as possible.

Sofie, Gertrude and Karl Langer in Vienna, 1928

The couple had started looking for places for their daughter three months earlier, when Karl had placed an advert in the *Manchester Guardian*, asking: 'Will a Philanthropist take a much-gifted Girl, 14 years old, daughter of an Austrian Jewish lawyer, as a foster child?'

The advert appeared on the same day and in the same column as the appeal by my grandparents for a 'kind person' to look after my father. But he had been luckier, having found foster parents and left Vienna weeks before *Kristallnacht*. Gertrude Langer was still stuck there.

It was fairly easy to find Dr Karl Langer, married to a Sofie Öhler with a fourteen-year-old daughter called Gertrude, in the synagogue records on JewishGen. And in the British archives there was an alien registration card, shaped like a luggage label, in the name of a Gertrude Langer, with the same birthday, 2 June. The card showed that in 1939 she was living in Maidenhead, Berkshire, proving that she had survived.

Family connections helped get her out. An uncle worked in the Jewish community's education department and placed her on the list for one of the first *Kindertransport* trains out of Vienna. The fact that she was the child of a prisoner in Dachau also gave her priority.

It was not clear from the records what happened to Gertrude Langer after Maidenhead. The first time I looked through the British archives there seemed to be no traces of onward move-ment. But within the space of a few months, newly uploaded documents unlocked the mystery. Gertrude's name appeared on the passenger manifest of the *Suwa Maru*, a ship of Japan's Nippon Yusen Kaisha line, sailing from Liverpool to Yokohama on 30 August 1940. She and nine other passengers, all European Jews, mostly teenagers, had booked passage to Shanghai.

The Chinese port city had come up several times in the records as I tried to trace the children from newspaper ads, but it was Gertrude's remarkable story that would lead deep into this little-known chapter in the Jewish experience of the Holocaust, an episode that would repeatedly take me by surprise. It was a cosmopolis where Jewish influence and economic power was arguably unmatched anywhere in the world. Shanghai was on the other side of the world from Vienna, which turned out not to be far enough away to escape the Nazis entirely. It was a life-saving haven which became a prison.

Putting Shanghai and Gertrude's name together into a search of US newspapers produced one striking result: the obituary of a Rabbi Theodore 'Ted' Alexander, who had died in October 2016 and was remembered in the *Jewish News of Northern California* as a 'progressive, welcoming leader'.

Born in Berlin in 1920, he had rescued a prayer shawl and a Torah scroll from the local synagogue as it was burning on *Kristallnacht*. He and his parents fled Germany with these salvaged relics and managed to reach Shanghai, where he met and married Gertrude Langer, from Vienna.

Gertrude had outlived him by just three years, but they did have a child, Leslie Alexander of Los Gatos, who had inherited her father's calling and become America's first female rabbi of a major Conservative Jewish synagogue, in 1985. Through one of her daughters, whose email address showed up online, I sent her an email with the *Guardian* advert attached on 11 January 2021. A reply came from Leslie Alexander herself within a few hours, just before midnight.

Leslie confirmed that she was the daughter of Gertrude Langer, the girl in the advertisement, and seeing it for the first time had left her 'surprised, shocked and very emotional'.

Gertrude had died in November 2019 without ever knowing about the advert, as far as her daughter knew.

'It would have been great to have shown her the ad and to have discussed what she knew of her parents' plans for her,' Leslie said.

Gertrude had not left a written memoir of her experiences, but she had given an extensive interview in a documentary called *Exile Shanghai*, made by an avant-garde German artist and film-maker, Ulrike Ottinger, about this obscure episode of Jewish history in China. In the film, Gertrude and Theodore sit side-by-side and tell their stories in a mix of German and English.

Gertrude left Vienna in December 1938. While some of the

children who boarded the trains at Westbahnhof were excited to be embarking on an adventure and escaping the Nazis, Gertrude Langer was weeping and terrified. She had never been anywhere on her own before, and her father was still in Dachau.

Her mood lifted though as soon as the train crossed into Holland, a moment of relief and liberation experienced by most of the refugee children who escaped by rail. Dutch well-wishers came on board and began handing out chocolate to the children.

When Gertrude reached Britain there was no specific family lined up for her, so she was placed among the unclaimed Jewish children, billeted in what was supposed to be a summer camp, except it was the middle of December and freezing cold. There was no heating, and the only warmth the children had was from hot water bottles.

Gertrude pleaded with the camp organisers that she be allowed to stay in London as she at least knew someone there, an aunt who had emigrated some years earlier. The relief committee agreed and she was one of a dozen children billeted in a large house funded by anonymous benefactors, where they were looked after by a team of carers who made sure they got to school and synagogue.

'They treated us beautifully,' Gertrude recalled.

Meanwhile the news came from Vienna that her father had been released from Dachau. Sofie had written to his foreign clients who had lobbied the Nazi regime and it had worked because, Gertrude said later, 'at that time, the German government was still interested in the opinion of people in foreign countries'.

In Dachau, Karl Langer had seen the brutality of the Nazis up close and he knew there was little time left to make an escape. One of the last resorts available was a visa for Shanghai. The Chinese free port did not actually require a visa for entry, but the Nazi authorities demanded to see one in order to grant permission to leave the Reich.

Word went around Vienna that the Chinese consul-general Ho Feng-Shan was issuing them freely, in defiance of orders to the contrary from his ambassador in Berlin. The thirty-seven-year-old Ho had grown up poor in rural China, and learned English and German at a free Norwegian Lutheran mission, before winning a scholarship to study economics in Munich.

He became consul in Vienna in 1937, and gave lectures on Chinese history and culture, befriending some of the city's Jewish intelligentsia and becoming keenly aware of the danger approaching from the north. Ho warned a visiting Chinese delegation: 'The situation now is like a fire in a paper bag and it is going to burn through . . . The consequences will be very dire, especially for the Jews.'

The Chinese ambassador in Berlin, Chen Jie, a pro-German diplomat, was outraged at Ho's liberal distribution of entry visas and attempted to have it stopped, even sending one of his embassy staff to Vienna to investigate whether the travel documents were being sold, but no wrongdoing was found. Ho argued that it was against foreign ministry policy to restrict visas and he continued to issue them to all Jews who applied.

On *Kristallnacht*, Ho remained on the streets, honouring an appointment to visit a Jewish oil executive in his home. Two Gestapo thugs arrived at the same time as the Chinese diplomat and he faced them down, refusing to show his identity documents before they showed theirs.

After he died in 1997, Yad Vashem named Ho as one of the 'Righteous Among the Nations'. In his translator's note to the English edition of Ho's memoir, *My Forty Years as a Diplomat*, his son, Monto Ho, said he acted 'naturally, almost routinely, as a decent human being'.

Ho issued nearly two thousand visas in total, and two of

them were for the Langers. Securing visa documentation was essential for them to leave the Reich, but Gertrude's parents still needed to get to Shanghai and that was not straightforward either. Ultimately, they had help from Gertrude's uncle in France who had connections in the shipping business, and got them passage on a ship that left from Marseille.

They had to wait more than a year for Gertrude to join them as it was near impossible to get tickets on ships to the Far East. It was not until November 1940 that she was able to book a berth on a vessel bound for Shanghai, as a result of late cancellations by other Jewish refugees, giving her just twenty-four hours' notice to get to Liverpool, from where the *Suwa Maru* was due to sail.

On board, there were eight children to a cabin, and Gertrude's berth was under the water line close to the engines. The engines started rumbling as soon as passengers boarded and the ship slipped its moorings. As it headed out towards the Irish Sea, Gertrude climbed on her bunk and fell into a deep sleep.

She had no idea how long she had been unconscious when she was suddenly woken by the air sirens echoing around the cabin. She looked up with a start, terrified, but her cabin mates were doubled up with laughter. The sirens that woke her had been the all-clear, and she had slept right through the air raid, which had been one of the worst Liverpool had ever suffered. Ships had gone up in flames around them but the *Suwa Maru* had switched off its lights and glided, a bulky shadow, out of the flaming harbour.

For the next few days, all the passengers had to keep their life jackets on constantly, as they crossed the Irish Sea to Dublin, stopped in Belfast before turning south to Lisbon and on through the South Atlantic, heading for the Cape of Good Hope. The Mediterranean and the Suez Canal were closed to them, so the only passage to China was around Africa into the Indian Ocean. The passengers had three months to get to know one another.

Many of her fellow travellers were the English children of colonial officials who had been at boarding schools, and whose parents were now panicking about a possible Nazi invasion of Britain. There were also Japanese nationals returning from Britain to a homeland that was, for now, still at peace, as well as a mix of South Africans and Indians, bound for ports along the way.

Gertrude got used to life on board, which was not that hard. The *Suwa Maru* was noted for its luxury. Charlie Chaplin had sailed on it to Japan in 1932. The food was particularly good, and she kept one of the lunch menus as a memento. It included breaded fresh lobster fillet, jugged hare à la Flamande and roast cushion of veal.

The passengers passed the time by playing shuffleboard and other deck games. There was no shortage of children for Gertrude to chat to, and they exchanged their short but often dramatic life stories.

'It wasn't as scary as it would have been had I been all alone among a lot of worried adults,' she said.

Gertrude's trip on the *Suwa Maru* was one of its last voyages as a civilian steamship. In 1941, it was requisitioned as a troop transport, which it remained until 1943 when it was hit by a torpedo from a US submarine and beached on a reef at Wake Island in the Pacific.

Gertrude finally arrived in Shanghai with little idea of what awaited her there. She had left in such a hurry when the berth became available that she had no time to contact her parents. But they were on the quayside among the crowds to embrace her, having come out to the docks to meet every ship arriving from Britain for the previous month.

By then, Karl and Sofie had already established themselves in Shanghai. Her father had been working as a judge in an international court set up to allow non-Chinese speakers to settle their own differences. It was all part of the bubble of Shanghai's International Settlement, run principally by British and American businessmen for their own advantage, which had been allowed its privileged existence by the Japanese occupation authorities since the fall of the city in 1937.

The Japanese had a complex relationship with the Jews. On the one hand, a Jewish financier, Jacob Schiff, the German-born president of Kuhn, Loeb & Co, helped finance the Japanese navy when other Western banks refused, contributing to the nation's victory over Russia in 1905. On the other hand, Japanese soldiers returned from that war with copies of the Protocols of the Elders of Zion, a fabricated depiction of a Jewish plot to dominate the world, and the conspiracy theory had wormed its way into some parts of Japanese society. In general, the Japanese were in awe of the Jews, and imputed great powers to them, particularly in Shanghai, which boasted one of the most powerful and remarkable Jewish communities in the world, one which could trace its roots to the nineteenth century and the arrival of two great Iraqi Jewish dynasties, the Sassoons and the Kadoories.

David, the patriarch of the Sassoon family, had come from Baghdad, descended from a line of Jews brought from Jerusalem by King Nebuchadnezzar as forced labour, at the beginning of the Babylonian captivity. The Sassoons had emerged as the wealthiest of the city's clans and in the late eighteenth century its Ottoman rulers accorded them princely status.

David Sassoon, born in 1792, was groomed to be a prince in Baghdad, but the whole system collapsed before he could inherit the role. In the 1820s, rifts between Ottoman factions broke out into open conflict, and when a victor emerged, he was no friend of the city's Jews. Sassoon was arrested in 1829 and had to be ransomed out of jail and then smuggled out of Baghdad at night in disguise for his own safety.

He and his family made their way to Bushehr and then to Bombay, arriving in 1832 just as the British East India

Company's trade monopoly ended and steamships were being introduced. It was a moment of opportunity for the quick-witted. The Sassoons flourished in the ensuing boom, and within a decade David was one of the richest men in India.

The secret of his success was, in a word, drugs. The Sassoons became enthusiastic participants in Britain's opium trade, shipping the narcotic into China in defiance of the ban declared by the country's imperial government.

The cynical inundation of China with opium led to the first Opium War and the 1842 Treaty of Nanjing, in which China was forced to cede Hong Kong to Britain and open five cities, including Shanghai on the mouth of the Yangtze, as free ports to international trade. Chinese law would not apply to Western traders there.

The Sassoon association with Shanghai began by chance. David Sassoon liked to go to the central post office in Bombay in person, to pick up business correspondence and listen to gossip. He noticed that a British competitor had begun receiving large amounts of mail from Shanghai, which made him wonder what his family was missing.

Shanghai in its 1930s heyday.

In 1850, the patriarch dispatched one of his sons, thirty-year-old Elias, to establish an outpost of the family business in the port, on the road running along the Yangtze known as the Bund, the word for embankment in Urdu, brought by the British colonialists from India.

Once he had set up shop, Elias began importing opium and Indian spices, and sending back silk, tea and animal hides. He bought his own warehouses, rather than renting them, maximising the profit. Some of the first telegrams sent in Asia were coded messages between the Sassoon brothers, discussing the opium price.

By the 1870s, the Sassoons controlled seventy per cent of the opium trade, displacing the Jardine Matheson company, and the family's fortune soared, to the outrage of at least one relative, Siegfried Sassoon, destined to be one of Britain's best known poets of the early twentieth century. He railed against his extended family's 'monstrous wealth' acquired from the 'dirty trading' in narcotics.

The Chinese Communist government later estimated that the Sassoons made the 2018 equivalent of $2.7 billion dollars from the opium trade. When many Western countries banned it in 1912, the family simply changed course, ploughing their drug money into property and business shares, doubling their investment again.

The other great Shanghai dynasty, the Kadoories, emerged from Baghdad in the wake of the Sassoons. Elly Kadoorie and three of his brothers were sent by their mother from Baghdad to Bombay to study in a Sassoon school, when Elly was fifteen. Starting out in business, he followed the Sassoon trail to Shanghai, making a fortune initially in the rubber industry and then in property, building Shanghai's most resplendent mansion, Marble Hall, and its grandest hotel along the Bund, the Majestic.

Victor Sassoon, David's grandson, had meanwhile become the International Settlement's most eligible bachelor, absurdly rich, monocled and urbane, and socially active despite having been nearly paralysed in a plane crash in 1915, flying for the Royal Naval Air Service.

He dissolved the family's assets in India in the late 1920s, in the face of the growing anti-imperialist movement led by Mahatma Gandhi, and focused them in Shanghai, where the threat of revolution appeared to have been kept at bay, at least for the time being.

Victor Sassoon competed with the Kadoories in the pursuit of decadent ostentation under Chiang's protective umbrella, building a company headquarters, Sassoon House, which, at nine storeys, was the city's tallest building, and then a hotel intended to outshine Elly Kadoorie's Majestic. He called it the Cathay.

By the mid-1930s, forty thousand tourists a year were stopping in Shanghai. Noël Coward wrote *Private Lives* in the Cathay Hotel while recuperating from influenza. Charlie Chaplin brought his wife-to-be, Paulette Goddard, to stay there.

The influence of the Sassoons and the Kadoories made Shanghai the stuff of legend for Jews fleeing pogroms in Russia in the early twentieth century. They provided jobs, housing, education and social services, although this newly established community was kept at arm's length socially by the two families, who saw themselves as part of the British establishment and distinct from the Russian Jews by class and language.

The first Jewish refugees from Germany and Austria arrived in November 1938, on board the luxury Italian liner, the *Conte Biancamano*. More than fifteen thousand had arrived by August 1939, most being sent to the Tilanqiao area in Hongkou District, which had been badly damaged in fighting between Chinese and Japanese forces two years earlier, and where conditions were miserable. Diphtheria, scarlet fever, tuberculosis, measles and typhoid spread unbridled among the immigrants.

Victor Sassoon and Elly Kadoorie organised medical services, board and lodging for the new arrivals. Elly Kadoorie's son, Horace, set up the Shanghai Jewish Youth Association, sponsoring vocational courses, sports and the arts, and at the same time established new refugee schools, taught entirely in English. Sassoon paid the entry fee at customs, and a reception centre was set up on the first floor of one of his skyscrapers, the Embankment Building, where each new arrival was given blankets, sheets, and a spoon, bowl and cup. A kitchen in the basement provided 1,800 meals a day. One of the Sassoon factories was turned into a hostel, and a vocational training facility was established for mechanics and carpenters.

Among those hired by Victor Sassoon was Ted Alexander, Gertrude's future husband, who was given a job as a purchasing agent. Ted had fled Berlin with his sister and parents, by train to Trieste and then by ship to Shanghai, with the family's gold and stock certificates concealed in a mattress and the lining of Ted's clothes.

On the crossing, no matter how rough the seas, his for-midable mother refused to let her three children leave the table at mealtimes, saying: 'In my family nobody gets seasick. We don't know when we will eat again or when we will have fun again,' she told them.

On arrival in Shanghai in March 1939, she turned to her son and told him: 'This is one of the capitals of sin in the world. You are eighteen years old. I am not going to tell you not to go to the bars. But you promise me if you have any relationship with a girl, the next morning you go to the doctor and get yourself an injection.'

Ted kept the promise and said he 'never had a problem like so many young guys'. Not long after the Alexanders' arrival, however, Ted caught sight of Gertrude, and after that, all other girls were irrelevant.

Almost as soon as she landed in Shanghai, Gertrude had set out to find herself a job. She had studied dress design and had a sketchbook of artwork to show to the dressmaker salons around town, including the fanciest, the Palace Hotel, one of the grand towers along the Bund. The owner took one look at her sketches and hired her.

'I was very proud of myself, as I was extremely young and should have been in school, but instead I had a very good job which I really enjoyed,' she wrote.

She would sit and talk to the clients and then sketch impressions of clothes for them, based on their ideas and what they looked like. In the city around her, a 'Little Vienna' sprang up as the new arrivals set up restaurants and cafes, quickly recreating what had been stolen from them in their home country.

This idyll of Vienna on the Yangtze was short-lived. The refugees' belief that they could outrun the war was an illusion. It could not be contained in Europe. On 8 December 1941, as the surprise attack on Pearl Harbor was underway, Japanese troops marched into the International Settlement in Shanghai, with barely any resistance. The US and UK had each kept a gunboat moored in the river with skeleton crews, mostly to maintain communications with London and Washington. The American ship was seized, and the British vessel, the HMS *Peterel*, was sunk.

The British regiments which had once garrisoned the International Settlement had been withdrawn in 1940, sent elsewhere in the empire, and the Shanghai Volunteer Corps, made up of a motley assembly of Scots in kilts, a Russian regiment and a Jewish company, was ordered to stand down as the Japanese marched in.

Ted Alexander was a volunteer, and with a foolhardy determination he attributed to his Prussian upbringing, he put on his uniform when he saw the Japanese arrive, taking his rifle and rushing out onto the street, where he was immediately disarmed. He counted himself lucky not to have been shot.

Japanese marines in tanks and armoured cars rolled into the Settlement and began patrolling the Bund. British and American residents were told to register at the headquarters of the Kempeitai, the secret police, which had been set up in one of the Sassoons' apartment blocks. There, enemy aliens were given red armbands, A for Americans, B for British.

A Japanese naval captain, Koreshige Inuzuka, was in charge of the takeover of the International Settlement. Inuzuka, like many Japanese officers, was a believer in Protocols-style conspiracy theories in which the Jews were all-powerful string-pullers in Western society and China too. He saw the Chinese leader Chiang Kai-shek, in particular, as a puppet of Jewish plutocrats and of Victor Sassoon in particular, and he arrived in Shanghai with the aim of recruiting Sassoon to the Japanese cause.

Sassoon played along with Inuzuka at first, spinning out talks, but the Japanese officer was insistent that the Sassoon empire be merged with a Japanese company in order to safe-guard it. When Sassoon demurred, Inuzuka started to make threats, and fearing imminent arrest, the tycoon quietly boarded a ship to India and slipped away.

After his very brief gesture of resistance, Ted Alexander was called in to the Cathay Hotel early in the morning to help shred Sassoon company documents, but Japanese soldiers arrived when he was halfway through the job and detained him and other company executives. Inuzuka then appeared, to pose triumphantly behind Victor Sassoon's abandoned desk.

Elly Kadoorie and his son, Lawrence, were held at Shanghai's Chapei internment camp, but Elly was allowed to return to the stables of his former grand residence, Marble Hall, where he would eventually die, in August 1944, a year before liberation.

The foreign residents of the Settlement were evicted from their houses, and most were interned in Lunghua Civilian Assembly Centre, a concentration camp established near Shanghai's airport. The writer J. G. Ballard was one of the children interned there, and his experiences were the inspiration for his novel *Empire of the Sun*.

After Japan signed a pact with Germany and Italy in September 1940, the Kempeitai began cooperating with its Nazi counterpart, the Gestapo, who were allowed to enter Little Vienna, a sight that must have been absolutely chilling for its residents who had travelled halfway around the world to escape the Nazi secret police. Within days of their arrival, a play being staged in Shanghai about Viennese Jews living through the Anschluss was shut down on Gestapo orders.

In July 1942, the SS arrived. The Wannsee Conference on implementing the Final Solution had taken place six months earlier, and the official visit reflected the Nazis' determination to make their programme of obliteration global.

The head of the SS delegation was Colonel Josef Meisinger, who had earned the nickname 'the Butcher of Warsaw' for his efficiency and relish in murdering Polish Jews.

'He was a frightening individual, a large, coarse-faced man with a bald head and an incredibly ugly face,' Walter Schellenberg, a senior SS intelligence officer, recalled.

Meisinger also had the remarkable distinction of having been disciplined by the SS for his brutality. He would have been court-martialled for these excesses, according to Schellenberg, but for the intervention of Reinhard Heydrich, the SS and Gestapo chief who chaired the Wannsee Conference, and who had been a friend of Meisinger since the early days of Nazi rule.

'Meisinger knew too much, and Heydrich managed to prevent the trial from taking place,' Schellenberg wrote.

Instead Meisinger was sent to Tokyo in April 1941 to be the liaison officer to the Kempeitai. He presented a range of solutions for the 'problem' of Shanghai's roughly twenty thousand Jews: either use them as slave labour in Manchuria or subject them to 'medical experiments' in a specially constructed camp on an island in the Yangtze River. Such were two of his suggestions. Meisinger's preferred plan, however, was to round them all up and put them on ships which would be towed out into the open ocean and sunk.

The Japanese naval authorities were taken aback. They were responsible for many atrocities, but this form of mass killing was several steps too far up the genocidal ladder for them. They argued for a compromise in which the Jews should be held in Shanghai for later use as possible bargaining counters. In February 1943, a 'Designated Area for Stateless Refugees' was declared in a three-quarter square mile area of Hongkou, and all refugees who had arrived after 1937 were given three months to move there. In practice, the order applied to all of the city's Jewish population. Barbed wire was put around the ghetto, and food rations were reduced to a starvation diet, eight ounces of bread per person a day.

'We had to move into a very primitive house,' Gertrude recalled. 'We thought it was really terrible that we had to live in this designated area and were unable to leave it except if we applied for a pass and we had to have a good reason to leave or else we were imprisoned. And it was in what was definitely the worst part of Shanghai, the part that had been destroyed in an earlier war by the Japanese and our living conditions were absolutely horrible.'

In the Langers' new home in the Shanghai ghetto, there were buckets in the alleys instead of plumbing, and in place of a stove there were little flower pots of charcoal over which everything had to be cooked. One of Gertrude's chores was to squat by the pots and keep their fires going with a Chinese fan, while holding the endemic mice and rats at bay.

The Japanese placed ammunition depots in Hongkou, in the

belief that the presence of a white Jewish population might act as a human shield, and because if there was a cataclysmic explosion, the mass casualties would be of less importance.

People were killed in the US bombing raids, but Gertrude said far more died from incarceration. Ghetto Jews were locked up for the smallest infraction, and once in jail invariably they would be bitten by lice, succumbing two weeks later to typhoid for which no medicines were available.

'People came out of prison after a two-day sentence and said goodbye to all their friends, because they knew they weren't going to be alive three weeks later,' she said.

Amid this steady attrition, Jewish life went on. Ted Alexander was ordained as a rabbi in the ghetto, and his family hosted regular literary and philosophical salons. The overwhelming majority of the ghetto's Jews survived their ordeal there, emerging thin and in rags, but alive.

When I went to Shanghai in 2016, the hotels built by the Sassoons and the Kadoories were still there along the Bund, but they were now overlooked by far taller glass skyscrapers whose constant neon glow reflected off the Yangtze. The old three-storey Ohel Moshe synagogue, which was the centre of Russian Jewish life in Tilanqiao, had been turned into the Jewish Refugees Museum. The British-built Ward Row prison, commandeered by the Japanese, where a short sentence could be fatal, was still there and functioning as Tilanqiao prison, behind its original squat concrete and brick gateway. After the war, the US executed Japanese war criminals there and the Chinese nationalist Kuomintang took it over and used it to lock up and execute Communists.

Mao Zedong's forces made a bid to fill the vacuum in Shanghai left by the retreating Japanese in 1945, but the Kuomintang prevailed, liberating three and a half million Chinese residents, six thousand Europeans, Americans and Australians at the Lunghua Civilian Assembly Centre, and twenty thousand Jews. The nationalist authorities of Chiang Kai-shek tried to maintain order and have everyone stay where they were, but the pent-up frustration in the ghetto was too powerful to be contained.

'We just didn't want to be confined any longer, and we just broke out of there as a group,' Gertrude said. The ghetto inmates then went to the other camps and had to coax their cowed prisoners into walking out. 'There were a lot of children in there and they were scared that the children might be harmed, and until we came and told them that they were safe and they could leave, they were afraid to come out of those horrible camps.'

As the Jews emerged from the Hongkou ghetto, the Europeans from internment camps, and Shanghai's Chinese population from the shelter of their homes, scores of US planes flew overhead, dropping leaflets telling them they were free.

'Everybody was . . . cheering the same planes that had bombed Shanghai, who were now welcomed because they were the liberators of the city,' Gertrude said. 'And it was a wonderful sight to see the people were laughing and crying at the same time and screaming and yelling and the whole city was celebrating. There wasn't a Japanese soldier to be seen. I have no idea where they were hiding, but they were totally invisible after having been everywhere.'

The day after liberation, Ted Alexander walked to the Bund in a shabby suit and shoes with holes in their soles, to represent E. D. Sassoon & Co, and reclaim its real estate empire. 'I looked awful,' he said, but he 'took possession of all our assets'.

The gambit could have gone either way; the struggle between the Chinese Communists and nationalists, which had never entirely stopped, restarted in earnest with the Japanese defeat, and Communist anti-imperialist ideas spread quickly across Shanghai. Some Western bosses returned to find their Chinese staff unprepared to accept the old status quo.

But Ted was welcomed by those Sassoon employees who had returned to their former jobs. He was put up in the royal suite at the Cathay Hotel, where he smuggled Gertrude in, saying she was his cousin, which raised some eyebrows when they got married the following year. The hotel's head chef returned and cooked Ted, Gertrude and other returnees a banquet, which was far too rich and substantial for their shrunken stomachs to digest.

Gertrude got a job working for the US army, painting signs saying 'Keep Out', 'Caution' and 'Do Not Enter'. She went on to work as a 'searcher' for the US army postal service, tracking down American soldiers who had moved posts so that, if they were still alive, their mail could be forwarded to them. They picked the right woman. Gertrude, who knew about being separated from family, was not going to let those 'poor people be without their mail', and threw herself into the task.

Gertrude and Ted were married on 9 June 1946. They and their parents and witnesses all signed a Chinese certificate without understanding a single word. It felt like home and their attachment to Shanghai ran deep but it was clear they would not be able to stay. Chiang Kai-shek's assurances that he had the Communist insurgency under control were obviously wishful thinking. His troops were defecting all the time.

The Sassoons and Kadoories had hoped that they would be able to do business with Mao's Communists as they had with everyone else, but they were rebuffed. When the revolutionaries took control of the city in 1949, they executed thousands of people in the Shanghai Canidrome, the dog-racing arena, on Mao's orders, making clear that those who had collaborated with the imperialists would be the first to die.

In the last days of the Kuomintang, the regime printed money to fund its army in an attempt to fend off the Communist advance, triggering a bout of hyperinflation. When Gertrude and Ted booked their passage to the US on the government-owned American President Lines, the cost was $740, but it had to be paid for in 'Chinese dollars' or yuan. It translated as 27 million yuan and the highest denomination note available was 10 yuan. The newly married couple had to hire a rickshaw to carry the bundles of cash. But between the time they had changed currencies in the morning to arriving by rickshaw at the shipping company, the yuan had fallen in value again and they had to go back to the currency exchange to get more money and another rickshaw.

They arrived in San Francisco on Yom Kippur 1947, and within a week, they both had jobs. Gertrude became a buyer at a fashion emporium, while Ted started off working in insurance but soon switched to the rag trade as well. He was a sales representative for women's clothes by day, and a rabbi in the evenings.

The couple found a small place in Oakland to live and were eventually able to house Karl and Sofie Langer there, followed by Ted's parents who had to wait longer for their US visas in a German resettlement camp.

Gertrude Langer, the fourteen-year-old advertised an inch or two below my father, went on to be a designer and couturier. She kept her notebooks from her days on the Bund in Shanghai, and a map marked with pins which traced her and Ted's extraordinary odyssey.

'They went on to create wonderful things out of their lives,' their daughter Leslie said. 'The thing to learn, that I learned and that my children learned, is that terrible stuff can happen, but if you can survive what other people do to you, if you can survive it inside yourself, you can still really thrive.'

9

Fred and the Trail to Auschwitz

THE METROPOLE HOTEL had all the glamour and elegance of late Habsburg Vienna, embodied in stone. It was a six-storey neo-classical palace on Morzinplatz where the old city touched the Danube Canal. It had been built in 1873 for the World's Fair that was held in the imperial capital that year, the twenty-fifth of Franz Joseph's reign.

The Metropole was a high temple of luxury, with a glass-covered central courtyard and 365 lavishly decorated rooms, a destination hotel for a famous international clientele. Mark Twain lived there with his family for eight months from the autumn of 1897 to the late spring of 1898, meeting the emperor, Johann Strauss, Sigmund Freud and just about every other Viennese celebrity during his stay.

In his absence from the United States, rumours circulated that the great writer had died, and the *New York World* cabled a reporter to commission a story with the instructions: 'If Mark Twain very ill, 500 words. If dead, 1,000.'

In response, Twain wrote to a curious journalist: 'The report of my death was an exaggeration', which was transformed by legend into 'Reports of my death are greatly exaggerated'.

The hotel's glorious past made it an irresistible target for the Nazis. It was something to be crushed and then erased. After the Germans marched into Vienna, the Gestapo commandeered the hotel for their headquarters. Its sheer size and location allowed the *Geheime Staatspolizei* (Secret State Police) to project dominance over the subjugated city.

As Jews owned the hotel, it was easy to confiscate – the proprietors were simply thrown into jail. The Gestapo could use the police cells a few blocks west along the canal quay, allowing most of the Metropole rooms to be converted to offices for its vast many-tentacled bureaucracy, though there were detention cells on the ground floor and basement of the building for high-value detainees.

The *Judenreferat*, the Jewish section, took up much of the third floor and set to work confiscating the records of the Jewish Community IKG, for use as a database.

The Schwarz family lived on Morzinplatz across from the Metropole and could see from their window when the huge red swastika banners were hung between the hotel's Corinthian columns. It was not a view they would have for long. A cordon was established around Morzinplatz to remove hostile elements, which included all Jews. So Alois Schwarz, a lawyer, his wife Helene, and their two sons, seventeen-year-old Fritz and four-teen-year-old Manfred, were summarily evicted with no compensation or alternative home offered. They moved in with Helene's mother on Schmelzgasse on the other side of the canal in the 2nd District, the old Jewish quarter.

Its slums had mostly been cleared in the nineteenth century when Vienna was rebuilt in grand style as the capital of a mighty empire, but a couple of ancient little houses survived, as if forgotten by the great cull.

The Schwarzes' new home, however, was an Art Nouveau masterpiece, with a circular marble staircase, and mouldings in the shape of intertwined flowers on the doorframe.

These were the last months the Schwarz boys would spend in Vienna with their parents, and Manfred stored away intense memories of them. Their fifty-year-old mother, Helene, was a beautiful woman, 'a real mother, energetic and with golden hands', and their father Alois, five years older, a civil lawyer, a man about town with a good reputation who suddenly had all that – livelihood, standing, respect and a vocation – stripped away from him. He was reduced to going from office to office looking for a way out. The city the Schwarzes had called home had become a vice that closed in on them with each passing day.

Fritz (later spelled the Dutch way, Frits), who was eighteen and had just passed his high school exams, was caught by a gang of Hitler Youth who handed him over to the local police and demanded that he sign an affidavit promising to leave the country by December. His father was summoned to the police station to sign it. Fred (as Manfred came to be called) had to leave his school, which he regarded as no great loss. He had never enjoyed it, preferring outdoor activities with the scouts. Those had been banned too. Former friends pretended not to know him at best, and at worst, had joined the Hitler Youth and sought him out to slap and punch.

That winter, he saw his first dead body. A man who had taken his life by jumping from the fourth floor of the stairwell in their building, lay in a pool of blood on the white marble floor of the lobby.

Fred worked in the family's clothing factory, learning how to use the machines, while spending much of his remaining hours in queues. After the Anschluss it was what Jews did in Vienna. There seemed to be no end to the documentation they required, especially if they intended to leave. Fred stood for hours for a new Reich passport in the crowds outside the Palais Rothschild which Adolf Eichmann had commandeered for his Central Office for Jewish Migration, the *Zentralstelle*, and then came back the next day and lined up again to have the obligatory 'J' stamped in it.

Then came the queues outside embassies looking for a route out. It was an enormously complicated and frustrating process. Austrians had been lumped together with Germans in a combined quota for US visas. But German Jews, who by then had five years' experience of Nazi rule, had applied earlier and taken much of the allocation.

On 3 September 1938, Alois Schwarz put an ad in the *Manchester Guardian*, offering Fred as an au pair.

'Fifteen-year-old Healthy Modest Viennese Boy, son of Jewish Vienna lawyer, grammar school education, several months training in machine knitting, seeks Home in English family to continue his education', the advertisement said. The name given was Dr A. Schwarz.

I read it eighty-three years later. Following its clues on the trail of Fred Schwarz and his brother Frits would take me in a completely different direction from the other advertised children, not outward and away, but sucked back on a winding course into the maw of the Nazi murder machine. It would turn out to be one of the most extraordinary accounts of endurance and survival I would ever come across.

Like all the adverts for Viennese children, Fred's was on the second page, alongside the listener's guide to radio programmes, which that day included some new film music by Arthur Bliss. It was listed in the extensive 'Situations Wanted' column, where countless Viennese Jewish couples offered to perform every kind of menial service in return for room and board.

It was one of the adverts that had stumped me at first. Putting the name Schwarz into JewishGen for Austria and the Czech lands (which were grouped together) produced over 3,600 results. That was enough to deter me the first time round, especially as not all the results were in chronological order. Taking a little more time, I found a couple of dozen Schwarz boys born in 1923 but only one born to a father whose name began with an 'A', who was a doctor. Alois Schwarz and Helene, born Quittner, had a son called Manfred, born 31 October 1923, so not quite fifteen when the ad was placed, but close enough.

There were traces of a Manfred Schwarz on Findmypast. com who had changed his name to Fred George in London, and another (or possibly the same man) who had registered as a company director in the UK, but had given Gudrunstrasse in Vienna as an address. But it was the wrong man.

However, broadening the search on Ancestry.com brought up another Manfred Schwarz, with the same date of birth as Fred, 31 October 1923. There was a German concentration camp record, which listed his parents' names, leaving no doubt that this was the right Fred. He had been arrested on 15 July 1942 in the southern Dutch city of Eindhoven, and sent to Westerbork, a transit camp in the north of the country for Jews and other prisoners. On 8 September 1944, he had been transferred to Theresienstadt, a Nazi-run ghetto and concentration camp in Terezin, in today's Czech Republic. Three weeks later, he was sent to Auschwitz, and there was another handwritten entry on his record after that: 'KL' for *Konzentrationslager* (concentration camp) 'Bu-' possibly Buchenwald, on 30 October 1944.

A second document came up under his name, a death notice for 5 January 2012 in Badhoevedorp, the Netherlands, suggesting he had survived that succession of Nazi camps. But it gave no hint of whether Fred had left family behind. I emailed the Jewish Community in Amsterdam, who confirmed that he was buried in the Jewish cemetery in Muiderberg, and that he had two children, Rolf born in 1946 and Madelon in 1950.

Dutch privacy laws made it hard to find Rolf and Madelon, so I contacted an acquaintance, Angelina Sutalo, whom I had known from the International Criminal Court for former Yugoslavia (ICTY) in The Hague and she asked her former colleagues in the prosecutors' office who she thought would have the necessary skills. They did indeed come up with phone numbers but they were no longer in use. Angelina spotted that Rolf Schwarz had written a number of books on psychiatry and volunteered to contact the publisher. An hour later she sent a WhatsApp message with seven exclamation marks. The publisher, Alex, played tennis with Rolf every other week and had passed on our message already.

Rolf wrote to me on 11 February 2021 to say that: 'My beloved father's name was indeed Manfred' and confirming the basic details of his life; he asked to see the advert, which had caught him and Madelon by surprise. Fred had not mentioned it to his children, and most probably had not known about it.

Rolf told me that his father had written a memoir of his odyssey from Vienna through the horror of the camps. Entitled *Treinen op Dood Spoor* (*Trains on a Dead Track*), it had been published in Dutch and translated into English by relatives in 2005, but the translation had never been published. He sent it to me by email.

Fred's book was an astonishing story of near-death and salvation, its matter-of-fact description of the camps written in the unflinching, urgent present tense, comparable to Primo Levi's *If this is a Man*. It is gruelling but also miraculous. You cannot help being changed by reading it, emerging at the end knowing more about what a human being is capable of enduring.

Trains on a Dead Track begins with the Gestapo takeover of the Hotel Metropole and follows his journey with his brother Frits through the worst horrors the world has ever seen, from which they emerged miraculously at the other end.

The boys' father Alois had placed the *Guardian* advert for Fred in September 1938, but Frits had required a more urgent exit route. There was an ultimatum hanging over his head, once he had signed a pledge to be out of the country by the end of the year after being detained by a Nazi patrol. Failure to leave would almost certainly lead to arrest and likely deportation to Dachau, and enough reports had filtered back by autumn 1938 for the family to know that their eldest son might not survive the experience.

A wealthy uncle, Hermann, who lived in Sarajevo, undertook to find a job for Frits in Messina, Sicily. It was impossible for a Jew to enter Italy overland, but with the right connections and the right person on the desk, you could fly via Venice. The family took Frits to the airport, but the bid failed. By the time they got back home, Frits was on the phone asking to be picked up. He did not have the right papers and was not being allowed to leave. They would have to find another route out.

At that time, there was a rumour going around Vienna that there were guides in Cologne who could smuggle Jews across the border into the Netherlands, where they would be allowed to stay. Reluctantly Manfred's parents agreed that was the best hope among a range of poor options for Frits.

Frits and Fred Schwarz as boys in Vienna, circa 1926.

The eighteen-year-old succeeded in crossing on the second try, and sent word of his arrival in Amsterdam. Fred was desperate to follow in his elder brother's footsteps and they had agreed Frits would leave directions at post offices or other drop-offs along the way. For their parents, having both boys in one place outside the Reich looked a safer bet, for all its risks, than waiting for a reply to the *Guardian* advert, so they reluctantly agreed Fred should make the journey, as long as he did not go alone. So they went looking for suitable travel companions.

Asking around among the families of other acquaintances, they found two eighteen-year-old boys prepared to make the trip with him: Ernst Hahn, a friend from the scouts, who was 'thin and tall as a tree', and Joschi Frisch, 'a jolly, fat fellow' who was the stepson of one of Helene's friends.

On 30 November 1938, their parents took the trio to the Westbahnhof.

'I felt too big for tears, but realised this meant the end of my youth,' Fred wrote. For him, as for all the other children fleeing Vienna, those farewells on the station platform were the pivot in their lives: not just the definitive cessation of childhood, but the end of security and certainty. In Fred Schwarz's case, it was the beginning of an ever-steeper descent into peril.

Fred and his two newfound companions Ernst and Joschi had a compartment to themselves and they began their journey in high spirits. Their parents had filled their bags with their favourite foods, and anyway Fred loved trains. It was the adventure of a lifetime.

They stopped in Cologne where they toured the city's cathedral, admiring spires that were even higher than St Stefan's in the heart of Vienna. As arranged, Frits had left a letter of instructions at the main post office, which told them to go to a Jewish coffee house opposite the burnt-out remains of the city's main synagogue and ask for a Mr Jacobse.

The plan fell apart at the first hurdle. In the cafe, the regulars told them that Jacobse had been arrested, and claimed he had also been a traitor. 'Go back to Vienna,' they told the boys. 'If it was possible to get to Holland, we would have gone long ago.'

The three boys sat down to work out what to do next. The idea of going home to Vienna seemed an unthinkable defeat, and they agreed that would only be an option under extreme duress. They went back to the train station, accompanied by a slim redheaded boy from the coffee house who wanted to join them, to study the map of the railway network.

The closest town to the Dutch border was Kaldenkirchen, almost touching the frontier, so they bought one-way tickets there, arriving just as it was getting dark. They had no plan of what to do and wandered down the main street hoping they would stumble across some clue that would point them in the right direction.

Sure enough, a sign appeared in front of them – the name of a pub in the town centre, which Fred remembered as being Zum Holländer, the Dutchman (now a fast-food restaurant famed for its chips called Zur Holländerin, the Dutchwoman). They breezed in, trying to make it look as if it was the sort of thing they did every day.

The place was almost empty, save for the publican and two men in leather jackets sitting at the bar. The publican asked the boys what they wanted and Fred blurted out that they were hoping to cross into Holland. Their naivety seems astonishing now but once Plan A had failed, they were totally unprepared for the journey they had embarked on. The publican nodded to the two men in leather who looked 'as though they had been waiting for us', and they took them straight to the police station.

The four boys were told to hand over their passports and money and were frisked, though all they had on them was some sliced sausage and squares of chocolate. Then there was a discussion between the plain-clothes men and a senior officer in uniform which was unintelligible to the boys.

After a few minutes, their passports and cash were returned to them and the officer told them they would be taken to the post office in order to send the money back to their parents. Then they were put in two sidecars alongside motorbikes driven by the men in leather, who sped off with their lights dimmed. The boys had no idea where they were going.

In the pitch darkness, the motorbikes stopped and the boys were told to get off. The plain-clothes policemen pointed at a building just visible in the distance. That was in Holland but it was a police station so the boys should steer away from it, and they should split up to be less likely to attract attention. They wished the young Jews good luck, climbed back on the bikes and drove off.

The boys decided to split into pairs: Fred with Joschi, Ernst with the redheaded boy from Cologne, and they set off in different directions. It was clear they had been left on the top of a hill, as after a few minutes' walk, Fred and Joschi could see a car's headlights and the grey ribbon of the Meuse river below them. But the descent was treacherous. They were near the brink of a quarry, and peering down the boys could at first not even see the bottom. There was no question of retreat, however, and they felt their way along the yellow stone quarry face, until they found a downward sloping path and then a muddy track that led to a paved road.

A truck approached and, taking a chance, they waved it down. It was only when it stopped and they could see it had Dutch plates that they knew they had succeeded in crossing the border.

The driver took them as far as Venlo, a border town straddling the Meuse, and stopping outside a shop front, he jumped out and rang the doorbell. A man appeared at the door and after exchanging a few words, the driver ushered the boys out, and drove away.

The man at the door did not seem overjoyed to see the unexpected guests, saying nothing but he let them in. Fred wished him a good evening in German, but Joschi ventured a *shalom* and the quiet man, to their great relief, said *shalom* in reply. He brought them fried eggs on bread and glasses of milk, the first substantial food they had eaten all day, and shook his head at the sheer recklessness of their adventure, telling them they were lucky to have stumbled on a truck driver whom he happened to know well. Local police patrolled the whole border zone under orders to send any refugees back.

Under Dutch law, once you had crossed the Meuse, or any other of the major rivers, you could register as a refugee and receive a temporary permit to stay. But because of that loop-hole, there were checkpoints at all the bridges. His advice to the boys was to give themselves up before they incriminated local people. They adamantly refused and got up to leave, but the Dutchman seemed prepared for their reaction. He told them to sit down and walked out, leaving them unsure whether to stay or flee. He could have gone to give them up to the police, but just as they were on the point of bolting for the door, he returned and informed them that arrange-ments had been made.

Not much later, a man and woman drove up in a large American car and told the boys to hide in the back under blankets as they passed through Dutch police checkpoints. Each time they were stopped, the woman, who was smartly dressed and expensively perfumed to distract inquisitive policemen, did all the talking.

It was three o'clock in the morning by the time they arrived in Rapenburg, in the centre of Amsterdam, at the address of a refugee hostel which Frits had mentioned in the letter he had left for the boys at the Cologne post office. They arrived to find him asleep inside.

It was 2 December 1938. In all, it had taken Fred just thirty-six hours from leaving Vienna to find his brother, despite the fact that the original plan had evaporated, they had been detained and he and his companions had had to navigate their way across the border in the dark, dodging police patrols in the middle of the night. It was a triumph of pure resolve and instinct.

Frits woke Fred the next morning so they could call their parents to let them know of his safe arrival. They then had him registered at the Committee for Jewish Refugees, where he was given a declaration that the Committee would guarantee his keep during his time in Holland. They took that piece of paper to the Dutch immigration office where he received a state registration card which legalised his stay, subject to conditions: he could not work, or go to school or leave the Amsterdam city boundaries, on pain of deportation.

Next they found Fred somewhere to stay, a cheap restaurant and hostel called Lohe's Lunchroom, which received 7.50 guilders a week from the refugee committee for every bed they provided. The food was good, the rooms were fine and soon Frits moved in from his hostel to stay close to Fred.

Together they wandered around the town, marvelling both at the poverty of the Jewish quarter but also the community's deep roots in the city, with its three major synagogues, three hospitals and a modern old people's home. A street collection for Jewish refugees in early December raised two million guilders. There was a community centre for the refugees in an old house where they could play ping-pong and shuffleboard, read the newspapers and spend their ten cents daily pocket money on coffee and cheesecake. Fred even enrolled on a painting course.

Over the next few weeks, more Viennese refugees trickled in across the border. Some had heard of Frits and Fred's success and followed the same route. They brought news from home about the increasing difficulties Viennese Jews were facing finding food, and how more and more of them were being rounded up.

★

The haven provided by Lohe's Lunchroom lasted little more than two weeks. On 19 December, a yellow card arrived for all the male refugee residents except Fred, inviting them to visit the immigration office. Frits and all the others made their way there, leaving Fred behind with the women. By the afternoon, they had still not returned, and by the next morning, the news reached the hostel that all the men and boys aged between sixteen and thirty had been forced onto buses and taken to internment camps. At fifteen, Fred had been too young and so had escaped the summons.

Frits and the others had been taken to Veenhuizen, a village in the north of the country that had an old penal colony of barrack-like cells, built in a square around a large central courtyard. Today it is the National Prison Museum. Frits wrote to Fred to say he was okay and not to worry, though in reality the conditions were dire.

In the first days of 1939, the internees were moved from various camps to a naval base outside Rotterdam, at Hellevoetsluis. There, at least, Fred was able to visit Frits.

Over time, the Dutch were better able to seal their borders against undocumented immigrants slipping through the smuggler routes, but some continued to find a way. One of the arrivals in early 1939 was a stocky man with a nose like a boxer's, Ignaz Feldmann, a famous defender and team captain of the Hakoah Vienna football team, who had played alongside my great-uncle Fritz. I have a team picture with Frits standing behind Feldmann, who would go on to play a vital role in the Schwarz brothers' story.

In May 1939, Frits was transferred to an open camp for under-eighteen boy refugees, the Dommelhuis, in Eindhoven in the south of the country, and Manfred left Amsterdam to join him.

The place was run by a wealthy local woman, the wife of the director of Philips electronics company, Mrs Verwey-Jonker, a small frail lady who went everywhere by bicycle and was the head of the refugee children's committee. She counselled the roughly hundred boys there on their prospects, either of emigration, or failing that, of vocational training. It was clear that the Schwarz boys had very little chance of the former, no visas having been obtained by any of the family, and so Verwey-Jonker set about fixing them up with jobs: Frits in a radio-electronics works, and Fred in a knitting factory called Tweka. Tweka even provided him with a bicycle.

The Dommelhuis (named after the nearby Dommel river) was owned, like much of Eindhoven, by Philips and had originally been a hostel for foreign workers. The company had put it at the disposal of the children's committee, which had made arrangements for football and gymnastics, as well as access to a swimming pool and cinema. For refugee children like Fred and Frits, it was a sanctuary, but a very temporary one.

When the war broke out in Europe in September 1939, the Netherlands initially sought to preserve its neutrality, as it had in the First World War, but mobilised fighting-age men as a precaution. At the Tweka works, some of Fred's fellow workers were conscripted while output was switched from bathing trunks to uniforms, but for some months nothing happened. Across the sea in Britain, they started calling it the 'phoney war'.

In January 1940, there was finally good news from the boys' parents: with help from uncle Hermann in Sarajevo, they had managed to cross the border into Yugoslavia, another of the illegal routes taken by Viennese Jews unable to obtain visas.

The trip was nerve-racking. Hermann had told them to go to the Yugoslav border and take the train to Zagreb. They were not legally allowed to buy tickets but were instructed to board without them and sit in the last carriage, where the lights would be turned off. Moments before the train began to move, the guard came back and handed them their tickets without a word.

On the Yugoslav side of the border they could hear officials working their way up the train towards them, demanding to see documents, but just before they got to their darkened carriage, they could hear a voice say, slowly and deliberately so the Schwarzes could hear: 'No one here any more. We can go back.' It had taken months, but Hermann had arranged everything.

Once they arrived in Zagreb, they were moved as part of a large group of refugees to the nearby historic resort of Samobor, where they were billeted in private rooms which were empty for the off-season. The rents were paid by a refugee organisation but new arrivals were supposed to help out with chores. Alois Schwarz taught English and chopped wood.

The 'phoney' phase in the war came to an abrupt end on 10 May 1940, when Hitler's forces invaded Holland with full *blitzkrieg* ferocity, ignoring its official neutrality. On that date, Fred and Fritz Schwarz were in Noordwijk, a small seaside town between Amsterdam and The Hague, to which workers in Eindhoven had been evacuated a couple of days before, and the boys woke up to the sound of German bombers flying low over the coast, being shot at by Dutch anti-aircraft guns from the beach. They watched the planes take a wide turn over the sea, part of a ruse to make Dutch defenders believe the real target was Britain, before making a sudden turn and swooping back to bomb The Hague.

With the invasion underway, the Jewish refugees found themselves in immediate danger from two sides: the new Nazi occupiers searching for Jews; but more immediately from Dutch police and soldiers on the lookout for German infiltrators in civilian clothes mingling with the local population.

Family friends organised a police escort to take the boys to safety, but the policemen instead took them to a temporary lock-up where they were holding Dutch members of the National Socialist Party. Fred and Frits protested but to no avail. The police just shrugged, and they were transferred with all the suspected fifth columnists to a stable in Haarlem to stay overnight. But their detention only lasted a few hours, as long as the remnants of Dutch resistance. At six o'clock on the morning of Wednesday, 15 May 1940, a Dutch officer climbed onto a box and announced that, in the wake of the blanket bombing of Rotterdam and the threat to do the same to Utrecht, the Netherlands had surrendered to spare civilian lives. The detainees were free to go.

There was silence in the stable, even from the National Socialists, and then a scramble. Deciding they could move faster without their suitcases, the boys went from door to door until they found someone willing to look after them while they searched for an escape route. They then ran to Haarlem station to get a train to IJmuiden, a small port straddling the North Sea canal that runs into Amsterdam, from where they hoped they could jump on a boat. They got to the train with minutes to spare and then ran down to the harbour, only to see a disappointed crowd who had had the same idea looking at a half-submerged ship that had been scuttled by the Dutch navy to block the canal from the Germans. The escape route to the sea was closed.

It soon became apparent that they were cut off by land too as German forces swept into Belgium and France and the British Expeditionary Force fled from the beach at Dunkirk.

Neutrality had neither saved the Netherlands nor the many thousands of refugees from the east who had sought shelter there. At the beginning of July 1940, the Nazi occupation authorities ordered all foreign and stateless people to report to Westerbork, a camp originally established by the Dutch for German and Austrian refugees, set in the bleak heathland of north-east Holland.

Westerbork was a compact village of white-roofed huts, just half a kilometre square, run by officials from the Dutch Heath

Society, an organisation set up in the nineteenth century for the purposes of land reclamation and agricultural development. The new camp inmates, including Frits and Fred, were made to spend all day digging soil and peat and planting lupins to put nitrogen into the earth.

In 1941, an apprenticeship scheme was started for younger inmates, and Fred tried electronics, blacksmithing and even interior design.

The temporary improvements inside Westerbork gave a misleading impression that their lives were stabilising. In the world outside, events were moving in the other direction, speeding towards the Final Solution. Fred was summoned to Amsterdam to register at the *Zentralstelle für Jüdische Auswanderung*, the Central Office for Jewish Emigration, the counterpart to Eichmann's office in Vienna, and he saw signs everywhere of how much the city had changed. Generations-old Jewish businesses had been shuttered, while signs on restaurants and cafes forbade Jews from entering. There were placards banning their presence in parks and other public spaces.

At the same time, to the south-east, life was becoming more precarious for the boys' parents. The Nazis had taken over Yugoslavia, installing separate puppet regimes in Croatia and Serbia. Alois and Helene Schwarz and some other relatives took refuge in a monastery in the Serbian mountains. It was clearly not a safe place to stay. The monks had been killed by pro-Nazi militiamen who were still roaming the area, so they moved south towards the sea, to a small town called Čapljina, along the Neretva river, in an area controlled by Italian troops who largely left the Jewish refugees in peace.

Alois and Helene tried to make a living in a rented house, taking in boarders, feeding them and teaching them English. Over the next two years they moved around the Dalmatia region, which Hitler had ceded to Mussolini, believing that as long they were in Italian-run territory, they were relatively safe.

Back at the Westerbork camp, by contrast, the Nazis were increasingly in evidence, arriving at the camp in 1942 to oversee the Dutch guards and begin a programme to expand its capacity by wedging metal bunk beds into the huts, until there was no more room to move.

On 14 July 1942, the camp was renamed the *Polizeiliches Durchgangslager Westerbork*, Police Transit Camp Westerbork. People from mixed Jew–Gentile marriages were ordered out, leaving 1,200 Jews in the camp. It had a new commandant, SS *Sturmbannführer*, Erich Deppner, from the *Sicherheitsdienst*, the SD, the Security Service of the SS, who replaced the Dutch administrator from the Heath Society. Three months before taking up the post, Deppner had overseen the murder of sixty-five Soviet prisoners of war, most of them Uzbeks. Later, he would take part in the slaughter of 450 Dutch resistance fighters, but largely managed to dodge justice. After five years in a Soviet prison camp after the war, he joined the Gehlen Organisation, an intelligence group of former Nazis set up under US auspices, and went on to work for the Federal German spy agency, the *Bundesnachrichtendienst*. He stood trial in 1964 in Munich for the murder of the Soviet prisoners, but not for the execution of Dutch resistance fighters or his role at Westerbork. He was acquitted and died a free man in 2005.

At Westerbork, Deppner immediately started organising transports to the east. All the inmates had to line up in alphabetical order and face him, answer a few questions about their profession and skills, after which he pronounced '*bleibt*' or '*geht*', stay or go.

Frits, who said he was a teacher, was told he would go, but he won an initial week's deferment on the grounds that he needed urgent dental work. Fred, an electrician and sewing machine mechanic, was told he would stay.

The next day, a hundred men and fifty orphans from the camp were marched off the five kilometres to the train station, along with 950 men who had arrived from Amsterdam for processing only the night before.

After that Westerbork became a transit camp for a thousand Jews a week, arriving from Amsterdam and other cities and dispatched on freight train transports, officially to Silesia. Most of the original inmates were retained to keep the operation running smoothly and maintain the flow of Jews eastwards.

'One becomes inured rather quickly and gets used to the daily course of events. In the end, the transports seemed no longer to touch you, especially as long as there is nobody you feel really involved with,' Fred recalled. 'But when you have found somebody, you try with all your might to save him or her from a departing transport. Only a few are successful.'

There were various ways of avoiding transportation: getting a *Sperre*, an exemption for your work or for your religion (if you joined the Dutch Reformed Church, for example). Temporary exemptions were also granted if you donated your wealth to the Nazis, if you had a visa to another country, or if there was an ongoing investigation into your lineage and exactly how many Jewish grandparents you had.

Westerbork inmates became adept at thinking up new items that could be made within the camp which could be claimed to be essential for its operation, like brushes, soap and barrels. That was the way Frits and other inmates were able to string out their exemptions. But each of these exemptions was temporary. There were no permanent guarantees in Westerbork.

Fred and Frits were moved to one of the newer, larger huts that held 270 people, with one toilet among all of them and just over one square metre per person.

In late 1942, reports circulated in the camp of the British victory at El Alamein, and German setbacks at Stalingrad, the first signs that a turning point had been reached in the war, but these were distant developments. The fight back against the Nazis could not come fast enough for Fred and Frits.

More than thirty thousand people had been transported from Westerbork by then and the Nazis were still trying to keep up the rate of two transports a week, on Tuesdays and Fridays. A branch railway line had been extended as far as the camp to make the process more efficient.

Everyone feared the train transports, though no one knew for sure what exactly happened at the other end. In 1943, Fred gave a pencil and paper to a girl leaving on a transport and asked her to describe what she saw on arrival. He told her to hide her note in a certain spot under a cushion in one particular, distinctive carriage. The carriage eventually returned and the note was there, hidden as arranged. It had been scrawled in a hurry.

'We are standing in a deserted landscape, not a house in sight. In front I see people getting out and getting into line. I see people getting into trucks,' the girl had written. 'The SS are coming nearer. They are calling through a loudhailer: get out. Line up in rows of five. Leave your luggage. This will come by truck. Those who don't want to walk can also go by truck. They are nearly here. I have to stop. Au revoir.'

These words are particularly ominous now, but in 1943 it was difficult to conceive of mass extermination from the vantage point of the Westerbork camp. Fred reasoned that the same words could have been written of arrival at Westerbork, but now at least they knew that the destination was not a city. It was somewhere out in the countryside, presumably another camp.

Partly at Fred's prompting, clothing manufacturing started up in 1943 in one of the big huts at Westerbork, to give him and as many inmates as possible continued employment exemption from the transports. The first items they made were blue overalls with red shoulder patches for 'penal cases'. These were rarely real criminals and were much more often Jews who had tried to hide but had been caught, often with the help of informants who were paid a few guilders for each Jew they turned in. Once designated, they were normally sent out on the next available transport, with very few exceptions.

Meanwhile, the carpentry shop made wooden signs to be put in the slots on the side of the wagons showing their sole route: Westerbork–Auschwitz, Auschwitz–Westerbork.

Later in the year, however, they were given a new destination to carve: Theresienstadt, an old citadel in northern Bohemia. The rumour was that Jews who had fought in the First World War would have certain privileges there, a rumour fortified by the fact that while Auschwitz transports used freight cars, trains to Theresienstadt ran with passenger carriages.

The stories created a dilemma for the inmates over whether it was better to stay in Westerbork, which was a known quantity but risked deportation to Auschwitz, or to take the gamble of a transport to Theresienstadt.

As Holland was emptied of its remaining Jews in 1943, a smaller detention centre at a castle in Barneveld was broken up and its inmates were transferred to Westerbork. One of them was a girl called Klaartje van Leeven, whom Fred and his friends took to calling Carry. When they chanced upon one another one day, Fred asked if she would like to come for a cup of real tea in one of the men's huts, and she agreed.

The next day she asked to be transferred to work in Fred's textile workshop, and started a side business making stuffed animal toys. From that moment, they would stay together as often as they could and suffered whenever they were separated. They developed a signature whistle to reassure each other that they were nearby and thinking of their partner, a refrain from *The Robber Symphony*, a musical film from 1936 directed by a Viennese Jew, Friedrich Feher, about a boy's adventures with a gang of bandits. It became their bond.

'It is remarkable: you live very fast in Westerbork; acquaintances soon become friends, boyfriend and girlfriend soon become lovers,' Fred wrote. The speed of life, he pointed out, was hardly surprising when either partner could disappear any day, swallowed by an eastward train.

A job came up in Amsterdam, demolishing machines in a now redundant matzo factory, for which both Frits and Fred were selected, a rare occurrence and possibly a mistake. Normally, the camp authorities preferred to send just one member of a family out of the camp at a time, so the others could be held as hostages, to deter all thoughts of escape.

Through his girlfriend, Frits knew about Dutch non-Jews prepared to hide them and began weighing the possibility of escape. Fred was not so sure. Reprisals would be taken against others in his hut and possibly include Carry and her family. In the end, the job changed and Frits did not go, so the dilemma resolved itself. Fred went alone and on the trip met a woman called Marja, the gentile wife of one of Frits's friends in Westerbork. She was trying to get her Jewish husband out and believed she had permission as long as he agreed to have himself sterilised. But she had heard something else that unnerved Fred. A colleague of her father's, an architect and builder, had told her that he had built gas chambers in Poland designed for mass killing, as the earlier experiments using carbon monoxide in trucks were not efficient enough. Fred concluded that the story, though detailed and specific, was too outlandish, and opted not to mention it to anyone back at Westerbork.

At the beginning of 1944, they celebrated Carry's birthday. Fred made her a ring out of coloured glass salvaged from the scrap of downed aeroplanes, to mark another year of survival together, as the war approached its end phase and the possibility of liberation drew nearer.

After the D-Day invasions, an upwelling of hope surged across the camp, but it soon became clear that a long gruelling campaign would be required to push the Germans out of Holland. The generals were thinking in months, but the Westerbork inmates had just days.

On 1 September, with the allies approaching the Dutch border, the camp commandant, SS *Obersturmführer* Albert Gemmeker, announced that Westerbork would be evacuated. On Sunday 3 September, a thousand inmates would be taken to Auschwitz. The day after that, two thousand would be taken to Theresienstadt (including prisoners transferred from Barneveld like Carry, and long-term inmates like Fred and Frits). There would be a third transport to Bergen–Belsen and three hundred prisoners would stay behind for maintenance.

Gemmeker ran Westerbork from 1942 to 1945, and in those three years, he oversaw the transport of eighty thousand Jews to concentration camps, later claiming he had had no idea what would happen to them at their destination. He served only a six-year sentence in the Netherlands, and though he was investigated for many years in Germany, he was never prosecuted there. He died at liberty in 1982.

Fred, Frits, Carry and her family used their camp connections to arrange travel in the same rail car, on a transport leaving on 4 September 1944. Climbing aboard was the moment they had spent their whole captivity in Westerbork dreading.

'The sliding door is closed, something we had seen from the outside, but from the inside it is terrible. Suddenly it is pitch-dark and you are incarcerated,' Fred wrote. 'The engine whistles, the train starts moving. We are on our way. Where to?'

The train stopped at Oldenzaal, near the Germany border, where a Dutch rail worker told them that US forces had reached Maastricht, a 250-kilometre drive to the south, too far away to save the two thousand Jews on the train, which rolled over the German border to Dresden and then, at the end of a thirty-six hour journey, to Theresienstadt.

Terezin, at the northern tip of Bohemia, was turned into a

fortified town at the end of the eighteenth century by the Habsburg emperor Joseph II to guard the bridges over the converging rivers of the Ohře and Elbe. The Nazis turned it into a ghetto and its adjoining small fortress was fitted up as a Gestapo interrogation centre and prison.

The prisoners were marched off the train and into the ghetto to be assigned living quarters. They had only been there a few hours when someone came up to Fred and Frits and seized their hands in excitement. It was their father's younger brother, Heinrich, who was wounded in the First World War and so had, in theory, an exemption against deportation. He lived in a corner of the ghetto with his wife Selma and their fifteen-year-old son, Herbert.

Carry and her family had been assigned to one barracks building, Frits and Fred to another, but they quickly found each other and wandered through what looked in many ways like a normal town. There were two-storey houses between the barracks, a high street, a square, a bandstand, a school and a cafe. In one direction, they could see green hills, and when they climbed up onto a grassy bastion they could look out over the surrounding Bohemian plains.

If you screwed up your eyes you could wish away the Nazi occupation and imagine yourself at peace in a historic town. The superficial normality was deliberately confected. The bandstand, the benches, the brightly painted signs were all props fabricated by the Nazi camp overseers ahead of an inspection by the Red Cross in June 1944. Immediately before the visit, 7,500 people had been deported to death camps to reduce overcrowding. Buildings along the route of the Red Cross tour were painted in bright colours and a pantomime of normality was conducted for the benefit of the visitors, with inmates sitting at outside tables being served proper food.

The charade was repeated for a propaganda film shot in August and September, showing Theresienstadt prisoners attending lectures, exercising, taking hot showers and generally leading a fulfilling life. Kurt Gerron, a German Jewish actor, singer and director, was allowed to hire a crew to make the film. Gerron thought that he and everyone he persuaded to take part would be spared deportation, but they were all sent to Auschwitz and murdered there in October 1944, including the children shown studying and playing in the film. A total of fifteen thousand children passed through Theresienstadt. Only one in ten survived.

Fred and Frits would only spend a few weeks in this false purgatory. On 28 September 1944, a transport was arranged for two thousand men: Dutch Jews and others, including those who had earned medals in the First World War. The Schwarz brothers were on the list, as were their uncle Heinrich and cousin Herbert. Carry and aunt Selma were left behind.

Fred took a last look at the walled town, as 'the dragon', the ribbon of green railway carriages, snaked its way towards the ramparts to devour them.

On seeing the train approach, Fred was all too aware that his feelings of fear and impotence had been experienced before by all those hundreds of thousands of prisoners he had watched shuffle past him over the years in Westerbork. Now it was his turn. He climbed aboard, and as the train pulled out he was overcome by fear and grief, but also by crippling exhaustion, and he fell into a deep, dreamless sleep.

He woke up in Dresden, where the passengers were handed postcards by the police and told that they could write back to relatives and friends still in Theresienstadt, but they could only write 'Arrived in Dresden'. No other text was allowed. To keep the inmates docile as they boarded the trains going east, they had to believe they were going somewhere where life and writing postcards was still possible.

★

Fred fell back to sleep and the next time he woke the train had stopped at a deserted, poorly lit platform, with a black-on-white station sign that said 'Kattowitz' – Katowice, the industrial centre of southern Poland which the prisoners had wrongly thought was already in Soviet hands.

A short distance away was Auschwitz–Birkenau where the train arrived at the end of September 1944, in the middle of the night, alongside other trains in a guarded shunting yard. Fred could hear shouting and moaning and there was a sickly smell that seeped through the train windows. The train was shunted through a gate and then lit up by powerful spotlights on a platform.

On the other side the prisoners on the train could see double layers of electric fence, huts and people in rags shuffling along rather than walking. This was Birkenau. SS men with whips were waiting on the platform behind a line of inmates in blue-and-white striped uniforms. Their job was to pull out the passengers from the train, while convincing them that their possessions had to stay on the train and would follow them to their residence. The SS men whipped the men in blue and white if they did not work fast enough, and whipped the new arrivals too.

The prisoners were lined up six abreast on the platform, from where Fred could see the dark mass of a building with a square chimney disgorging dense billows of black smoke, lit up every few seconds by a fiery glow emanating from deep within the building. It must be the boiler house, he thought, constantly working to keep the camp warm.

The column of prisoners was broken into twos, and then driven forward by shouts and frequent whip-blows, until the head of the line reached an SS *Obersturmführer*, who asked some basic questions before pointing to the right or left.

The pair of prisoners immediately ahead of the Schwarzes were their friend from Westerbork, Leo, and his father. Leo was sent to the right, but his father was sent to the left, so Leo pleaded to be allowed to stay with the old man. The *Obersturmführer* laughed and said '*Aber natürlich*', allowing Leo to go to the left.

Fred and Frits stepped up and were both sent to the right, where they were ordered to stand to attention and wait under the smoking chimney until dawn broke. Fred was standing between Frits and Ignaz Feldmann, the Hakoah Vienna soccer player who had been at Westerbork with the brothers.

An SS *Unterscharführer* with a pronounced Viennese accent asked them if anyone had a relative who had gone to the left, and someone said yes, his uncle had gone that way. 'Do you know where he is now?' the corporal asked, laughing. 'Look up there at the smoke. That's him, he's just been burned. What else should one do with you filthy dirty Jews?' He roared with laughter to see the horror on their faces. By insisting on following his father, their friend Leo had accompanied him to his death.

The surviving prisoners were marched along the edge of the camp, with woods to the left and the wall of barbed wire and watchtowers on the right, as a breeze blew sand and dust in their faces from the desolate plain. They came to a brick building where they were told to strip, keeping only shoes and a belt. In Fred's case it was a scout belt Carry had given him. Their hair was chopped off by other prisoners, they had some form of reeking disinfectant poured over them, which was rinsed off with showers before they were sent out onto a lawn outside to drip dry in the autumn wind.

When they were standing there one of the new arrivals walked to the electrified wire and grabbed it with both hands. But nothing happened. An SS man climbed down from a watchtower and guided him back into the line.

'Sometimes one learns more in a few minutes than in years,' Fred wrote. In particular, he had to learn how to survive in a vast industrial enterprise dedicated to murder.

Some of the prisoners had intact blue-and-white uniforms. These were the *Sonderkommando*, whose job it was to sift through the property of the new arrivals and to wheel piles of bodies from the gas chamber to the crematoria. Every three months, half the commando was gassed and replaced by other inmates, so if you were chosen, you had another six months to live. The question was whether that would be enough to carry you through to the end of the war.

On 7 October 1944, after Frits and Fred had been in Birkenau for a week, the *Sonderkommando* in Crematorium IV revolted, knowing they were about to be liquidated and had nothing to lose.

In the weeks before, women in the munitions factory within Auschwitz, the Weichsel-Union-Metallwerke, had smuggled out small amounts of gunpowder at a time, wrapped in paper or cloth, which was channelled to the *Sonderkommando* in all four crematoria. The plan had been to blow them all up in unison, but the *Sonderkommando* in Crematorium IV could wait no longer. Their time was up.

There had never been any real prospect that the revolt would lead to escape. Realistically, it had been an effort to exert some control over the time and nature of death, with the added prospect of taking some Nazis down into the abyss. With just one crematorium's *Sonderkommando* rising up instead of four, its impact was even more limited. Some 250 prisoners were killed in the revolt, and another 200 executed afterwards, including the four women who had smuggled the gunpowder.

Not long after the rebellion, the *Kapo* for the Schwarz brothers' hut arrived with three men in duffel coats and hunters' hats with chamois brims. Feldmann was summoned and ordered to nominate a hundred workers. Fred and Frits, his fellow Viennese inmates from Westerbork, were among those he picked. The brothers had not been there long enough to be tattooed with an Auschwitz-Birkenau number on their forearms, so a stamp and pad were found and the name of their new employer, the HASAG munitions plant in Leipzig, was printed on their forehead. It was a rare ticket out of Auschwitz-Birkenau, and Fred spent the next few days doing all he could not to touch his brow, terrified it would rub off.

Finally, a whole week after they had been stamped as company property, the workers were marched out of the camp. Ignaz Feldmann had saved their lives, at least for the time being.

Fred and Frits were among the very few ever to experience what it was like to leave Auschwitz-Birkenau, a dreamlike inversion of the process of arrival. They were escorted back to the brick building they had entered through, given a shower and a random selection of clothes, and marched outside the wire to a waiting freight carriage. They had been in Auschwitz-Birkenau for exactly one month.

Their destination was the Meuselwitz slave labour camp, a subsidiary of Buchenwald camp, which supplied workers to a nearby munitions plant. By the end of 1944, it had 1,666 prisoners, of whom 1,376 were women.

Compared to Auschwitz-Birkenau it felt like a reprieve. To start with, there were straw pallets to sleep on. There were proper toilets and showers, and they were given their own enamel mug, bowl and spoon. In place of the SS and *Kapos*, they were guarded by an old man from the *Volkssturm*, conscripted by the Nazi regime in its death throes. The first day on the job was 31 October, Fred's birthday. He was twenty-one and had already spent nearly five of those years in the camps.

The work involved making machine tools with lathes, and also repairing nearby railway lines when they were hit by allied sorties. One day, the plant was bombed in an allied raid, igniting the ammunition store which exploded in the quarters housing about five hundred Polish women prisoners, killing scores. The next day, Fred spotted their body parts on the back of a truck covered in tarpaulins.

At the beginning of April the workers were gathered together and told that the allies had captured Buchenwald and that the Meuselwitz plant would be handed over in an orderly fashion within a few days. For a few hours, perhaps a day, it seemed likely that liberation was finally imminent, but then there was a change of plan. The remaining prisoners were roused from sleep in the middle of the night and marched to a train made up of coal wagons, guarded by the SS and *Volkssturm*.

These were the volatile last days of the war. The Soviet army was approaching from the east, US troops from the west, with the ever-shrinking remnants of the Thousand Year Reich in between. The Schwarz boys' jailers were making hourly decisions about their prisoners, in which they weighed up their orders, the need to eliminate witnesses against their own survival and the impulse to drop everything and run.

The train laboured south-east to Chemnitz and then over the Czechoslovak border to Graslitz, stopping and starting to negotiate bottlenecks caused by allied bombing of the rail network. When it was halted outside the town the train was strafed by allied fighters, killing some SS guards. A few of the prisoners on board seized the opportunity to escape, but the Schwarz brothers hesitated, and were left to wonder whether there would be another chance.

In fact an opportunity arose just a day later, when the Nazi guards decided that the train could advance no further, and the human cargo was lined up and marched away along a road that zigzagged up a forested hillside. When the road made a turn close to some thick bushes, the brothers made a run for it, working their way through the undergrowth, moving upwards and away from the town as much as possible. It was a spring morning, the war was on the point of ending, and it was the first time they had run free for three years. But it was a short-lived liberation. Even in the final moments of the Nazi regime, it commanded loyalty from many Germans. They were caught by a vigilante woodsman and returned to their guards.

They were fortunate not to be executed on the spot. Rising desperation was making the SS guards and the *Volkssturm* nervous and unpredictable, but at the same time careless. Fred and Frits escaped again that same night, 22 April, hiding in a shed while the prisoners were being loaded onto trucks. But once again they were recaptured, by a local Gestapo official, and put to work digging an anti-tank ditch, before being loaded with other forced labourers onto a local train which took them fifty kilometres east to a town called Komotau (Chomutov in Czech), only a few kilometres from Theresienstadt.

The longer they survived, the greater their chances of escape. Discipline and order were breaking down, the distinction between labourers and slaves was blurring. In Komotau, the Schwarzes presented themselves at the labour exchange as itinerant German workers and were given new identity cards. With that simple act of bureaucratic subterfuge they became legal, able to move around as if they were Germans, and they set off cross-country to the west, trying to find the Americans before the Soviet advance overtook them. That is how they ended the war, on the road posing as itinerant workers, when Germany surrendered on 7 May 1945.

As the news spread, freed prisoners of war and concentration camp survivors scrambled to get on a train headed west to the town of Karlsbad (Karlovy Vary) on the Czech–German border. Overnight, the cruel hierarchy of the Nazi years had been inverted, and it was Germans who were at the bottom of the pile. When Red Army soldiers arrived, they took all the Germans, as well as any Soviet citizens they could find, off the train, and more ex-prisoners took their places. When it finally left, latecomers were hanging from the sides, and Fred and Frits had to struggle to find spaces.

Karlovy Vary was an old spa town of genteel hotels and nine-teenth-century townhouses set among wooded hills along the

River Ohře. The Americans had taken it over and when the Schwarz brothers and their fellow escapees bedded down on the main square, it was under the shadow of a US tank, the first they had ever seen.

The next morning they were registered and given breakfast and Fred caught sight of some recent US magazines, including one with General Dwight Eisenhower, the allied commander, inspecting the horrific remains of Buchenwald.

Standing alongside him was the squat figure of a former inmate who was showing him around. It was Ignaz Feldmann. He had survived, but learned at his liberation that the rest of his immediate family had been killed.

The trip homewards from Karlovy Vary was interrupted with a severe case of typhoid which ripped through the mass of freed inmates, and the brothers collapsed in the town of Plauen on the German side of the Czech border. But after a few days' recuperation the US army put them in a car with an American driver and a doctor, and then an ambulance for the last stage of the journey home. They drove through abandoned battle-fields, where early summer flowers were beginning to bloom, and then the ruins of the German industrial heartland along the Rhine, and finally over the Meuse close to where they had crossed into Holland illegally seven years earlier.

The roads and the buildings became more familiar with every passing minute, and as they entered Eindhoven, they began to recognise faces. The town's inhabitants were clearing up the rubble and other refugees were trickling back.

A registration centre had been set up, and Fred went to fill in the requisite forms. As he emerged he happened to glance up the road and caught sight of Carry walking towards him.

'A pale beige shirt and a very wide brown-beige skirt, sunglasses, shoulder bag, she looks terrific,' he wrote. 'We see each other at the same time, we are both running and almost bumping into each other, but our lips find each other without fail.'

Fred and Carry Schwarz, circa 1945.

The survival of the Schwarz family was one of the small miracles of the war. Within moments of Fred and Carry's reunion, Frits arrived with the news that their parents, Alois and Helene, were safe in Egypt.

Fred and Carry went to her parents' house in The Hague, where they stayed in separate rooms until they married in 1946, but well before that, Fred would climb through the window to her bedroom, and that was where their first child, Rolf, was conceived.

In Westerbork and Theresienstadt, Fred and Carry's time in private had been scraped together in minutes and occasional hours. But from the moment they found each other again in Eindhoven, they would have another sixty-seven years of each other's company. When Fred died in January 2012, Carry would hold on for just another three months.

IO

Defiance and Aunt Malci

M Y DAD'S AUNT, Malci, was our last living link with
Vienna. She was an eccentric figure on the fringes of
our lives, to whom we children would write monthly letters
in schoolbook French, the language we just about had in
common. She spoke no English and we spoke no German.

Her full name was Malvine Schickler, Leo's younger sister
and the only member of the family to return to Vienna permanently after the war. Every few years until the 1980s she would
visit us and we boys would be told to hide away our various
toy guns, as a gesture of discreet compassion for a woman who,
we were told, had lost her husband and son in the Holocaust.

I have a memory of her arriving on our doorstep, a small
figure with a crooked nose and staring, somewhat asymmetrical
eyes. She dressed traditionally in a dark green coat, lace-up
brown shin boots, and an oddly jaunty little Tyrolean hunter's
hat of a muddy colour with the rim turned up at the back.

During these visits, she was happy enough to sit at our
kitchen table, benignly observing the noisy life of a family of
four children. She would smile at us, often it seemed on the
verge of tears, and try out a handful of English words.

Her home in Vienna was a cell-like one-bedroom flat in a
seven-storey block in Favoriten, the 10th District, some miles
south of the centre, where she led a life of extreme frugality.
I had the feeling she turned on the heating in winter only on
those rare occasions she had visitors. When we arrived on our

first family trip to Vienna in 1975, she made arrangements which resulted in a highly ascetic form of tourism. We slept on heavy-duty metal bunks in a student hostel, and had meals in a college cafeteria.

In the early 1990s, the last years of her life, I was working for the BBC and the *Guardian* in Warsaw, a city in which there is a shrine to the murdered of the Second World War every hundred metres. It was the fiftieth anniversary of a series of awful Holocaust milestones, which required travel to Auschwitz-Birkenau to attend sombre commemorations.

In the same period, I saw a crowd of elderly folk, their pensions eroded to dust, chant 'down with the Jews' outside the cabinet office in Warsaw. There were no Jews in the cabinet and less than ten thousand in the whole country of thirty-eight million, but the memory of three million Polish Jews slaughtered by the Nazis was like an amputated limb that would not stop itching.

'The Jews here are no longer a nation, but a nomination. You nominate as a Jew anyone you dislike,' said Konstanty Gebert, a Jewish journalist then working for the new independent paper *Gazeta Wyborcza*.

Just as many Polish Catholics died as Jews, so they had been victims as well as witnesses to the slaughter, and sometimes beneficiaries, taking over Jewish property after the deportation of the owners. There was a miserable mix of guilt and resentment at feeling guilty after having suffered so terribly themselves. The legacy of the Holocaust was encrusted in the fabric of the city under the accumulated black soot of the Communist decades.

From Warsaw I was sent to cover the wars in Croatia and Bosnia, which would often involve travel through Vienna, where I would stay a day and two and visit Malci. We would meet at her apartment and then amble very slowly in the direction of her local Chinese restaurant, stopping every few minutes for her to lean on her walking stick and catch her breath.

As I remember it, the restaurant was dark and wood-panelled, the food was awful and her plaintive calls for service – '*Herr Ober!*' – were often ignored by the surly waiting staff, all of them white Austrian middle-aged men. Vienna was not a city of immigrants.

One cold autumn day we walked back to Malci's flat halfway up a modern block and she made me tea. We talked about her early years in Vienna at the beginning of the twentieth century, and she took me by surprise by starting to sing a song in Yiddish, a language I had no idea she spoke. In that moment a different person seemed to appear for a few moments, maybe a glimpse of Malci as she had been before the Anschluss and the war, with a flicker of joy in her eyes.

There were pictures of a boy and girl in wooden frames in her living room, Mordechaj and Chana, whom she had lost many years before. Mordechaj was a handsome lad, with dark blond hair and a robust build. I was aware that the Nazis had killed him but unsure of the details. Nor had I any idea what had become of Chana, also a beautiful child with a wide smile below a head of thick auburn curls. My probing was gently deflected and I learned nothing at all about their father, Elias.

I came away from her Vienna apartment convinced I had caught sight of a fragment of an untold story, but it was another two decades before I would begin to unearth that story in the Vienna archives. That is where she had left her mark.

Her big brother, our grandpa Leo, had thought clearly enough and acted fast enough to get my father and grandmother out of Austria and to flee himself, just in time. But Malci had taken a different path: she had stayed in Europe and resisted.

Young Malvine had been the rebel in the family all along. She had started out like Leo, attending trade school and learning bookkeeping, so she could one day work in the family shop, but when she was twenty-one, she took her life in another direction, steering sharply off the road that had been laid out for her.

She met Elias Mayer Schickler, a man eleven years her senior from Kolomea in Galicia, the easternmost corner of the Austro-Hungarian empire. It is now Kolomyya in western Ukraine. The records show Elias as the son of Chana Schickler, but no father is mentioned. It was a society of shtetls and small towns. The Habsburgs had acquired Galicia in the partition of Poland in the late eighteenth century, and it became a haven for Jews fleeing pogroms in Russia. They flourished there, particularly the black-hatted Hasidim who trace their spiritual origins in the mystical Judaism of ecstatic prayer, and devotion to a charismatic leader, the Rebbe.

The Galician Jewish community doubled in the second half of the nineteenth century and was 900,000-strong by 1910. They were ten per cent of the total population but nearly sixty per cent of civil servants and judges. The main town, Lemberg (Lviv today), was a centre of Yiddish literature and learning.

After the First World War and the fall of the Habsburgs the region was a geographical scrap, left over from the dismemberment of the empire, and fought over by Poles, Romanians, Ukrainians and the Soviet Union, ultimately becoming part of Poland.

Galician Jews, surely among the world's longest suffering and most bitterly persecuted peoples, were caught in the middle and subjected to pogroms by both Poles and Ukrainians, with the survivors being swept away decades later with far more efficiency by the Nazis. Over a million and a half Ukrainian Jews were killed in the Holocaust.

Elias Schickler had managed to find a way out of Galicia. He fought for the Austro-Hungarian empire in the First World War, earning a silver medal for courage under fire. That gave him the right to move to Vienna, and he arrived in the aftermath of the war with his young wife, Hudi.

In Vienna the couple had two children. Chana was born in

February 1919, and Mordechaj in December 1920. Elias found work as a boiler repairman, and like many demobilised soldiers, especially from the east, became involved with revolutionary communist politics. Disastrous military defeat left Vienna in ferment. Demobbed soldiers like Elias were inspired by the Bolshevik Revolution in Russia and the uprising in Berlin. The German insurrectionist leaders, Rosa Luxemburg and Karl Liebknecht, emerged as heroes. Galician Jews were in the vanguard of the movement in Vienna, far poorer than the assimilated bourgeois 'old' Jewish families, and they converged on the capital infused with Soviet influence from the east and infuriated by their experience of the trenches. There were waves of strikes and protests, but the Social Democrats refused to support an all-out revolution, confident that they would win parliamentary elections. Ultimately, the end of the Habsburgs was bloodless. Karl I simply renounced participation in the affairs of state.

The city became *Das Rotes Wien*, Red Vienna, run by Social Democrats who launched vast social housing and public sanitation works. It felt as if a new society was being forged, but amid the tumult and dislocation, Elias's wife, Hudi, cracked. In 1921 she was admitted to a hospital for the 'care and cure of the mentally ill and for nervous disorders' in Steinhof, western Vienna. The sanatorium, on the edge of the Vienna Woods near the village where Gustav Klimt was born, had been designed as a utopian alternative to the cruel, cramped warehousing of the mentally ill. It consisted of sixty buildings set in gardens and parkland, and was described by one Viennese art critic as 'a white city sparkling in the bright summer sun . . . crowned by the golden dome of a white marble church'.

In the 1940s the Nazis would turn this architectural attempt to humanise mental care into a crime scene. The inmates were subjected to medical experimentation and 7,500 of them were killed, many of them children. The brains of hundreds of the victims were kept in glass jars at the hospital for decades. They were only buried in 2002.

Hudi's medical notes are still there among the Steinhof files in the Vienna city archives. She was found wandering the streets with no shoes, claiming to hear voices saying her children had been murdered. When asked who had killed them, she replied: 'Society' and then blamed Elias.

'She sits in an armchair with a scowl on her face. She only reluctantly answers questions when they are asked loudly,' the notes record, saying in conclusion that the twenty-three-year-old Galician woman was 'mentally weak' and should be detained at the Steinhof at her family's expense.

Hudi would remain locked up there until 1929, when her uncle, Moses Hersch Sorger, asked for a letter from the hospital authorities to enable him to obtain travel papers to come to Vienna to collect his niece and take her home to Obertyn, just a few miles from Kolomea.

'According to what I hear from Vienna, the only thing my niece, Hudi Lea Schickler, needs to be liberated from is your institution,' Moses wrote. There are no records of Elias visiting her or making any attempt to contact her. When he met Malci in late 1921, he had two young children in his care, but was legally single. His marriage to Hudi had been rabbinical and had not been recorded by the dying imperial bureaucracy.

Malci and Elias married in May 1922, seven months after Hudi had been detained at the Steinhof. A few weeks before their wedding they formally renounced their Judaic faith and declared themselves *konfessionslos*, without religion, though their real shared faith was communism.

Within the space of a few months, Malci had gone from a single young woman destined to work in the family shop to a desperately poor stepmother of two very young children, with a new ideological home in the form of the rigid framework laid down by the Communist Party, and a husband who turned out to be only a passing presence in her life.

Elias Mayer Schickler is recorded as being resident in Vienna until 1923, when the authorities listed him as leaving 'for Palestine', which was then ruled by the British under a League of Nations mandate. There are no records of Elias arriving in Palestine, however. The only traces I could find of him were a fleeting appearance in Belgian police immigration files in Antwerp in the mid-1920s, and then a string of French articles from 1928, with headlines about the expulsion of a Bolshevik agent. Three paragraphs in, it was clear that the agent in question was Elias.

The accounts in the newspapers were all similar, being based on the same police briefing. Elias told his interrogators that he had come to Paris in January 1927 to perfect his French and work as a journalist. The head of general intelligence, Guy Lebreton, claimed that this was just a cover story, and that Schickler had among his belongings coded communications and letters from militants from various countries demanding money and instructions. Lebreton, a Doctor of Law and military veteran from central France, was fifty-three and a year away from voluntary retirement. This was one of his last grand coups. In his telling, Elias was 'one of Moscow's most important agents'. He had been caught in possession of an unfinished report to Moscow indicating that he had been sent to France to assess the state of the French Communist Party, the police alleged, and by this account Elias had been unimpressed with his Gallic comrades.

'In a bitter tone, he criticised the softness of the party leadership, and noted with great concern the success of Poincaré [then in his third term as prime minister] and the many failures of communist platforms, which the masses refused to adopt,' the press report in *Le Matin* said, describing Elias as a 'major player' and claiming that members of the French party's central committee 'trembled under his iron rod'.

Elias had been arrested leaving his flat on the Boulevard Arago, apparently a hotbed of leftist agitators, 'in the company of his mistress', a Mademoiselle Jablonowska.

The Communist Party organ, *L'Humanité*, unsurprisingly, gave a dissenting view, accusing the police press of spinning a story worthy of a 'serialised novel'. Elias according to their account was a Communist activist and had been expelled for that reason alone.

'This veiled repression of foreign workers is a hateful scandal which should end as soon as possible,' the paper declared.

The whole story took me by surprise. When I was growing up, Elias had been a name without an accompanying story. He was just Malci's husband who died. Nothing more was said about him, and indeed that entire generation of our family were portrayed as people of little consequence, but here was Elias making the news in all the French dailies. We seemed to have a spy in the family, albeit a rather unsuccessful one.

Elias was not charged but ordered out of the country. *Le Matin* reported that he and Mlle Jablonowska were deported to Munich, an odd destination as he was originally a Polish national and an Austrian citizen. After that, Elias disappeared. I found no more trace of him in the Austrian archives, nor does he show up in the list of twenty Schicklers from Kolomea murdered in the Holocaust. The closest approximation to a clue I could find was buried in French literature.

The Austrian-French novelist and psychologist, Manès Sperber, was born a few miles from Elias, just outside Kolomea, and his family also fled to Vienna during the First World War. Like Elias, he renounced his faith, initially joining a socialist Zionist movement, Hashomer Hatzair, before graduating to the Communist Party.

After the Nazi takeover, Sperber went to Paris, a few years after Elias's deportation, where he worked for the Communist International, the Comintern. Even if Sperber had not met

Elias, it is almost impossible that he should not have heard about him. They had followed the same path.

After the war, he wrote a trilogy about those times called *A Tear in the Ocean*, in which the leading protagonists lived lives like Sperber and Elias, moving between Galician villages to Vienna, to Paris and back. They had one eye out for the authorities and the other on their comrades for any signs of doubt in the Party and in Moscow. They hid in safe houses and changed names, and one of them was recalled to Moscow and executed.

If Elias Schickler swapped identities and died under an assumed name, that could explain why he vanished from the records. Or the summons could have come from Moscow and he never returned.

Malvine 'Malci' Schickler, circa 1930.

Whatever really happened to Elias, our great-aunt was left behind in Vienna with two small children, Chana and Mordechaj. Malci held on to the name Schickler to the end of her life – I wrote the name dozens of times on letters and postcards without a clue about its dark, mysterious weight. Whether she held onto it out of loyalty or administrative convenience I have no idea. Chana and Mordechaj both dumped it as soon as they reached adulthood and reverted to their biological mother's name, Sorger.

When I first saw that surname surface in the Vienna archives it triggered a memory of a joke Malci had once told me about how, when she had married Elias Schickler and took on his children, people had warned her of *Borger Sorge*, roughly meaning 'money worries'. It must have been grimly funny to her by the time she passed the joke on to me. There had been no money, and a lifetime of worries.

Malci brought the children up in her adopted Marxist faith, sending them off to Young Pioneers, Communist scouts, from the age of eight. Both of them would devote their short adult lives to communism. After the Anschluss, Chana secured a UK visa as a maid to a family in Glasgow and stayed in Britain for the duration of the war, getting married in 1940 to another refugee, Helmut Gustav Legler, a Czechoslovak communist.

Malci and Mordechaj moved to France soon after the Nazis took Vienna, with the help of Communist Party contacts who found them a room in the Hotel Nollet in Paris, where the French painter and poet Max Jacob, friend of Picasso and Modigliani, had once lived. Mordechaj took the less conspicuous name of Martin and went to vocational school, which led to jobs in a series of electronics factories around Paris to support them both.

In the spring of 1940, with the Germans closing in on Paris, they moved again, this time heading south, to Tarbes, near the Spanish border, where Mordechaj found work in a Renault plant. With the fall of the capital and the establishment of the collaborationist state of Vichy France in the southern half of the country, both mother and son joined the

Österreichische Freiheitsfront, the Austrian Liberation Front, a network of Austrian communists run from Paris and Brussels. They were affiliated to a cell centred on Lyon and led by the Czechoslovak-born Oskar Grossmann, a leading figure in the Austrian Communist Party who had fought in the Spanish Civil War, and his second-in-command, Paul Kessler.

Kessler's role in the underground cell was that of a master-fixer, organising safe accommodation, weapons caches, forged identity documents and ration cards.

The group, about 130-strong, became an important arm of the French Resistance, in particular of the Communist group, the Francs-Tireurs et Partisans (FTP). The Austrians' language skills were a valuable asset, allowing them to eavesdrop on the Germans, and they found jobs in Wehrmacht and SS offices, posing as French workers.

Tilly Marek, who was part of the Grossmann-Kessler group, described the stress involved in remembering your *légende*, your cover story.

'Everyone who lived illegally in the time of fascism and fought against it knows the many difficulties and dangers connected with the issues of accommodation and personal data alone, the sheer nervous strain of living abroad over many years, with different names, different dates of birth, parents, professions and biographies, quite apart from the burden of making sure you did a good job, fulfilling your mission,' Marek wrote in notes she made after war, which I found on a handful of type-written pages in the archives.

Mordechaj was already juggling a handful of different names. He had traded Schickler for Sorger. He went by the name Martin in France, while his family, friends and comrades called him Motti, a diminutive form of Mordechaj. On top of that, the Resistance gave him forged identity papers in the name of a Frenchman, André Vandroux, a *monteur* (machine fitter or installer) from Lille.

All these layers of identity were not enough to stop him being caught. Under the Vichy regime, the hunt for Jews was steadily ramped up under Nazi pressure and police raids in Lyon became increasingly common. Those deemed to be suspect were ordered to lower their trousers to show whether or not they were circumcised. The numbers of arrests, deportations and executions were constantly rising.

Mordechaj was swept up in a raid and sent to the Gurs concentration camp. Before the war, the French government had established the Gurs camp near the Spanish border, initially for political refugees and members of the International Brigade fleeing Spain. In early 1940, even before the fall of Paris, the French government began using it for detaining Jewish refugees as 'enemy aliens'.

Once the Vichy regime took over Gurs, the number of inmates soared and conditions worsened considerably. It was built on a swamp, and under the rain it became a morass of mud. Mordechaj was detained alongside Dolly Steindling, a fellow member of the Grossmann-Kessler group who gave a description of life for the inmates in his post-war memoir *Hitting Back*. This passage is particularly hard to forget:

'The lice, in astronomical numbers, were the worst. People who were ill, weak or had lost their lust for life were almost consumed by them. You could sometimes find articles of clothing hanging on barbed wire or in front of the barracks in which millions of lice were intertwined. When I first saw them it made me vomit, despite my hunger and empty stomach.' In the harsh winter of 1940–41, cold and starvation became the serial killers, accounting for several hundred inmates.

After a few months, both Mordechaj and Steindling managed to escape. In his book, Steindling described how he got out with the help of members of the local Basque resistance, and it is reasonable to assume they played a role in Mordechaj's escape too. Security was lackadaisical, and local workers were allowed to come and go, offering a way out for inmates disguised as Basques in a phalanx of departing labourers.

Once they had returned to the Grossmann-Kessler group, both Steindling and Mordechaj were assigned to a unit known as TA, for *Travail Allemand*, German Work. It involved infiltrating Nazi institutions, the most likely way in the resistance to get yourself killed.

'Being one of the infiltrators was an act of death-defying courage,' Tilly Marek wrote. The Gestapo automatically executed anyone caught in such a role.

Steindling was sent north to the English Channel coast, to blend in with the French workers building the concrete emplacements of Hitler's Fortress Europe.

In 1942, Mordechaj was ordered back into the heart of the Reich. Playing the role of André Vandroux from Lille, he registered at a German-run recruitment centre as a French migrant labourer looking for work, and he was assigned to the Hermann Göring steelworks in Linz, one of the biggest industrial concerns in Austria, which had become vital to the Nazi war effort.

Malci stayed behind, but in November 1942 life in Lyon became significantly more risky when German forces occupied Vichy territory, no longer willing to trust the collaborationist regime after French naval crews scuttled their fleet off the coast at Toulon. With the Nazis directly in charge, it became far more dangerous for a foreigner even to be seen, and Malci was hidden in a nunnery, the Convent of Les Soeurs de Saint Régis in the small town of Aubenas, 170 kilometres south of Lyon.

There were a third of a million Jews in France at the start of the war. Three-quarters of them survived, compared to only forty-five per cent of Jews in Belgium and twenty per cent in the Netherlands. That striking statistic is due in significant part to the role of convents and other havens provided by the Catholic Church, particularly in Vichy.

Malci and Mordechaj's comrade, Tilly Marek, emerged from

the war with a rosy view of the French populace in general. 'We were above all lucky to have worked within the framework of the French resistance movement, which was sustained by the anti-fascist attitude and the will to resist of the majority of the French people. It allowed us to live and fight despite everything,' she wrote. 'It was the simple people, the caretakers, those who rented us rooms, the shopkeepers and others who in France were seldom, if ever, willing to run to the Nazi police to report "suspects". They enabled us to hold out a relatively long time in difficult circumstances and make a modest contribution to the fight against Nazi barbarism.'

At the Hermann Göring steelworks in Linz, Mordechaj's mission was to collect information, sound out workers for signs of dissent, disseminate information about what was happening in the war and ultimately lead unrest or acts of sabotage. There were thousands of foreign workers from more than thirty nations working at the plant. Paid migrants like Vandroux worked alongside forced labour, including slave workers from the nearby Mauthausen concentration camp.

The plant is now owned by the Voestalpine company, which has funded research into its wartime past. There is a data entry in the archives for André Vandroux, describing him as a Lille locksmith who was hired as a welder, starting work there on 18 December 1942. His employment stopped abruptly on 10 June 1944.

That was the day the short, fictitious life of André Vandroux came to an end. The Gestapo and the Linz police arrived at the factory asking for him by name. They knew who he was before they arrived. He was bundled into a car and taken to the Linz police station, held for a couple of days and then transferred to the converted Hotel Metropole on Morzinplatz in Vienna, the biggest Gestapo headquarters in all of Europe.

Malci went to her death convinced that her stepson had been betrayed by a comrade in Vienna who had been responsible for coordinating resistance fighters posing as migrant labourers. That was what she told a researcher many decades after the war.

That must have been a bitter suspicion to carry through the second half of her life, but there is strong evidence that it was not true. In his memoir, Dolly Steindling said the whole Austrian network was rolled up after Oskar Grossmann, the leader of the unit, was captured in the late spring of 1944. Under the codename Lucien, Grossmann was by then running the whole TA operation in the south of France. He had a rendezvous on 27 May with another member of the network (identified by Steindling only as 'P') at 10 p.m. at a tram terminal in Lyon. P was late and while Grossmann was waiting, the last tram of the night arrived, filled with German soldiers.

As they emerged a French resistance unit threw grenades and opened fire with machine guns. Grossmann was hit in the eyes by shrapnel and blinded, unable to flee. When the Gestapo went through his pockets they found enough to make them suspicious about how he had happened to be at the scene of the attack.

In Steindling's version, Austrian Gestapo officers were able to trick Grossmann into thinking they were comrades who had come to visit him in hospital for a chat, casually mentioning the nicknames and *noms de guerre* of TA members, thereby eliciting vital information from him.

'It was a satanic plan, conceived by devils,' Steindling wrote. 'When they could get nothing more out of him, his life was meaningless to them and he was murdered. Lucien could not have continued living had he known what he had done in good faith.'

It is an extraordinary story, but presumably the only source for it would have been Gestapo agents. I was sceptical. Grossmann would have known he was in custody or under surveillance and, as a tough and experienced operator, would have been immediately suspicious of unknown men turning up at his bedside wanting to chat about his resistance cell.

*

In a reading room in Vienna, I came across evidence of another, equally tragic but more convincing, explanation of how the Austrian network in southern France was destroyed, and how Mordechaj was tracked down and murdered.

The Archives of the Austrian Resistance are behind a modest glass entrance opening on to a courtyard in Vienna's old city. The foyer is lined with display cases, a *Schutzbund* flat cap in one and a feathered *Heimwehr* hat in another, duelling mementoes of the 1934 civil war. The blue-and-white striped uniform of a concentration camp inmate hangs limply in another glass box, alongside code books and pictures of fallen resistance fighters.

In the small reading room upstairs, an archivist laid down a small pile of buff folders on a table in front of me containing everything they had on the Grossmann-Kessler ring and its demise, including extensive notes by Tilly Marek. There was also Paul Kessler's prison diary, and the more formal, letter-headed reports marked *Geheime Staatspolizei*, the Gestapo, whose job it was to track down and destroy the unit and everyone in it.

Marek had drawn up a list of the members with abbreviated descriptions and deployments. Against Malci's name she noted: 'South of France, mother of "Motti", survived.' Mordechaj's entry reads: 'South of France, known as "Motti", murdered.'

With this list, Marek appended some observations, which she described as 'a sketch that is a modest contribution to the history of the European resistance movement and a rather incomplete depiction of the activities of Austrian citizens in the French and Belgian resistance movements'.

By 1943, the Austrian resistance had made itself a sufficient irritatant to the Nazi authorities in France to merit a special operation. A three-man team of Gestapo officers was sent from Vienna to Paris, bringing with them files of fingerprints, mug shots and potted biographies of left-wing activists who had been on the books of the Austrian police in the pre-Nazi era. The Gestapo team was led by *Sturmscharführer* Eduard Tucek. It was a relatively junior rank to lead such an important operation, but Tucek had earned a reputation for his brutal interrogation methods in Vienna so was put in charge. In June 1944, his team achieved a breakthrough.

A courier, whom Marek identified as the 'hapless Paula Draxler', a former nurse volunteer with the International Brigade in Spain, arrived in Paris from Lyon carrying a handbag with a false bottom. Draxler's partner, Leopold Hagmüller, a leading member of the Austrian resistance in France, had entrusted her with delivering secret documents to the underground leadership in the French capital. But in an astonishing breach of secrecy rules, he had included a list of names, cover names and addresses of underground members who had been sent into Austria disguised as French migrant workers.

Draxler's train was delayed so she missed her first rendezvous with her contact. The directive in such circumstances was to come back at the same appointed hour the next day. But in a second fatal breach of tradecraft, she went instead to a safe house run by the network, which had already been discovered and was being watched by Tucek's team.

'She ran right into their arms,' Marek's report notes.

'From the material that was found on her person, the Gestapo were able to get a lead on the whole Lyon group, and through that they were able to destroy the work of the TA resistance effort,' Marek said.

Paula Draxler was tortured 'in a bestial fashion' and when she was confronted with the fact that her capture had led to a string of arrests of her comrades, she took her own life by throwing herself out of the window of a toilet in Gestapo headquarters.

'She had a four-year-old daughter,' Marek noted dryly, in conclusion.

A few days after Draxler's arrest, the Gestapo arrived at the Hermann Göring steelworks looking for André Vandroux.

I found the Gestapo account of Motti's last few months in a letter from Morzinplatz 4, the site of the former Hotel Metropole and the most feared address in the city. The letter, dated 13 October 1944, is from Gestapo *Kriminal Kommissar* Höfler to the chief physician of the Steinhof sanatorium, Dr Huber, concerning the case of Martin Israel Sorger. The Gestapo bureaucracy had automatically stripped him of the name he was born with, and added the generic Hebrew middle name.

Motti was described as a 'blacksmith's assistant, stateless, Jewish, single, former Linz resident, high security prisoner'. By the time of his transfer to prison he had been in Gestapo custody for more than three months, and Höfler was asking Huber to keep him alive.

'He suffers from diphtheria. Please keep me informed of his progress by telephone. Since Mr Sorger is an important political prisoner, can I ask you to make sure he is kept secure and to monitor him as far as conditions allow. It is forbidden for him to have visitors of any kind or any form of written communication.'

The next entry on the file was a message to the Gestapo from Dr H. Bertha, the medical director of the infectious diseases section at the Steinhof.

'We would herewith like to inform you that Mr Martin Sorger, born 4th December 1920, who became a patient on account of diphtheria on 11th of October 1944, died on the 17th October 1944 at 8:45am. Cause of death: paralysis of the heart muscle. Toxic diphtheria.'

A post-war affidavit in the same file, signed by Paul Kessler, said that before delivering him to the Steinhof, the Gestapo had tortured Mordechaj at Morzinplatz for four months.

★

The Hotel Metropole is long gone. It was bombed in the war and the wreckage was demolished in an effort to eradicate any memory of it. The police lock-up where Gestapo detainees were held is still there though, a great white wedding cake of a building alongside the canal, distinctive for its round turret on one corner.

The Gestapo chief for Austria and the region, Franz Josef Huber, emerged from the war with no damage to his person or even his career from his wartime actions. He spent no time in prison and was hired by West German intelligence soon after the war was over. Tucek, the man who tracked down, tortured and killed Mordechaj and his comrades, was sentenced to five years' imprisonment by a French military court, but only served one year. Proceedings against him in Austrian courts were suspended in 1947, resumed in 1956 but then abandoned after an amnesty for former Nazis in 1957. The Austrian state paid his legal fees. The crimes committed by Tucek and his team in Paris, Lyon or elsewhere were never brought to court.

I can never know what Mordechaj's last weeks were like. The only source available that could help me imagine is the story of his immediate superior in the resistance, Paul Kessler, who had been picked up at his Lyon home in the same sweep of resistance fighters as Mordechaj, days after Paula Draxler's arrest.

'A large number of policemen climbed over the wall into the garden, started shooting into the windows and broke down the front door,' he wrote in a typewritten account preserved in the Resistance Archives. 'As soon as I was arrested, I was punched in the face in front of my family, tied up with string like a parcel and taken to Gestapo headquarters at Place Bellecour in Lyon . . .

'There I was immediately surrounded by a group of Gestapo men, who began to take turns to beat me. Their expert blows hit me in the face and head, so soon I was bleeding from my nose and mouth and was knocked out several times . . .

'To check if I was conscious they pulled out tufts of my hair and burnt me with matches. They would throw me naked on the floor and throw buckets of water on me, leaving me for two or three hours. I would come to, shivering.'

The Gestapo threw Kessler into a bathtub and filled it with ice water, pushing his head down until he was on the point of drowning.

After six weeks of this treatment in Lyon, he was transferred to Gestapo headquarters in Paris on Rue de la Pompe, where he was tortured for another four weeks by Tucek and his men.

He was made to stand in front of a firing squad and told to talk or die, and on other occasions pushed up against a wall with a pistol to his head. Each time, he said he would rather die. In fact he tried to take his own life as Paula Draxler had. He made a run for an open window but was caught by the guards when he was halfway over the sill. He also tried cutting his wrists in his cell with a splinter of wood, but was foiled by a guard dog posted at his door, which started barking when it heard his movements.

A sign declaring him a threat of suicide and escape was stuck onto his cell door, and the guards woke him up every hour at night to check he was still breathing.

Kessler somehow survived the ten weeks of Gestapo torture and was transferred to Fresnes prison in the south of Paris where French resistance fighters and British infiltrators from the Special Operations Executive (SOE) were being held. In August 1944, after the allies broke through in Normandy, the Gestapo started massacring the Fresnes inmates, dragging them out into the courtyard and gunning them down. The killings continued every day until the prison and the survivors were eventually liberated at the end of August by a French armoured division.

Kessler lived because he was transferred with other Austrian prisoners to the Drancy transit camp in north-eastern Paris just before it was his turn to be shot. On 17 August, as French and US forces were approaching Paris, he was among fifty inmates of mixed nationalities to be selected for a transport east to Buchenwald.

Before he left, however, someone in the resistance passed him a loaf of bread with chisels baked inside it, so he and a handful of other inmates were able to cut a hole in the floor of their cattle wagon and escape just as the train crossed the Belgian border. They walked back, over several nights, to Paris.

Liberation rolled across France, driving back the Wehrmacht and ending four years of occupation, but for many Jewish survivors, it also swept away the last scraps of hope and brought a terrible finality. They found out about the deportations and death camps, and sooner or later the names of those they loved would appear on a list, or in a terse letter.

When the area around Lyon was liberated in the first days of September 1944, Malci was able to leave her shelter in the convent for the first time in two years. Mordechaj was still alive, barely, in the Gestapo cells. She would have found out quickly from the remnants of the Grossmann-Kessler network that he had been arrested and taken to Vienna. She would have known he was being tortured. And it is a fair guess that she would have heard about his death on 17 October not long after it happened. Vienna was not liberated for another five months, so she had to wait in a refugee camp in France before she could go home to search for his body.

The Austrian capital was not as badly damaged as parts of Berlin and other German cities, but about a fifth of it was demolished by allied bombing, and the food supply had broken down. It was a struggle to survive.

The Third Man, which Carol Reed directed in the defeated and dangerous city, became my favourite film from the first time I visited Vienna, but I had watched it over and over for years without realising that our Malci had been one of those desperate Viennese survivors depicted as the movie's silent chorus, competing for shelter and scraps to eat among the ruins.

Among the mementoes Malci bequeathed me, there was no picture of Mordechaj, an absence I felt more deeply as I became consumed by his story. He was my father's cousin, and it seemed a shame his picture was not on our wall at home, and that he had been mentioned only in passing.

The story of the Jews in the Holocaust is usually told as a binary tale, of murder or survival, and those were the alternatives for many of the children in the *Guardian* ads and their parents. The children mostly survived, but those parents who left their departure too late were often deported and killed. Yet there was a third path, active defiance. It was the road not often taken, and even less frequently remembered. But it was the road that Malci and Mordechaj took. They retreated as far as Vichy France and then turned round and resisted.

The Austrian Jewish resistance movement was small but it had a disproportionate impact. It stands out as an act of defiance alongside the Warsaw ghetto rising in April 1943, in which thirteen thousand Polish Jews died. The fighters knew they had no chance against the SS, who turned the ghetto into an inferno, one block at a time. But that was not the point. The point was that for once the Nazis were not allowed to determine the time and place of Jewish deaths.

Our step-grandmother Vally had a cousin in Ohio, Kurt Thomas, born Kurt Ticho in the Czech town of Brno, who had been one of three hundred prisoners to escape from Sobibor in October 1943, the greatest camp breakout of the whole war.

I was based in Poland fifty years later and I was hoping Kurt would come for an anniversary reunion of survivors, but he could not face going back to the place where his father, mother and sister, Max, Paula and Marianne, were murdered.

'I cannot help them. To get there to face the mound of soil on which now grass grows makes no sense to me,' he told me on the phone from Ohio. After the Nazis seized Czechoslovakia, the Ticho family were sent to the Theresienstadt camp, then to Trawniki, a camp in Poland, and then a nearby ghetto at Piaski. Kurt was put on a work detail at a nearby farm, where the farmer stealthily supplied him with extra food, which he was able to smuggle back to his parents and sister in Piaski. They were deported to Sobibor while he was at work in the fields, and he came back to find their hut empty. He never saw them again. By the time he was moved to Sobibor, at the end of 1942, they were long dead.

Built right on the Soviet border, Sobibor was one of three main extermination camps devised by the SS as part of *Aktion Reinhard*, which put the slaughter on an industrial scale with all the science and know-how the Nazis had acquired.

The administrative area incorporated buildings which had belonged to the Polish forestry department, and there was also a farm. In the summer of 1942 it had undergone 'beautification' works to give it the superficial charm of a Tyrolean village, to reassure new arrivals. The extermination area with gas chambers, *Lager III*, was set back in the woods behind a fence. Any inmate suspected of having seen the interior was immediately executed. Kurt once caught a glimpse of a building with a sign claiming it housed 'baths'.

Sobibor needed some six hundred slave labourers to keep it going, and Kurt was given a job sifting through the clothes of inmates who had been gassed.

The catalyst for the uprising was the arrival of Soviet Jewish prisoners of war in early October 1943, and planning began with the Polish underground cell which was already there. The plan involved killing as many of the guards as possible one by one and quietly so that the alarm was not raised. The deputy commandant, SS *Untersturmführer* Johann Niemann, had a 4 p.m.

appointment at the tailor's workshop. Kurt saw him walk in knowing he would never walk out. He was trying on a leather coat from a gas chamber victim and as the tailor told him to turn around to see how it fitted, Niemann was struck on the back of the head with an axe. Another early target was a Ukrainian guard who arrived in the camp on a bicycle and was wrestled to the ground and stabbed by a group of young boys. Kurt dragged the body away and hid it in a narrow space between two barracks. Then a group of thirty men emerged from the carpentry workshop with the task of taking apart the gates to the outer section of the camp, where the SS armoury was located. The plan was to grab the weapons and march out as an armed unit to join the partisans.

The carpenters' effort to storm the gates failed, and they bolted along the perimeter to a section of eight-foot-high barbed-wire fence opposite a mined meadow and started to climb over it with an improvised ladder they had knocked together in case they could not break through the gates. A soldier in the guard tower began shooting but came under fire himself from a prisoner who had got hold of a gun. Kurt took that moment to make his run to the wire and climb, the second from last over the top, and began crossing the meadow. Another prisoner urged him to run, but he said: 'I don't run any more. I am a free man.'

He told me: 'We felt a great desire for life and freedom and an urge to rid ourselves of the humiliation inflicted upon us and, until then, accepted, because of the constant, systematic terror.'

Kurt reached the forest on the far side of the meadow, where other escapees were forming into groups to flee. He ran with another prisoner, a fellow Moravian. After a few hours they slept on a pile of pine branches and woke in the morning to the sound of cowbells. They started walking westwards, sleeping in haylofts and begging for food along the way. The pair separated after a few days. Kurt headed back to the village near the Piaski ghetto where the Polish farmer who had provided food for his family hid him in the loft of his barn. He remained there, in a small space too low to stand up in, until June 1944, when the Red Army arrived, and Kurt left to join a Czech military unit.

As he left the farm, his Polish host urged him not to pass through the village, 'because if the villagers found out he had saved a Jew they would kill him'.

Kurt had stayed in touch with his benefactor ever since. Instead of flying to Poland for the fiftieth anniversary, he told me he would send money to the farmer so that he and his wife could visit their son, who was then at university in California.

Escape was about dignity as much as it was about mere survival for Kurt. Having been humiliated countless times as a camp inmate and slave labourer, defiance was the only way of reclaiming his humanity, whether he lived or died. That is why, when he reached the meadow outside the wire at Sobibor, he did not run, but walked towards the forest.

I could only hope that Malci felt that same sense of dignity. Kurt Thomas had moved to America, where there was reverence for the survivors. Malci had to fight constant bureaucratic battles to secure some respect for Mordechaj. She herself sought no more recognition other than as his mother. In a way, she served a life sentence, condemned to outlive almost everyone she loved.

Motti's death under torture wasn't even to be the last blow inflicted on her. Her other adopted child, Chana, whom she had raised from the age of two, had moved to Prague after the war with the man she had married in Manchester, Helmut Gustav Legler, a Czechoslovak.

They were loyal Communist Party members and he was sent to China to represent the regime in Prague, accompanied by

Chana, now known as Hanna. Their posting was the reason we had Chinese wall hangings at home when growing up. Hanna had given them to Malci, who had passed them on to us. It was another instance of our upbringing amid objects suffused with tragedy of which we were totally unaware.

The Leglers returned to Prague in the early 1950s, part of the Czechoslovak Communist Party elite, but in 1954, no more than a year or two after their return, Hanna took her own life. As with Mordechaj, Malci saw personal betrayal as being the cause of death. She told my mother she blamed her husband for cheating on her. But Legler's descendants, when I tracked them down in Germany and sent an email, had a different version. They remembered Hanna as a beautiful and kind person who was devastated when the Czechoslovak Communist Party, to which she had given all her faith and allegiance, turned against its own Jewish members.

The leadership, with Stalin's encouragement, staged a show trial in November 1952 in which the main defendant was Rudolf Slánský, the Party's first secretary. The country's president and his personal friend, Clement Gottwald, sacrificed him to save himself in the face of Stalin's demands for a purge. Ten of the other thirteen defendants were Jews, accused of a Zionist-Imperialist conspiracy in league with the US and Israel. They all pleaded guilty, and eleven of them, including Slánský, were hanged in December 1952.

For Malci, her daughter's suicide was the last twist in the unravelling of her life. My brothers, sister and I were, unwittingly, her sole supply of joy, a burden no child can possibly comprehend or sustain. At her death in 1994, after living on the most meagre rations for decades, she left us four children thousands of pounds' worth of Austrian shillings in accounts recorded in little red savings books, and a safe deposit box containing gold coins bearing Franz Joseph's familiar visage.

To obtain access to the box I had to show an account number, and the password Malci had given me some years before, whose emotional weight I would not appreciate until nearly three decades later – the code that had failed to protect her son: Martin–André.

11

George and the Return to Vienna

GEORGE MANDLER WAS the first of the *Manchester Guardian* children to go back to Vienna. In 1942, he was living with his parents in New York, working as a hospital lab technician while taking night courses in chemistry with the intention of earning a degree and then joining the family leather business. When he turned eighteen, however, those plans were shelved and George enlisted.

He did basic training in Camp Barkeley, just outside Abilene in Texas, which is where he became an American, awarded citizenship as a reward for joining up. His initial assignment was to the US Army Medical Corps, which gave him nightmares about being deployed as a stretcher-bearer on some Pacific island, where the casualty rates were brutal and life expectancy very short. But then someone told him that, as a fluent German speaker, he could request a transfer to military intelligence and the European theatre.

The response to his application could hardly have come any later, arriving just as he was on the point of shipping out across the Pacific. Under his new orders he was not to board the waiting troopship with his fellow draftees, but to board a train heading east, across the entire country, to Camp Ritchie in the Blue Ridge Mountains outside Hagerstown, Maryland, where George arrived in May 1944.

The trainees at Ritchie were a mix of German and Austrian refugees and second or third generation descendants of earlier immigrants. From 1942 until the end of the war, more than eleven thousand soldiers were trained at the base, the Army's first central school for intelligence and psychological warfare. They became known and celebrated as the Ritchie Boys and two thousand of them were Jewish refugees like George.

They were taught how to interrogate prisoners of war, to find out information about the enemy's order of battle, practising on fellow recruits and even captured Germans. There were courses on how to interpret aerial photographs of front lines and how to spot booby traps while making their way through a life-size replica of a German village, complete with wooden German tanks. They learned how to creep up behind a sentry and kill him silently, and how to fire a machine gun or a carbine.

The British were meanwhile training a similar force, a commando unit in the British army, dubbed X Troop by Winston Churchill, which consisted of about ninety Jewish refugees from the Reich who had been schooled in counter-intelligence and combat. They fought at Sword Beach in the D-Day landings in Normandy, at the Rhine crossing and into Germany. At the end of the war, twenty-three-year-old Lieutenant Manfred Gans from the north-western German town of Borken took a bag full of grenades, rations and a jeep with a British driver, and drove the whole way across Holland and Germany and over the Czechoslovak border as far as the Theresienstadt concentration camp, which had just been liberated. He ran from one half-dead inmate to another giving his parents' name, and by some remarkable piece of luck, they were still alive, though his father was by then so starved Gans could have passed him on the street and not recognised him.

The Ritchie Boys, the US version of X Troop, also had a critical impact in the last stages of the war, providing more than sixty per cent of the actionable intelligence gathered on the battlefield in Europe. German-speaking refugees like George Mandler were at the cutting edge.

In September 1944, after four months' training, George was made an interrogator and document examiner with the rank of sergeant. He was despatched across the Atlantic in a converted tanker to Britain and then a landing ship for the week-long trip across the Channel and up the Seine to Military Intelligence headquarters in Le Vésinet on the western edge of Paris, a former sanatorium whose previous occupants had been the Gestapo.

George had a freewheeling role. Military intelligence teams travelled around the battlefield in their own jeeps, independently of regular units, and wore no rank insignia, so they acted as if they were officers when they came in contact with enlisted men.

George's three-man team set off on his first deployment on New Year's Day 1945, as the Germans unleashed their second big push in the Battle of the Bulge, in the depths of that year's historically cold winter. The unit was sent to Mulhouse, near the German–Swiss border, where captured German soldiers were brought for interrogation.

'The major tactic we used derived from the very strict German discipline,' George wrote. 'We would point out that the soldier was now subject to American Army discipline and that he had to follow officers' (our) orders just as he did in the Wehrmacht . . .

'Most of the time this tactic worked surprisingly well. When it did not, a favourite ruse was for one of us to put on Red Army insignia, be designated a Soviet liaison officer, and threaten that the PW [prisoner of war] would be handed over to the Russians if we did not get the information we wanted.

'We hardly ever threatened force and never used it,' George stressed.

'With captured officers, the tactics were entirely different. We greeted them as fellow officers, offered them cigarettes and coffee (and sometimes, when necessary, even some brandy) and then settled down to discussions of their units and the action they had recently been in.'

George recalled the case of a German major from a tank battalion at a point in the battle when his unit desperately needed intelligence on enemy armoured formations. The major was badly wounded but Mandler had permission to talk to him briefly before surgery. He made him an offer: 'Tell us what we want to know and you go into surgery, don't tell us and I can cancel the surgery.'

The bluff failed. The major still refused to talk but was immediately transferred to the operating room nonetheless and survived.

The closest George said he came to real danger was when a German rocket attack hit a street he was in, and killed two American signals men he had been talking to only minutes earlier. He also came under fire a couple of times when he was doing 'quickie' interrogations at the front.

George ended the war in the 221st CIC (Counter Intelligence Corps), which seems to have been something of a brains trust. Its commanding officer, Don 'Doc' Senter, had been close to completing a PhD in social anthropology when he joined up. George described him as 'attractive, smart, easy to get along with, and always concerned for the welfare of his team'.

Another officer in the unit, Frank Manuel, stepped in to save George from a possible court-martial for having an accident in his jeep while on an unauthorised jaunt in Munich. Manuel went on to become a distinguished historian at New York University, a biographer of Isaac Newton and a specialist on the history of Utopian thought.

George called this team 'the ablest group I encountered in the army'. His fellow privates and non-commissioned officers were Lucius 'Smitty' Smith, a Baltimore lawyer, Gerard 'Brains' Charig, another lawyer, from New York, whose primary concern seemed to be 'that his somewhat left-wing views should not be confused with the communists'. Two others, Robert Maxwell and Andy Olson, went on to become foreign service officers. At twenty, George was the youngest.

There was no question the Ritchie Boys had a wealth of talent. In Hanover, not far from George's unit, the resident team was led by another exceptional Jewish refugee, just two years older than George: Sergeant Henry Kissinger, who would be awarded the Bronze Star for his work tracking down Gestapo officers and saboteurs.

In 2009, Quentin Tarantino made the film *Inglourious Basterds*, in which a team of American Jewish soldiers make their way through Germany killing and scalping Nazis until finally killing Hitler and Goebbels in a cinema. It is a revenge fantasy in which the Jews mimic the lethal techniques of the Nazis, and I found it almost unbearable to watch for its glibness and light-hearted exploitation of violence. I would much rather have seen a movie about George and his intelligence team, who appear to have been every bit as effective as Kissinger's unit but somewhat more nomadic and informal in their methods.

'We had a fine time,' George recalled fondly. At one point in their wanderings, they even managed to acquire a French chef, René, an officer who volunteered to cook for them when they helped liberate him from a prisoner of war camp in Germany.

'He had nobody to go back to, had been chef in a very good Paris hotel, and wanted the opportunity to spend some time with the Americans,' George wrote.

'As we moved into a town, René would go ahead, requisition a villa and household help, and then "go shopping".'

This involved bartering US rations of staples like flour, sugar and salt for fresh German meat and vegetables. René was also a fine pastry chef, and commandeered the team's wine supplies from stately homes. The unit ended up pulling a trailer behind their jeep as they made their way across Germany, full of carefully packed vintage wines.

At the end of the war, 221st CIC was diverted to doing investigative work for the allied military government in Germany, often pursuing suspected war criminals hiding under aliases.

One of the team's tasks was to evacuate the Kaiser Wilhelm Institut in Halle, one of the great German research institutions and the precursor of the Max Planck Institute. Halle was just outside Leipzig and was about to be handed over to the Soviet zone, so the orders were to get the scientists out to the West before the Red Army arrived. George and his team had to put them on a cattle freight train going west, a somewhat ironic task that afforded them a certain amount of grim satisfaction. Much of their work involved screening German prisoners of war before discharging them into civilian life. Each had to fill out a *Fragebogen*, a long political and personal questionnaire which was a central feature of post-war German life. There were strict guidelines on rank: no one was discharged who was above the rank of major in the *Sturmabteilung* (the SA Brownshirts), corporal in the *Waffen*-SS, or who had belonged to the Gestapo, the SS 'death's head' units who ran the concentration camps or the *Reichssicherheitshauptamt*, the Reich Main Security Office, which played a central role in implementing the Final Solution to rid the Reich of Jews.

In the summer of 1945, George's unit was sent on a mission which would transform their remaining time in Europe. They were ordered to accompany a combat patrol to flush out a *Werwolf* nest. *Werwolf* units were special forces volunteers, mostly from the SS, who fought behind allied lines in the last months of the war. The Nazis had not made any concrete plans for a rearguard force to fight the occupation, because the Führer refused to hear of any talk of defeat. But nonetheless a mythology had grown around the rumours of *Werwolf* units lying in wait in the forests, and it lived on well after the war. In the James Bond novel *Moonraker* the villain Hugo Drax is a former *Werwolf* commando.

George and two other members of his team, also German-speaking refugees, were pursuing a suspected *Werwolf* group. They followed a US army patrol into the wooded hills, making sure to stick to the paths that had been cleared of mines, until they reached a hut said to be a *Werwolf* hideout. The combat soldiers took a glance around and then it was the turn of the intelligence trio to have a closer look, check for booby traps and winkle out any useful intelligence.

There had indeed been some SS officers hiding in the hut, and they appeared to have departed hurriedly, leaving behind a locked box, which was gingerly opened. Inside, underneath a batch of the SS unit's documents, were bundles of Reichsmarks. A hundred thousand marks in fact, equivalent to about $600,000 now. The men looked at each other.

'Never was there a thought that this money should be turned over to anybody at all – we were refugees from the SS and considered the money justifiable restitution,' George wrote. They split it three ways.

With his take, George bought some paintings and jewellery and an Amati violin (like Stradivari, one of the great violin-making families of Renaissance Cremona).

Some years later, he gave the violin to a girlfriend who was a musician. Much of the jewellery was stolen in a burglary in California. His considered response was 'easy come, easy go' but he managed to hold on to some of the pictures, which reminded him of his 'single act of *Wiedergutmachung*' (restitution).

Shortly before the end of the war, George fell in love with a German woman, a twenty-one-year-old war widow called Anneliese Gustke. It was against the rules, but that did not stop them. They set up home in her Munich flat and he got a car on to which he stuck military intelligence plates. Every time they were stopped by military police, he would say he was taking Anneliese in for questioning. They got away with it.

In his book, there is a picture of her, a beautiful dark-haired woman standing against a snow-covered landscape in a winter coat holding the puppy they adopted.

At the time it felt to George like a relationship that would last a lifetime but it petered out after he was shipped back to the US in April 1946. Having been uprooted once, taken across the Atlantic by happenstance and then back again, he had a fatalistic attitude to the tides on which he floated.

'In the end, the story of a life is a story of contingencies,' George concluded, and that was true for many of the children from the classified ads. Once torn away from their moorings, they were carried along in the torrent of life in wartime.

George Mandler, as a young boy, circa 1934.

Alfred Rudnai was advertised on the second page of the *Manchester Guardian* on 12 January 1939. 'Will any family offer Temporary Home Austrian refugee boy, 14: most urgent', it said. A British family replied and he was eventually reunited with his mother, Margarete. She had secured a visa as a domestic worker and found herself a job as a housekeeper in Wallasey, across the Mersey from Liverpool; there was a place for Alfred in the local grammar school.

Alfred's first paid employment after leaving school was as a hotel doorman, 'a lovely job,' he later recalled, but it did not last and he moved on to factory work for a company fashioning waterproof raincoats.

Margarete Rudnai had meanwhile found a job in the fashion trade in Oxford, where she rapidly made a mark with her Viennese seamstress skills, making dresses for local women for the celebration of a royal visit. She persuaded Alfred to move in with her and work for a military tailor. Once Alfred was in Oxford, she introduced him to a professor of Ancient Greek, whose wife was one of her customers. The professor in turn encouraged him to apply for a place at St Catherine's Society (which later became an Oxford college).

Towards the end of the war, Alfred Rudnai joined the Royal Air Force in a Lancaster bomber squadron, initially as an engine mechanic in one of the ground crews, but within weeks he had found himself in a Lancaster up in the skies over Germany thanks to chance and a little aerial improvisation.

'They were fitting radar to the Lancaster planes, for which they had to cut out holes in the bottom,' he recalled. 'But the radar equipment was late arriving, and they couldn't just leave the hole so they made an additional belly machine gunner's nest there and I did that job because I'd done a machine gun course as part of my training, so I told them to fix me a seat there and I could be the belly gunner.'

The war in Europe was entering its final act by the time Alfred took to the air, and allied bombers were focused on the last strongholds of the Reich east of the Rhine. Alfred's squadron was now based on an American-run airfield on German soil. But the Luftwaffe was still able to put planes in the air, and on the handful of sorties in which Alfred took part, his plane came under fire from German fighters.

As well as fending off attacks, he found his own way of participating in the bombing runs, filling empty cans with rubbish before take-off and dropping them on German targets, an idiosyncratic, and largely symbolic, act of retribution.

After the war was over, Alfred stayed in Germany, working for the RAF Chaplain, who was opening 'moral leadership centres' in Germany to instruct young men and women serving in the RAF on how to interact with the German population. Rudnai taught a course in Hamburg, and while he was there he was naturalised as a British citizen.

He was offered promotion to a junior officer's position, but he preferred to stay a sergeant, arguing it was better to be a big fish in the sergeants' mess than some small fry in the officers' mess.

George Mandler was in Germany at the same time and, like Alfred, remained a sergeant. He was on the point of being made an officer but as the war was over the army stopped giving 'field promotions'. It was just as well, George thought. If he was promoted he would have had to stay longer in Germany, and anyway as a full staff sergeant he had all the clout he needed. It allowed him, in particular, to get a travel permit to go back to Vienna to look for any surviving relatives.

The journey would involve travelling through the Soviet-occupied zone, but the US authorities, to his surprise, granted the permit. They just advised him not to stop for anything and try to avoid breaking down along the way.

'I was scared shitless driving across the Russian zone because in those days, we never knew what the Soviets would do to an American soldier,' George said. 'Not that they would kill him, but they could arrest him, take the vehicle.'

George reached Vienna unhindered, but it was a freezing trip in an open-top jeep across recently silenced battlefields, alongside columns of displaced people trudging homeward.

Vienna itself was pockmarked with thousands of bomb craters. The bridges were down, and many of the gas and water pipes were cut. More than twenty per cent of Viennese homes were damaged or destroyed; some 87,000 flats were not fit to live in.

Amid the chaos, George was able to track down a small handful of surviving relatives, an uncle, aunt and one of his cousins, Suzi. They were joyously reunited, but at the same time George discovered that many of his relatives had been killed, including seven of his cousins, all girls, and their parents, with whom he had spent his childhood holidays.

'The shock of those immediate post-war years, when I learned about the death in the camps of my relatives as well as of many friends and acquaintances, shaped me permanently,' George wrote. 'I do not tolerate confrontation with death anymore. It leaves me therapeutically untouched – I cannot and will not deal with death.'

To try to explain himself better, George characteristically retold a joke, about two British agents who survived a German death camp. Shortly after returning to Britain and civilian life at the end of the war, they came across a funeral procession. They both started to laugh, uncontrollably, to the astonishment and disgust of those around them. They just could not believe there was 'all that fuss for just one corpse!'

'I avoid funerals and avoid discussing or reacting to people's death. The strategy protects me, though it obviously makes my friends and relatives uneasy, if not unhappy. I am frequently embarrassed, but it is a scar that helps protect the wound,' George wrote. 'I carry the Holocaust with me and object to being told that I have to be reminded about it. So, I do not read Holocaust books or see Holocaust movies. I know – and that is enough.'

I think Malci sought to protect herself in similar ways. She presented a diagnosis of 'severe vascular and nervous disorder', most probably the consequence of the continued stress of living and hiding in France. When she visited Leo and Vally in

Shrewsbury many years later, she would have panic attacks, convinced that she was on the point of death. It was the reason we had to hide our toy guns when she came to visit. But there would have been no protection in 1945 when she returned from France to Vienna and picked her way around the wreckage, in all the places where she had once played with the children, and where she had to face all those neighbours who had come out to cheer for Hitler in 1938.

She found a two-room flat near the Prater amusement park, which provides the setting for a pivotal scene in *The Third Man*, where Harry Lime, the villain played by Orson Welles, looks down from the zenith of the giant Ferris wheel and contemplates the insignificance of his fellow human beings.

Malci's old apartment and furniture had been confiscated under the Aryanisation programme, and she was unable to get them back. The small family summer cottage in woods at Kaltenleutgeben, south-west of Vienna, had been destroyed by the Nazis.

Much of the correspondence in her file at the Resistance Archives consists of her letters to various associations of victims of political and racial persecution in the years after the war, asking for some form of restitution so she could rebuild her life.

In post-war Vienna, she struggled to secure official recognition for Motti's wartime sacrifice, which was both about respect and income, as it qualified her for a meagre survivor's pension. She had Paul Kessler and other veterans sign affidavits on Mordechaj's role in the resistance, his torture at the hands of the Gestapo, and his subsequent death.

'She raised her stepson Mordechaj Martin Sorger from the age of one, and cared for him just like her own child,' one affidavit said. There was a signed note from the city's Communist leadership that Mordechaj had 'fought under the framework of the Party for a free and democratic Austria'.

Malci also secured a statement in French from the Forces Unies de la Jeunesse Patriotique (United Patriotic Youth Forces), a Communist-led French resistance group, certifying that 'Martin Sorger-Schickler (*nom de guerre* André Vandroux) was . . . sent on a mission for the French Resistance to Austria, was arrested by the Gestapo and died as a result of torture in Vienna, in October 1944.'

Malci appealed to have Mordechaj exhumed and reburied in a memorial to the resistance, but no action was taken. He is still in the Central Cemetery, in the fourth section, set aside for Jews who died in the 1930s and after.

Malci's flat near the Prater park was barely habitable and her pleas for somewhere better to live led nowhere. A handwritten note on her application for accommodation in June 1947 baldly concludes: 'still nothing'.

The awful truth was that the circles of power in Vienna had remained little altered by the military defeat of Nazism. In the aftermath of the war, the republic which emerged from the ruins declared Austria to have been the first victim of Nazi expansionism, and therefore to have nothing to atone for. The overwhelming bulk of demobbed Austrians who had fought in the *Wehrmacht* were a far more potent political force than a handful of returning Jews and resistance fighters.

Former soldiers, whether willing combatants or not, were seen as equal – if not primary – victims and their interests were aggressively promoted by veterans' groups, and in the jostling for benefits, the line between *Wehrmacht* veterans and former Nazis was blurred.

Their stories 'formed a layer of remembrance that all but stifled the memory of the victims and the survivors of the Holocaust', wrote Oliver Rathkolb, a University of Vienna history professor, in his book on the period, *The Paradoxical Republic*.

The first post-war chancellor, Karl Renner, a veteran Social Democrat, argued against a rapid restitution of property confiscated by the Nazis, saying that it would risk an inward flood of 'Jewish masses'. The attitude taken was that as Austria was a victim of Nazis, those seeking restitution should turn to Germany for recompense, not look to Vienna.

The policy of hindering the return of Jewish survivors had the full support of the occupying powers. In 1943, the Soviet Union, the US and UK issued the Moscow Declarations, signalling their intention to reinstate an independent Austria after the war, and recognising it as 'the first free country to fall a victim to Hitlerite aggression', laying the foundation stone for 'first victim' ideology.

Such was the state of denial in Austria that when Hollywood descended on Salzburg to film *The Sound of Music* in 1964, the city authorities initially refused permission to hang Nazi flags from buildings or have actors in German uniforms crossing the square, claiming absurdly that Salzburg was never Nazi-controlled and swastikas would not have been on display. It was only after the producers threatened to use documentary footage of enthusiastic Salzburg crowds welcoming German troops that the authorities relented.

In retrospect, the film was a publicity coup for Austria, conveying the impression that in its heart the country was anti-Nazi. It became a huge hit, but I cannot remember my dad or any of my Austrian Jewish relatives expressing any enthusiasm for it.

The post-war powers wanted stability above all, and believed that the way to achieve this was through reconciliation between 'Red' and 'Black', the left and right who had fought the civil war in 1934, rather than delivering justice for the victims.

After the war, Dolly Steindling, one of the other surviving members of Malci's resistance group, was allocated an empty flat in Vienna's 19th District which had belonged to a Nazi dignitary who had fled with his wife after the fall of the regime. 'After 1948, he considered the political situation to be safe enough and returned from the security of western Austria,' Steindling recalled. The Nazi sued to reclaim his flat and won the case in court. Steindling, together with his pregnant wife and small daughter, were forced out. 'What more needs to be said?' he asked wryly.

By 1949 any semblance of de-Nazification had been abandoned, and former Nazi party members were being welcomed back into positions of power. Nazi war criminals were acquitted by Austrian juries in the 1960s and after his election in 1970, the Social Democrat chancellor, Bruno Kreisky, who had Jewish roots, thought it was so important to appease the far right that he appointed four former Nazis as ministers, including a former SS *Untersturmführer*, Hans Öllinger. Under pressure Kreisky dismissed Öllinger, but defended the other three.

Like most of the survivors, Leo refused to go back, but Erna, our grandma Omi, could not settle. In Britain, she was a maid, but in Vienna she would be a shop owner once more, so she pursued a restitution case in a Viennese court, winning Radio Borger back by striking a deal that involved waiving the right to other forms of recompense, like the return of the exorbitant taxes the family was subjected to when they fled. Leo thought she had been duped and continued to press for those taxes to be repaid in a correspondence that only ended when the Viennese authorities declared that the relevant files had been lost. Omi's return and their financial disagreements ultimately led to their divorce.

After their wedding in Manchester in 1957, our parents went on their honeymoon to Austria, taking a trip to the mountains and then to Vienna, where Omi had booked them a room and got them tickets to the opera. It eventually transpired that Leo and Malci had paid for everything, as Omi was broke. Her efforts to revive the shop were a failure, and she was a poor manager. Her son was appalled when he took his bride to see Radio Borger to find the office in chaos with piles of bills and receipts lying around in disorder.

He was furious with his mother and the fury hung over the whole trip. It seems an odd choice of destination for a honeymoon anyway. The last time he had been there he had been chased through the streets by Brownshirts and traumatised for life. It was not as if he had gone to exorcise those memories with his new life partner. Wyn cannot remember him talking about his childhood experiences, only his rage at his hapless mother. Robert most likely felt obliged to make the detour to Vienna to introduce his bride to Omi, but he clearly did not relish the trip.

The final act in Omi's abortive return to Vienna came when she met a man who convinced the fifty-eight-year-old divorcee that he had a way of beating the odds at the casino in Baden. It turned out, to the surprise of no one else, that he did not. The house, then as now, always wins but Omi had borrowed money, using the shop as collateral to support his scheme. It was a disaster. In January 1960, Malci lent her funds so she could skip town and evade her creditors.

Omi arrived in London on the day my sister was born, turning up at the hospital in Stamford Brook with £15 in cash. There was no spare room at our house. My mum's mother, Annie, was already living with us, and Omi was not prepared to return to the scene of her failed marriage in Shrewsbury. So she moved into a small flat in a council block in Swiss Cottage, which became her permanent home until the stroke that felled her some twelve years later.

The first time I ever went to Austria was on a family trip in 1976, which was my father's second post-war visit and the first since the honeymoon in 1957. We took the car on a ferry, camped overnight in Germany and then drove to Vienna. I can remember walking around Landstrasse peering through the window of what was formerly Radio Borger, which by then was a stationers, and gazing up at where the family flat used to be. In the park where young Bobby used to play, two huge concrete towers, the size of ten-storey blocks of flats, had been built during the war as air-raid shelters for civilians and a platform for anti-aircraft guns. The flak towers' walls were three and a half metres thick and they proved impossible to destroy after the war, so they stayed, taking up half the park, abandoned war veterans brooding darkly over the neighbourhood, good for nothing except as a canvas for graffiti.

The rest of the visit was taken up by tourism, walking around the gardens of the Schönbrunn Palace on a hot summer's day, visiting the grand art gallery and sitting on an old *Wehrmacht* tank parked outside the military history museum.

If our father had an emotional response to taking his four children around his old haunts, a surge of proud defiance perhaps at both having survived and produced a family, he did not share it with us. I recall the underlying mood as slightly melancholic, which lightened considerably when we went to the mountains to spend a week in the house of family friends. Our father never returned to Vienna.

Other children from the *Guardian* ads had a similar allergic response. One of them, Ernst Schanzer, who was advertised in November 1938 as 'well-bred' and a 'good sportsman', was given a place at a Newcastle commercial college when he reached Britain before being interned on the Isle of Man and eventually evacuated to Canada.

His parents and his brother Peter were unable to get a visa to the UK, and instead escaped as far as Latvia, where they were arrested by the invading Soviet troops. In 1941, they were deported as enemy nationals to Siberia, where both his parents died in the gulags. Peter survived six years of near starvation and bitter cold and made his way back to Vienna after the war, but the Canadian embassy denied him a visa, suspecting – with no evidence – that he had gone soft on communism while in the camps. Instead, Peter emigrated to Australia and it was decades before the two brothers met.

Ernst became Ernest Schanzer and a renowned Shakespearean scholar, moving to West Germany where he became a professor of literature in Munich. He never married, but had friends and girlfriends, who would come to admire the clematis he cultivated on his balcony. During the holidays Ernest would often travel with his closest friends, fellow academics from the university, but would always turn down invitations to nearby Vienna.

Siegfried Neumann was one of the very few who returned to the city after the war to live and study there, but it was unbearably hard, cohabitating with the ghosts of his parents and the grandmother he adored who had accompanied his violin playing on an old upright piano. 'Of the thousands of Vienna's Jewish citizens only a few hundred were now living in Vienna,' recalled Paula, who visited her brother in their home town in 1946. 'I felt I had returned to a graveyard.'

Fred Schwarz professed no problem at all going back to Germany and Austria in adulthood. By his daughter Madelon's account, he showed no resentment. His revenge was to be happy and alive, travelling around the carcass of the Reich, which had once tried to kill him. He came back for holidays while Hitler and all 'the bastards' were consigned to the septic tank of history.

The relentless cheerfulness bewildered and frustrated Madelon, who felt more resentment than her parents. She thought perhaps it was second generation syndrome, something she had read about in a Dutch magazine, in which the symptoms of trauma manifest themselves in the children of victims. Her parents were sceptical: 'How can you suffer from something that doesn't bother us.'

As a family, they only went to Vienna once but travelled half a dozen times to a small lake in Carinthia where Fred had gone to scout camp before the Anschluss. Along the way, he would regale his children – Madelon and her older brother Rolf – with stories of his experiences with their mother and uncle Frits, who had gone through all the same horrors. His resolutely light tone and the heavenly mountain scenery were at dramatic odds with the dark subject matter, which may be why Madelon and Rolf could remember very little of them, while being able to recall what they ate on the journey in perfect detail.

Frits and Fred had very different relationships with the past. Frits never went back to Germany or Austria if he could possibly help it, and he never talked about it. When Fred wrote his memoir, *Trains on a Dead Track*, Frits's children learned much of the story for the first time.

On one occasion Fred and Carry took their friends to see the place where they had met at Westerbork. And in 1993, as research for his memoir, Fred and Carry took Madelon and her partner Adriaen on a long trip to visit all the places where they had found themselves during the war.

They visited Theresienstadt, Terezin in the Czech Republic, which was largely unchanged. Its German signs had not been painted over, and Carry could show her daughter the attic where she had lived. They saw the place where she had watched Fred being loaded on the train to Poland. They went to Auschwitz-Birkenau, tracing the route he took from the train, being sent to the right, rather than the left towards the gas chambers, the showers and the lawn where they were supposed to air dry. Fred showed them the remains of the latrines, a block of concrete with holes in it. He stressed how there was nothing with which to clean your backside, not even grass. Back home in Holland, he made sure there was always plenty of toilet paper, as well as generous supplies of soap and shampoo. 'Enough for a decent hotel,' Madelon noted.

According to George Mandler it took at least a generation for Germany to look its Nazi past in the face, starting in the 1970s. But it took much longer in Austria. 'The allies in world war two gave Austrians the umbrella of the myth of Austrian liberation, that Austria was a "victim" of German aggression,' he said. It provided an alibi and eased any internal pressure to seek redemption. 'They considered and treated Austria as an occupied and conquered country, which surely it was not. The Austrians thus had the gall and privilege to consider themselves as victims of, rather than participants in, the Hitler regime.'

The rehabilitation of Nazis in Austria reached its zenith with the election of Kurt Waldheim as president in June 1986 despite the publication of evidence that he had lied about his war record and had been a special missions staff officer in Yugoslavia and Greece from 1942 to 1944, in such close proximity to mass killings that he must have known about them.

It was only after widespread international revulsion and a diplomatic boycott of Waldheim that any sort of introspection began in Austria over the blind eye it turned to Nazism. That did not stop the rise of Jörg Haider, the far-right leader of the resurgent Austrian Freedom Party, entering a governing coalition for the first time in 2000.

George Mandler felt a visceral reaction when he visited the city of his birth. 'Today, as I observe the people in the street, they look and dress much like the Viennese who threw me out of their country (thus being prevented from doing worse),' he said. 'It is only in Austria and by Austrians that I have been subject to antisemitic remarks.'

On one of his visits to Vienna in the 1970s, George sought out the boy who had been the chief Nazi party agitator in his class at school in the 1930s. His name was Joseph and in the post-war decades he had risen to become an eminent professor in the University of Vienna's medical faculty.

When George called out of the blue, Joseph immediately recognised his name and cheerfully asked him around for coffee. He arrived at Joseph's house and was welcomed in. The two old school mates sat down and exchanged small talk about what had happened to the students and professors in the war. George waited for the other man to raise the question of his own past and perhaps utter a word of remorse about his misguided youth, but there was not a hint of self-reflection.

George had expected Joseph to feel awkward. Instead, it was George who felt uneasy. He could have quizzed Joseph about his past, but could not bring himself to do so. If the other man did not take the initiative, what was the point? George got up and left and the past was left unacknowledged and unaddressed.

Malci felt the same oppressive burden of history when she ventured out onto the streets. I remember going to see her in 1992, at about the time Kurt Waldheim was leaving the presidency. We were making our slow progress to the local Chinese restaurant when Malci took one of her breaks to draw breath. She cast a baleful glance at the passers-by, her neighbours.

'*Ils ne changeront jamais*,' she hissed. '*Ils sont toujours les mêmes.*' (They will never change. They are still the same.) They were the same people who had been happy to see her and everyone she loved simply disappear.

Nonetheless, she had chosen to live among them. It seemed to me she was past caring, having decided after 1945 to lead an existence rather than a life – one that had completely lost its savour. I came to understand that I had only known the husk of a woman, her emotions numbed years before I was born.

Malci died in February 1994. The sole reference to her passing that I could find in the records was in a 1994 edition of *Der Neue Mahnruf* (The New Reminder), the newsletter of Austrian Communist Holocaust survivors, which had also printed annual congratulations on her birthday.

'The Favoriten district group laments the death of Comrade Malvine Schickler, who has died at the age of 94. She was the surviving relative of Martin Sorger, the victim of racial and political persecution who perished at the hands of the Gestapo in Vienna, on 17 October 1944,' the short obituary said.

I kept coming back to the city even after Malci's death broke my last living blood link. In late 1994, I was posted to Bosnia for the *Guardian*, so packed up all my possessions in Warsaw and drove south, stopping in Vienna on the way. In the years that followed, it was somewhere to stop off and change planes and pick up supplies. Being witness to another genocide in the centre of Europe answered questions about how it was possible for such large numbers of people to be slaughtered among all the trappings of civilisation.

It made such questions redundant. The amphetamine cocktail of flags and maps, myths and fear was being stirred again.

My job brought me back to Vienna in 2015, to cover the international negotiations over Iran's nuclear programme, which gave me plenty of time to wander the streets. Each time I came back to the city, I would visit 103 Landstrasse Haupstrasse, where Radio Borger used to stand, and each time I came, the place seemed to have taken a further turn for the worse.

When we first visited as a family, it was a stationer's shop; when I came as a journalist to see Malci, it sold discount women's clothing; and when I returned to research this book, it was derelict and closed off with chipboard, covered in posters for a clown show and some neat graffiti claiming: 'Jesus is the only saviour'.

The site appeared to have been cursed since Aryanisation, which gave me some satisfaction.

On my most recent visit in the summer of 2022, I felt much more at ease in the city, halfway to belonging. That was in part because I was unearthing more of the family's roots and in part because I had come bearing an Austrian passport. In September 2019, Austria's parliament passed a law that allowed descendants of victims of Nazi persecution to apply for citizenship. I applied in early 2021, and on 13 July I received an email from the exceptionally friendly lady at the consulate to tell me I had become a citizen.

'Congratulations on behalf of the entire staff at the Embassy and welcome to our Austrian Family!' she said.

The state which had stripped my father and grandparents of an important part of their identity had restored Austrianness and Europeanness to me, after it had been taken away by Britain, my father's haven, which had succumbed to its own ambivalent nativism and xenophobia.

As Britain seemed to wallow in self-deception, Austria was beginning to face truths that mattered to me, about the fate of its Jews. The view of the Anschluss as being an act of Austrian martyrdom was in decline, along with the belief that the country had been Hitler's first victim. Vienna's Jewish past was no longer invisible. In 2021, a new memorial was erected in a park near the university, an oval of marble wall segments inscribed with the names of 64,450 Austrian Jews who were murdered.

'We looked away for too long until we realised our role as perpetrators of the crimes and the historical responsibility that comes with it,' the country's chancellor, Alexander Schallenberg, said at the opening.

I spent a summer afternoon walking around the 'Wall of Names' finding my family members and those of the other children from the *Guardian* ads, and reaching out to touch them. Around the city, brass cobbles had been inlaid into the pavements, marking the addresses which had once been Jewish homes. They were called *Stolpersteine*, stumbling stones, the idea of a German artist, Gunter Demnig, suggesting that one should not walk blithely over the ground where such an atrocity had taken place without stumbling over an uncomfortable historical truth.

George Mandler's relationship with the country of his birth improved when he discovered early in 1998 that the Austrian government had made it possible for him to reclaim citizenship without taking up residence in the country. He was taken aback however by one of the questions on the application: What evidence did he have that he actually left Austria in 1938? His answer was simple and instinctive: 'I am here and alive!'

12

Lisbeth and the Will to Live

IN JULY 2015, my mum, youngest brother Bias and I took the train to Caernarfon for Nancy Bingley's burial. She had died nine years earlier at the age of 101 in Surrey but it had taken that long to arrange for her to be interred next to her husband, Reg. He had been waiting there alone for sixty-three years, on a hillside graveyard above the Menai Strait where, on that summer's day, a fierce breeze was blowing in from the Irish Sea and bending the coarse, long churchyard grass.

There were a few dozen mourners at the graveside, most of them octogenarians who had been her pupils at the county school, and her adopted daughter, Christine Robertson, who had flown from New Zealand for the ceremony.

After the coffin had been lowered into the earth and the rest of the work had been left to the gravediggers, we walked to the church hall and reminisced about the extraordinary Bingleys and their open, kind, talkative home.

I asked Christine to define her mother, and she thought for a while and wrote this: 'A truly remarkable character, kind, gentle but firm with a lovely sense of humour, considerate of others, loyal, reserved but not shy, an agnostic, a socialist, a teacher but above all else, a philanthropist.'

The Bingleys had not only offered to take Bobby Borger in, they had taken the train to London and camped out on the steps of the Home Office to make sure the paperwork for his visa was done in time.

They, and all those who welcomed refugees from the Nazis and provided them with shelter, were as much evidence of that 'finest hour' as the Spitfire pilots in the Battle of Britain, it seemed to me. What good is one without the other?

I would only discover long after her death quite how disturbed Nans was by my father's suicide. She had been driven her whole life by the desire to save and enrich as many lives as she could. She and Reg plunged in, working out how to afford it later. But Robert's was one life which ultimately defied salvation.

None of the other children I could find from the *Manchester Guardian* ads had taken their own lives, but looking through their recollections and talking to their descendants, a common thread emerged. They all carried a burden from Vienna: the weight of loss and the guilt of survival.

For George Mandler, the experience of forced migration and the reliance on strangers for survival left its mark on him for decades afterwards.

'I kept meticulous and repetitive notes of the names and addresses of anybody who I met and who played any kind of role in my life – fellow students and teachers, passing (and lasting) girlfriends, and chance, but impressive, acquaintances,' he said.

'This behaviour of holding on to everybody I ever knew, however slightly, clearly was a reaction to what I had lost. I was trying very hard to rebuild a community for myself,' George wrote. 'I had tried to create a new life and a new social surround by holding on to all these people, to replace my loss of a home, a place and people of reference.'

Whatever imprint his experiences had left on him, George was always aware that they were the luxuries of survival. When reminded of family and friends who had been killed, he wrote, 'I literally shudder at the thought of my own escape.'

He would daydream scenarios in which history is inverted

and he is caught by the Nazis while others escape: 'I wonder where on a range from courage to craven surrender I would have emerged and I do not know.'

The burden was heaviest for those children who had been put aboard the train at Vienna's Westbahnhof by parents who were unable to escape and follow them.

These children had arrived as young teens in Britain bearing the responsibility of having to save their mothers and fathers through the bureaucratic machinery of a new country, in a foreign language they hardly knew. Every day they did not succeed was a day when a parent could be beaten up or sent to Dachau, maybe never to return. They were racing against the momentum of events in the Reich and had just a few months to succeed. By September 1939, when Hitler invaded Poland, and Britain and France consequently entered the war, the western escape route was blocked and the cord with which the children held on to their parents was cut, along with their hopes of ever seeing them again.

Gertrude Batscha had tried desperately to find sponsors to offer jobs and financial guarantees to her parents, pleading with her host family, the Partingtons, to help. No one stepped forward for her in those critical months in the first half of 1939, as the doors of escape steadily closed. Adolf and Vally Batscha were trapped in Vienna, from where they were deported in 1942 and murdered in a pine forest outside Minsk.

Gertrude, who became Yehudith Segal in Israel, had a life-time to wonder how things might have been different and carry the guilt of continuing to live while 'the thread of their lives has been severed . . .

'We did not suffer from cold and hunger and therefore our suffering does not come close to the suffering of the children of the ghettos and camps. That's why we did not often tell our story,' she said.

This sense of unworthiness was another common theme

among the children from the ads. With the exception of Fred Schwarz, they had not been in the camps themselves, so they felt they had no right to express the pain of what they endured. George Mandler had an argument with his sister Trudi about it. She thought of them both as 'Holocaust survivors', but he thought that was a claim which 'denigrates the true survivors who emerged from the camps'.

That did not mean, however, that they were left unmarked, George conceded. 'The rest of us who did not share their suffering lived under the shadow of the Holocaust, and it has coloured our lives.'

One of the emotional legacies for George was a feeling of distrust, not just in people but in a wider national community.

'After 14 years of being an Austrian – a patriot with a feeling of belonging and an identification with a small country full of symbols and ways of identifying with it – I was suddenly told that I was no longer wanted, that I was no longer part of that entity or idea,' he wrote. 'I felt betrayed, lied to, and rejected. That sense of betrayal has stayed with me ever since . . .

'And so I left behind my country, my family, my friends – never again to trust fully, never again to feel truly at home.'

When his first marriage broke down in 1956, he realised that it was probably his fault and went to see a psychoanalyst, concluding that he was being dogged by two basic fears, of betrayal and inadequacy.

'In part, I was working through an adolescence that the Nazis had postponed, and between the 1940s and the '50s, I achieved some degree of adulthood,' he reasoned, adding that 'the sense of inadequacy was, in part, due to my status as a Jew, a second-class citizen, in Vienna . . .

'I now began to accept myself as on equal footing with others.'

As with so many of his writings, I wondered if he also spoke for my father. Both were academic psychologists, and it seems not imposible that they could have met at a conference. I like to think they did and feel that they would have got along – atheist, social democratic psychologists who had grown up in the same district and fled Vienna within a few days of each other.

They had the same analytical approach to life, the great difference being that Robert never seemed to turn that analysis on himself and wonder how he might have been affected by his experiences of the Anschluss. Perhaps he was therefore doomed never to entirely escape that sense of inadequacy or betrayal, or leave behind his stolen adolescence.

Like George, my father was wary of patriotism and nationalism in his adopted homeland. 'I don't trust any politician who tries to get to me through my gut, rather than my head,' he once told me.

The issue that drew him into political activism was Britain's first national referendum, in 1975, on whether the UK should stay in the European Communities, the forerunner to the Union. He felt safer in a country that looked outwards and grounded itself in shared European ideals, rather than looking inwards and backwards to a sense of belonging rooted in blood and soil.

Many of the children in this book saw their parents for the last time on the platform at the Westbahnhof, and went through what Gertrude Batscha had called her 'slow orphanhood', living with the steadily growing probability of their family's death for years before it was finally confirmed, with a letter listing names, dates and places of death. Gertrude talked about the loneliness of drifting in that bereft state among strangers who often did not understand or notice profound grief.

'You have no one who really cares about you with whom you can share the worries and the grief and the joys in addition to the incessant longings for your family,' she wrote. 'You have to be solely responsible for all the decisions of your life.'

Gertrude described it as a loneliness that 'got in your limbs'.

From time to time in the early years of separation, Gertrude would feel resentment flare up that, in saving her without managing to save themselves, her mother and father had somehow abandoned her.

'In difficult moments we are angry at the parents who sent us to freedom, and think that we would rather die with them as long as we are with them,' she said. In her worst misery, she felt that a shared death would have been 'a price worth paying'.

Paula Neumann said that life afterwards had been balanced on a knife-edge. She and her brother Siegfried also lost both parents. Their father Karl died in Buchenwald. Their mother Berta, who had put them on their train from Westbahnhof, was deported to Minsk in November 1941 and was killed shortly after.

'To this day, I see my parents, also my grandparents, aunt and uncle clearly and vividly in my mind's eye,' Paula Neumann wrote in her diary. 'I have felt the terrible pain at their loss throughout all of the years, today no less than when I lost them as a little bewildered, unhappy child of nine years old.' Paula describes a lifetime trying to maintain an emotional balance between the gratitude for having survived and the 'horror that has never left me . . . I can never get away from it,' she concluded. 'Death will be my only release.'

With time and luck, gratitude eventually got the upper hand over horror for many of the children from the adverts. They had their own sons and daughters and grandchildren, each time adding to the number of lives their parents had made possible. Gertrude hoped that, as her parents approached their end, being led through that Belarus pine forest towards a trench, they were able to draw comfort and strength from the thought of the generations that would survive them. She believed the parents who put those advertisements in the paper and gave up their children were not victims but saviours.

'I hope never to know such desperation as [that which] prompted them to decide to part with me and send me away alone,' she wrote. 'The countless Jewish parents who did this belong undoubtedly among the unsung heroes of our history.'

Reading that, I imagined Leo, my quiet frugal grandfather with string for a belt, standing on the Westbahnhof platform as a younger man installing his wife and son in a compartment on the train to Hoek van Holland, and saw him anew in heroic form.

He placed the advert for his son, my father, in the *Manchester Guardian* on 3 August 1938, one of the first such ads. He had seen the threat and acted on it long before other Viennese Jews. Those who hesitated, thinking their plight would somehow improve, would have another chance to save their children when the *Kindertransport* began at the end of 1938, but they were much more likely to leave them orphans.

'They clung to an opportunity that was suddenly given to them like a drowning man to a lifebuoy. They brought their children to the train station and there they parted,' Gertrude wrote.

Like Gertrude, I thought of my own son, half-formed and wide open to hurt at the age of eleven, and what terror I would feel putting him on that train. Would I have been able to hide my own fear from him? Would he have cried and clung on to me as I tried to leave him in his compartment, or held firm, looked resolutely forward and embraced the adventure of his solo journey? I pictured my dad, in his pre-teen form in such a railway carriage, and reminded myself that he and the man who wrote the suicide note were one and the same.

My brothers and I scattered our father's ashes in the garden of the cottage Leo had bought in the Shropshire village of Grinshill. The old man had imagined at the time that he had carved out a corner of English rural loveliness for his family in eternity. Our mum lived there for a few years after selling the family house but grew lonely and moved back to a flat in London.

We could no longer afford to keep the place in Grinshill and it was sold, along with its ash-fertilised garden, to a neighbour.

We did not quite leave him there. The dead do not take to being left behind and his demanding presence accompanied me through life, making unsolicited judgements on the mistakes I made, while remaining elusive about himself. I found it hard to pin down just who he had been or the nature of our relationship. When I had a son of my own I became conscious that I was trying to be a different sort of dad. Robert had eventually come to interpret his paternal role principally as an academic mentor and disciplinarian. I would climb the stairs to his study most weekday evenings to present my homework and would on occasion be required to do press-ups for the maths problems I got wrong.

He was not a complete martinet. He took a tennis lesson or two so that he could coach us children on the local courts. On one occasion, when my sister and I were about to host a teenage party at home and found the toilet blocked, he plunged his arm deep into the pipe to remove the foul obstruction, an act of selflessness that earned an indelible place in my memories. And on the occasion of my first devastating break-up with a girl, he took me out to the pub and used both his paternal and psychological skills to reframe my perceptions, showing me that I was not as pathetic as I felt myself to be, and that the girlfriend had had multiple flaws I had hitherto failed to recognise.

For the most part, however, there was a subcutaneous restlessness to him that often manifested itself in resentment of our comparatively easy lives and plentiful leisure. He had grown up in tougher times, and when we were not studying, he would be sure to find work for us. At the cottage in Grinshill much of our time as children was assigned to heavy-duty gardening, like digging down under the roots of rotten trees so they could be removed. Among ourselves we would call it Grimshaw, which sounded more fitting.

He once took my younger brother Bias to the family allotment near his university, and left his eleven-year-old son there alone for a whole day with a list of chores to complete, while he went to teach.

I had been completely compliant with his fixation on academic achievement, but we fell out over politics, particularly after he left the Labour Party for the newly founded Social Democrats in 1981, a schism I believed, in my teenage certainty and high-mindedness, weakened the left in the face of the radical right-wing government of Margaret Thatcher.

The intergenerational squabbles were quite natural. What was unnatural of course was his act of abandonment, especially of his two younger sons, still half-formed in their mid-teens. The reasons set out in his suicide note seemed flimsy at the time, and vacuous as justifications for the shock wave that would reverberate through decades and generations, to places we could not imagine.

We maintained only fitful contact over the years with our half-brother, Alex, whose existence our father had revealed to us only posthumously. He had grown up musically talented, a trait Robert had hoped for in us, and became a singer in stage musicals before settling for the more predictable life of a schoolteacher when he had a daughter himself.

As I was writing this book, I wrote to Alex to let him know and to ask his thoughts, and his reply took me by surprise with its vehemence.

'I won't lie, Julian, the revelation of what happened to our father hit me very, very hard. I honestly felt it changed my entire life overnight, as odd as that might sound considering I never knew him,' Alex wrote in an email.

'I can't really explain it, but I'd always felt there was some great overwhelming sadness in my life hanging over me, and when I found out about Robert's suicide, it all made sense. I admit I have struggled with suicidal feelings and depression for a good deal of my life; the first time I remember wanting to end it all I was only ten years old. Admittedly, that was probably due to the fact my mum was a bit of a bully and tyrant, and made me extremely unhappy growing up. She was a very bitter and angry woman. Again, when I learned of Robert's suicide, a few more pieces fell into place on that front too.'

Alex's email made me feel ashamed. I had not even tried to imagine what legacy he would have had to carry through life. When I had returned from foreign postings to work for a while in London, he came to see me at the *Guardian* offices to talk about journalism as a possible career change. I wrote afterwards to ask if it had been useful but did not get a reply and failed to probe deeper, quite possibly because of a sense that it would involve matters I had spent more than half a lifetime avoiding.

In his email, Alex said: 'Yes, I have always been sad that my own father never wanted to know me, and angry that he abandoned me in this world, but I imagine that feeling is amplified a hundred times for his children that he did actually know and help rear. I think the fact I never knew him is a saving grace. But although I am neither religious or superstitious, I have often wondered whether trauma can in fact be carried in genes.'

Alex and we four, Robert's other children, shared the same genes and perhaps the way they were expressed under the impact of his terror and trauma. Like Alex I had often felt the presence of a trap door lurking under my daily life, left behind by an unseen past. I dealt with it when I was young by travelling. When my dad died in September 1983 I was on the point of leaving for Lesotho, in southern Africa, on an economics fellowship. I put off my departure for a month but in the end I left anyway, and the next eight years were mostly spent in Africa, first as an economist then, once the two-year stipend was over, as a journalist. I spent the next twenty-one years away from Britain.

From the small sample of men and women who emerged from the *Manchester Guardian* ads, there did seem to be a pattern suggesting that families of those who chose silence suffered more. Alice Hess and fellow Vienna survivor Richard Schoen had chosen that route for most of their adult lives. 'I realised I was also profoundly affected by the Holocaust. I too experienced anxiety and depression,' their son, Dennis, said. He and his brother Ronald were always aware that part of their role was to replace lost relatives.

In later life, Richard and Alice began to talk more about their past. When they were in their sixties, Dennis even managed to persuade them to attend a Holocaust survivor event in Washington. If they lived long enough, most of the children who had been advertised came to the conclusion that silence suffocated their relationship with their own children and left them powerless in the face of creeping Holocaust revisionism and denial.

Towards the end of his life, George Mandler began to fear the forgetfulness of the world around him, that the horror of those years would be 'lost to social consciousness.

'That is why those of us who barely avoided them must continue to refresh the memory of what happened and continue to bear witness,' he wrote.

Once Fred Schwarz had written his memoir, his astonishing tale of surviving Theresienstadt and Auschwitz, he took the book on the road, giving readings at schools and colleges. He was looking for younger audiences, with the idea of building a bulwark against the drift back towards the collective madness of the 1930s.

At the same time, with the help of his wife and fellow survivor, Carry, he continued to uncover more material, including examples of Dutch acquiescence in the destruction of the Jewish community. He found an exchange of letters in which Queen Wilhelmina complained about a camp being built to intern Jewish refugees, but only because it was going to be too close to the royal palace of Het Loo.

I wrote this book in the twilight years of the survivors. George and Fred and almost all the *Guardian* children had died years before, along with the last of the Holocaust generation. Their voices, amplified by the power of being eyewitnesses, have fallen silent, and other voices have crept in in their place to scratch away at moral certainties.

I had despaired of finding any of the *Guardian* children alive. When I was researching an article on the subject for the *Guardian* in early 2021, I thought I had discovered a survivor in Karl Trommer, who had gone to Palestine under the British Mandate, become Akiva Trommer, and joined the special forces, the Palmach, fighting for Jewish statehood. At ninety-one years old, he seemed to be alive still, online at least, with an address and phone number. I called and his son answered. I was two weeks too late. Akiva had just passed away. I offered my condolences and emailed a copy of his *Guardian* advertisement.

Returning to the archives for this book, I dug a bit deeper, looking again at some of the names I had failed to trace, scouring the various genealogy websites to see if I had missed something.

The first time round, I had not thought it worthwhile to look for anyone called Weiss as it was such a common name, but with a little more time I saw that if I set the date of birth range quite narrowly, I could filter down the field considerably.

On 27 August 1938, Wilhelm Weiss had placed an advertisement calling on an English family to take care of a twelve-year-old girl, a 'clever child worthy of support'. The arrangement would be 'temporarily without payment' but the advertisement promised that her 'parents will join her later and settle the financial part of the education'.

The closest match was a Wilhelm Weiss, married to Rudolfine, who had a daughter, Lisbeth, born in February 1927. She was still eleven when the advert was placed, but Wilhelm may have thought she would be close to twelve by the time she arrived in Britain.

Lisbeth Weiss did make that journey, leaving documentary traces as she arrived in Britain and then, on 22 May 1940, set off across the Atlantic on the *Samaria*, an ocean liner that was part of the Cunard-White Star Line. In the US she had married a man called George and had become Lisbeth Ruderman, living in the New York area. There were no signs of any obituaries.

On 13 January 2021, I emailed all the Rudermans I could find in the New York area and within a day I had a reply from Tom Ruderman, who worked in the Anti-Defamation League, who wrote: 'Yes, Lisbeth Weiss Ruderman is my mother. Would you like to chat?'

He confirmed that his mum, who was Lis to her friends and family, was alive, healthy in mind and body and was willing to talk to me. And so, on 23 January 2021, she appeared on my computer screen, and I found myself light-headed with happiness, struggling to express just how grateful I was to see her, a heart still beating, mind still sharp, and memories still intact of the world my dad had been born into, the place I had been straining to imagine.

Lis was a slightly built woman who appeared even smaller because the tilt of her computer camera put her face at the very bottom of my monitor, but by the time we had finished talking, over three long sessions, it was as if she filled the screen. She was gracious, dignified and insightful, humble and author-itative at the same time, as eloquent a spokeswoman for the power of hope and determination as I could have ever imagined.

Lis had been born three months before my dad and lived on the other side of the old city, in the 9th District, a couple of blocks from the Danube canal. Like my father, she was an only child, the focus of sheer adoration. The family dry goods shop was named Lisbeth's after her. 'The concentration on me was enormous,' she said.

Seeing her *Manchester Guardian* advert, and reading for the first time how her father Wilhelm had described her, the 'clever child worthy of support', was overwhelming for her. They were words no doubt agonised over before being consigned to the page. Unburied eight decades later, they were still fresh and raw for the daughter they were intended to save.

'To this day, I cannot understand where they got the chutzpah to advertise for someone to take me, and to let me go,' Lis said. 'I just didn't think that they had been that aggressive about doing something. So I'm amazed about that and I'm grateful.'

The Nazis had been running Vienna for five months by the time the advert appeared, but she said: 'Nobody knew what was coming.'

No one could know what was coming because it was beyond imagination.

The first time young Lisbeth was aware of this darkening shadow over her life was on her eleventh birthday, 20 February 1938, which was totally ruined by Hitler's speech to the Reichstag on that day.

'For the first time I could remember, there was no party, no nothing. Everybody stayed glued to the radio to hear his speech,' Lis remembered.

As the only child in the family, she was used to being the centre of attention but on that day 'Hitler took the stage away from me.'

Hitler talked about Germany and Austria being one people with a common history, accompanying the fraternal rhetoric with fratricidal threats.

'Germany is not a warlike nation. It is a soldierly one, which means it does not want a war but does not fear it. It loves peace, but it also loves its honour and freedom,' the Führer declared in his affected, staccato manner.

After the speech was over there was a family discussion in the Weiss household. Lisbeth's uncle, Martin Ziegler, the undeclared but undisputed leader of the family, announced that 'there was nothing to worry about'.

'Hitler will never come here and if he ever does, we'll be long gone,' Martin assured them.

'So you can see there was no concept of how close things were, how dangerous things were at that point,' Lis said.

Life for the Weiss family began to change. On Fridays they would go to her grandmother's house for the usual family dinner, but on 18 March, the first Friday after the Anschluss, uniformed Nazis stopped them.

'They didn't ask us if we were Jewish. I don't know if they could tell or not, but they wanted to know where we were going,' she said. 'There was a sense of doom, of fear, of not knowing.'

Jews were at first moved to a different floor at her school, and then to a different school altogether, in another district. She saw Jews being arrested, signs daubed on shop windows, declaring them to be owned by 'dirty Jews'.

Lis remembers stepping through the classical portico entrance of the Hotel Metropole with her father and sensing the 'awe and fear' hanging in the stultified air of the Gestapo headquarters. One day she recalls being picked up from school by her mother Rudolfine and walking home past groups of Jews on their hands and knees being made to clean the pavements.

'They had small brushes. I can't remember if they were toothbrushes,' she said. 'And there were people standing around, people enjoying this.'

'The swastikas, the Nazi flags appeared in windows and

rooftops all over the city, instantaneously,' Lis remembered. 'It was unbelievable.' She watched from her fifth-floor window as the German tanks rolled along the streets, and saw the welcoming crowd of her neighbours. 'The Viennese were cheering wildly. There is no question about that,' she said.

For the Weiss family, *Kristallnacht* began with a phone call from uncle Martin, with a cryptic message. He was sorry to hear Willi, Lisbeth's father, was so sick, Martin said. His advice was to take some aspirin and go to bed to sweat it out, as he might be having guests.

'What he was telling us is that the Nazis would be coming into Jewish homes, and my father should be in bed and sweating, looking real sick,' Lis said. 'That saved him.'

The SA Brownshirts did indeed arrive later in the day and asked for the man of the house, so Lisbeth's mother led them into the bedroom.

'I remember that very clearly. I remember the knock on the door. I remember the brown shirts and the swastikas,' she said. 'They came to get him, but he was in bed, sweating from all the aspirins he had taken, and they left him.'

'I think that was a turning point. Once that had happened and people were really sent to concentration camps in relatively large numbers, although there was not an inkling of understanding of what was ahead, people did start to talk and think much more about leaving. There had been some discussion about leaving before, but the attitude was: this will blow over. They will leave. Why should we leave? And if we're going to leave, let's go somewhere as close by as possible.'

'But, as I got to realise later, nobody wanted us,' Lis said. 'Nobody opened their doors to us . . .

'I've thought back a great deal and I'm amazed at how readily I accepted everything that was happening. I don't know if that was simply my personality or if the situation forced it on me.

But I was quite accepting of what was happening, or not accepting but living with it: that's the way it is.'

Her parents did not tell Lis about the ad in the *Manchester Guardian* until there was a reply, from a family in Oldham.

'My mother told me in her usual very tactful way, and said: you don't have to go, but we think you should go,' Lis recalled. 'I don't know where they got the strength to do what they did but I think it's just totally amazing.'

Before preparations could even start to send young Lisbeth to Manchester a relative got in touch from Norwich where he had already found haven, and where he had helped persuade twenty-five Jewish families there to each take in a Jewish child from Vienna. Would the Weisses like to send Lisbeth?

'The Manchester people were not Jewish, and everybody felt it would be better for me to stay in my religion,' she said. The Manchester family's offer was politely declined, and a picture accompanied by a few words about Lisbeth was sent to one of the Jewish families in Norwich, the Brenners.

That was in late November 1938, and after that, things happened fast. Over the course of December and January, the family duly queued to get a passport for Lisbeth and then to get the requisite 'J' stamped in it, and the other documents needed to exit the Reich. A couple of pieces of jewellery, a bracelet with the Star of David and a locket with her parents' portraits, were sewn into a jacket. On 1 February, the day of departure, the family had lunch together at Lisbeth's grandmother's house, and then her parents took her to the Westbahnhof.

Her mother was to accompany her as far as the German–Dutch border, but she had to say goodbye to her dad on the platform.

'I can see my father now. Running along with the train, he was pulling out his handkerchief and crying. That I remember very well,' she said.

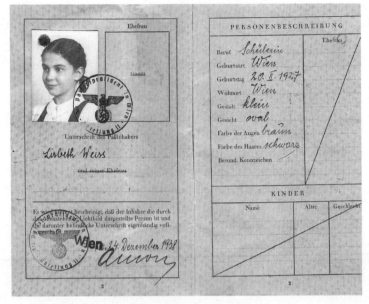

Lisbeth Weiss's passport.

Lisbeth's mother Rudolfine tried to cram in as much parenting as she could in the few hours they had together on the train, 'trying to explain things like the facts of life', before she had to get off at the frontier. There was a woman in the same compartment who was also bound for England to be a maid, and she assured Rudolfine that she would watch over Lisbeth for the rest of the journey, and also help look for jobs for Lisbeth's parents on arrival.

Her mother reluctantly got off the train, to make her way to Nuremberg where she was to spend the night with relatives before returning to Vienna. After she had gone, the corridor filled with German border guards and customs officials checking papers, but they too eventually left, and the train started moving again, into the Netherlands.

'I was out and I do remember a sense of freedom,' she said.

'There was more curiosity than fear at that point. I'd never seen the ocean and I was about to get on a ship and cross the Channel.'

When Lisbeth Weiss arrived at Liverpool Street on a February evening, Lily Brenner was there to meet her. She was with a German Jewish boy who was already staying with a host family in Norwich and whom she had brought along as an interpreter. Lisbeth had taken just three months of English lessons before her arrival and Brenner had no German.

By the time they reached the Brenner home in Norwich, on the strikingly named Unthank Road, it was the dead of night, and Lisbeth was struck by how bitterly cold it was inside the house. Lily Brenner turned on an electric heater though it made scarcely any difference, but having helped the girl into her pyjamas, the Englishwoman let her sleep with her in her bed the first night so she would not feel cold and alone.

She was a forty-nine-year-old widow, her husband, Max, having died in a car accident some years before.

'I thought that was really something,' Lisbeth said. She did not feel homesick until three weeks later, but then it hit like a boulder and she wrote to her parents pleading to be allowed to return. 'I don't care what happens,' she told them. 'Whatever happens to you will happen to me.'

Lisbeth was so distraught, Lily Brenner called a rabbi to talk to her and reassure her, as well as the relative who had first helped to put the Weisses and the Brenners in touch. The crisis passed. More Viennese children arrived in Norwich, including one of Lisbeth's former classmates, she started school, quickly learning English, and that summer her uncle Martin, aunt Seraphine and cousin Susie arrived, renting rooms nearby.

Lisbeth, the only child, found herself part of a larger family, with Lily's son Victor, a couple of years older, and daughter Minda, three years younger, with whom she developed an instant bond.

Almost everyone in Vienna lived in flats, but the Brenners had a house with a garden, and an apple tree for Minda and her to climb on.

'We were inseparable, and that was nice for an only child. So there were compensations,' she said. The two women still write to each other today, eighty-four years on.

Lisbeth's temporary sense of security and belonging on Unthank Road was upended again once the war started, and Lily Brenner's married daughters returned to Norwich from London with their husbands and children to escape the German bombers. She was abruptly informed that she would be moved into another home.

'I remember very clearly being in school and being called to the office because somebody was coming into the class to talk to them to see what other family would like to take me,' she said.

At the time she took the sudden ejection in her stride but in retrospect she is astonished.

'They had no business doing that. As far as I'm concerned, now as an elderly adult, I would have had me sleep on the floor rather than put me out.' When she returned to Norwich after the war, the two daughters met her at the train station and the first thing they did was to apologise for her eviction.

A local family, the Nimmos, took her in for a few months, but then the Brenners' son-in-law thought she should be in a Jewish household, so she moved in with his family, the Rosens, who had small children, down the road from Lily Brenner.

'I was delighted to have these little siblings to look after, and I felt perfectly at home,' she said.

Like George Mandler, Lisbeth Weiss started working on ways of saving her parents almost as soon as she arrived. She wrote letters, asked everyone she met whether they knew of any jobs her parents could do.

'You should have seen me. I was aggressive: "Where should

I try? Where should I go?"' she said. 'But I guess I didn't have the right connections.'

Her uncle Martin Ziegler had bought tickets for the whole family to travel to the US, but her parents had to get out of the Reich first. Wilhelm had been born in Poland, and the waiting list for visas for Polish-born applicants was the longest.

Getting visas to Britain involved learning new skills. Lisbeth's mother took a course in making corsets and bras, my grandfather's eventual profession.

'They were going to keep trying. People were crossing the border illegally and walking into Yugoslavia and places like that,' Lis said. 'They talked about doing something like that, but they never tried it. I don't think my parents were what you call adventuresome. They were regular bourgeois people.

'The fact that they sent me out, I would say, was one of the big accomplishments of their life – that they had the strength and the wisdom to do that. Now we have great-grandchildren. It is mind-boggling.'

There was a limit to the risks Lisbeth's parents would take because some part of them hung on to the notion that the Nazi regime was a passing phenomenon. It was a hope born of an ingrained belief in right and wrong, and normality.

'They had this definite feeling that this was a very temporary thing. That's how my parents talked about it. This can't go on. It will end and she'll come back.'

Meanwhile Lisbeth and her parents wrote each other letters, and they called on two occasions: once unsuccessfully, to wish their daughter a happy Passover, but she was out, gone with Minda to synagogue, and a second time when she was in. It was the last time they talked, and Lis racked her brains many years on, trying to recall what was said: most likely enquiries about health and wellbeing, how she had spent her time with Minda and her brother Victor. None of them knew it would be the last time of course.

But then on 3 September, with Hitler having invaded Poland, Britain declared war, and her parents were trapped behind enemy lines, unable to leave.

In the spring of 1940, US visas came through for her uncle Martin, aunt Seraphine and her baby cousin Susie. By then, Martin, like almost all Austrian and German refugees, had been interned, but he was released from camp on the Isle of Wight after only a few days when he could prove he had a visa and tickets to emigrate to the US. Children were not allowed to make the Atlantic crossing without their parents, but it was unthinkable to leave Lisbeth behind. They all went to the US consulate in London to plead their case and she cried in front of the consular officer, who made an exception.

On 22 May 1940, they boarded the *Samaria* from Liverpool. All the passengers and crew wore life vests for the first few days as the ship zigzagged across the Irish Sea and then the open Atlantic, dodging German U-boats, the constant changing of course contributing to Lisbeth's sea-sickness.

When the *Samaria* arrived in New York, Lisbeth woke up early with her uncle Martin to see the Statue of Liberty. The American family who had signed an affidavit to underwrite their visas met them at the dock, having organised a place for them to stay in the Bronx for their first few nights in the United States. It was an unusually hot early summer, much hotter than the new immigrants were used to, especially in the crowded, gritty, Bronx.

When their sponsor family asked them to visit their home in Laurelton, a suburb in Queens, they invited Lisbeth to stay for the summer. Martin and Seraphine found a room to rent nearby, and the family began their American life there. But of course it was only half a family.

Lisbeth was able to exchange letters with her parents again as America was not yet at war with Germany, and her uncle

Martin continued to look for ways to get her parents and grandmother out.

At one point it appeared that Lisbeth's father's number was about to come up for a visa as he was called to the consulate for a medical exam. But after that he seemed to fall to the back of the line again. His number, it appeared, had been sold to someone able to pay to jump the queue. Then Wilhelm Weiss was sent to a labour camp, and the family in New York had to scramble to wire affidavits to Vienna to help get him out. Through it all, her parents' letters continued to exude confidence that they would somehow escape and join Lisbeth and the others in America.

There was an expensive route through Cuba, and by 1941 Martin had secured visas and tickets for them, but before they could leave Vienna, the Japanese bombed Pearl Harbor, and Germany entered the war on Japan's side against the US. The last exit route was cut off.

There were a couple more letters through the Red Cross after that, and then they ceased. On 27 May 1942, Lisbeth's parents, Wilhelm and Rudolfine, were deported from Vienna to Maly Trostenets, a collective farm outside Minsk, Belarus. Lisbeth would never find out exactly how they died.

Many perished in the cattle wagons on the journey. As each train arrived, prisoners were stripped of any remaining valuables, a few were selected for forced labour on the farm and the rest were driven immediately to a forest a few miles away, lined up at the edge of a pit and shot from behind by the *Einsatzgruppen*, SS death squads. More than ten thousand Austrian Jews were killed there.

A little later in the same year, Lisbeth's grandmother was transported to Minsk from the Theresienstadt camp, and died there too.

Lis would only discover the basic facts of what happened to her family many years later. At the time, she was aware of the peril they were in, but her aunt and uncle sheltered her from the worst. Martin and Seraphine (Finny as she became in America) had somehow managed to bring a trunk of Willi and Rudolfine's possessions out of Austria – pictures, mementoes and clothes – and it was stored in the attic in Laurelton. One day, they started giving the clothes away.

'I didn't need much more proof of what had happened. They were trying to protect me, I guess, and didn't come out and tell me. But that's when I broke down. Especially when I saw [they were giving away] my mother's favourite dress.'

The incident hammered a wedge in Lis's relationship with her aunt and uncle, who had done so much for her and stood in as parents.

'I think I was torn by loyalties,' she said later. 'There must have been a wish in me, way down, that I could be adopted, and that I could just forget the past completely. But on a much more conscious level, I knew that I could not give up my loyalty to my parents, and so there was a conflict.

'But the whole atmosphere in those days was to forget the past, to assimilate, assimilate, assimilate, to be all-American. There was no pride in heritage . . .

'In those days, it was enough just to be American, and to forget. That was one way of dealing with the past. You can call it denial. For the survivors who experienced the horrors like the camps, it was certainly a way of dealing with it, and also an inability to talk about it for quite a while, and I think in our case it was just the need and the desire to make a new life and push back the past,' Lis said. 'It was certainly not losing respect or feeling, but not talking about it a great deal. I don't remember having pictures of family members out particularly in those years. I think it would have been too painful.'

In New York, Lisbeth earned money from tutoring and working in department stores, which helped cover some of the expenses when she went to a local college to study French and psychology. Her uncle Martin paid the remainder. Unable to find a job at that time and with those qualifications, she then went to business school and learned to be a secretary.

She moved closer to the city and rented a furnished room, but then realised she did not enjoy being a secretary and so moved back to Martin and Finny's in Laurelton to save money so that she could go to New York University to take a teaching degree.

She met her husband George Ruderman when she was teaching elementary school in the 1950s in Stamford, Connecticut, sharing a house with two other teachers, one of whom was from Montclair, New Jersey, George's home town. On election day on 6 November 1956, as Dwight Eisenhower was in the process of beating his Democratic challenger, Adlai Stevenson, this teacher's parents came to visit; they were sitting there when the mother started staring at Lisbeth and just said 'George!' That was it. On returning to New Jersey, this woman called George's mother.

'A few weeks later, George and I were engaged,' Lis said. The matchmaker came to their wedding but died soon afterwards.

Lis temporarily gave up teaching soon after they married, and focused on motherhood, giving birth to three sons in five years in Montclair.

The past could still ambush her though, like the time in the early 1960s when she received a postcard giving the date of her parents' deportation to Maly Trostenets. 'It came at me one day with no warning. That was a bad, bad time.

'I waited to go back to Vienna until I felt ready,' Lis said. 'And I had some psychological help, which I needed periodically, and I decided I was ready. My aunt tried to stop me from going. She was worried that it would be too upsetting. But I knew I had to go.'

It was 1980. Lis was fifty-three and she had been married to George for twenty-three years. They went on a European vacation, but when it came to Vienna, she insisted she go on ahead and spent three full days alone in the city of her birth.

'I had to experience it.' She went to her school, and walked the route back to her former family home, and went to sit in a cafe around the corner from the family's old apartment.

'To be honest, it was not very emotional. I don't remember angst, or anything like that,' she said, adding that she was 'a little taken aback' by the absence of her own emotion. But then again, she had moved to Britain and shuttled around different homes there without any substantial reaction.

'That's probably why I needed some psychological help afterwards. Yes, dig it up a little, because I had pushed it down.'

The apartment block where the family lived had been bombed and rebuilt with shops on the ground floor, but the communal arched entrance and central courtyard remained the same. On one trip back Lis went in with her granddaughter and stood on the spot from where she would yell up to her mother asking permission to go out.

'I always kept hoping I would find somebody, whether it be the concierge whose son I played with – anybody . . . I kept wishing that I would meet people that I had known and been able to show my American citizenship. But I did not have the opportunity.'

All the other people had long gone, the stones were new, but the empty space between them was still the same.

She shared my aunt Malci's view that there had been no magical transformation. They were still the same people who had hounded her out.

'I had a very cocky attitude. I would speak German without an accent, and since I was an American that puzzled them. I never explained anything to anybody,' she said. Her attitude was: 'Here I am, even though I am the only one left in my immediate family, but I made it.'

She found the flat in Leopoldstadt across the Danube canal

on Obere Donaustrasse, where her parents had shared a single room with relatives after being evicted from their family home and where they had spent their last days.

By the time George arrived, Lis was able to be a tourist again and see the sights with him, and show him places that were important to her. She was determined to see her trip as revisiting her childhood, which had been a happy one, rather than a return to the horrors of what came after the Anschluss. On the whole that seemed to work.

Like our father, Lis had wrapped Vienna and her past in silence. Just as my dad aspired to be bourgeois and British, she just wanted to be 'the all-American wife and mom and woman'. She had pictures of her parents in her bedroom but what happened to them was never discussed when her three boys were young. But as they reached adulthood, she realised they had to know something about their background.

I wondered if our father would have reached the same conclusion if he had lived longer, at least long enough to meet his grandchildren. Maybe they would have changed his perspective, and he would have seen the broader arc of our family's history. Lis found that it brought no sudden catharsis but rather required constant work. 'We are still struggling with it,' she told me.

She helped set up a Holocaust education committee in the Jewish Federation in Bridgeport, Connecticut and became its chairwoman, talking to local schools about the way the subject should be taught.

'That's how I got myself to look back,' she said. She still has to calibrate her relationship with her own history, limiting what she reads or watches on television.

'Part of the reason is that I don't really know what happened to my parents,' she said, so that any portrayal on the page or on the screen rushes into the vacuum about her parents' end, leading her to speculate once more: 'is this what happened to them – is this how they suffered?'

'I just decided that at some point, I don't need to hurt myself over and over again,' she said. 'I want to lead as normal a life as I can to deal with the trauma and deal with my past, but not let it run my life. That's been my philosophy in the past few years.'

Many of the children from the *Guardian* ads had sought to find the same kind of balance, realising that the past can trap you if you spend too much time there, or control you if you spend too little. Floating between the two is some sort of freedom and happiness. It is a place our dad did not manage to find, and perhaps he never looked for it, doubting it even existed.

For us, his early life had been a blank space, a dark silhouette set against the backdrop of the 1930s. The conversations with Lis, the memoirs left behind by some of the other *Manchester Guardian* children, reflected light and colour and lit up at least an imagined version of what had been left undescribed in our lives.

What Nans told me when our father took his life rattled me and left me confused for years, a reminder that I had grown up really not knowing him, and was missing the key to understanding how he made his decision. He had chosen not to stick around to meet my son and all his other grandchildren. His contemporaries, who had left Vienna on the same trains and gone through worse, had not taken the same path. Lis's son Tom sent me a picture of her on a beach looking out to sea beside her great-grandson, named Wilhelm after her father. My immediate thought was that there could have been pictures like that of Robert. I had told myself and others that I held nothing against him, and it had not been true.

The writing of this book unearthed my resentment of him but also brought its antidote. The lives of those advertised alongside him taught me things about him.

In particular, the research led me to a revelation about his final days, of which I had been entirely unaware. It explained why, when I called Nans that day in 1983 to tell her that her foster son was dead, her response, that he was Hitler's victim, had been so adamant.

After he left our home for the last time my father had driven straight to Nans' house in Woking. He arrived unannounced and found she was not in. She had gone away for a long weekend to Wales. Robert was taken by surprise – Nans rarely left home – so he just sat there.

Her daughter-in-law, Doris, was getting off the bus on her way back from the shops when she found him in our old dark blue family car, parked in the driveway. She asked him in for tea and biscuits and he stayed, in no hurry to leave, repeating what a shame it was that he had missed Nans. In the end, he got up and reluctantly drove away, and a few days later he was dead.

He had not gone to friends who had only known him as Robert, Englishman, psychologist and lecturer. Instead he had sought out Nans, who had known him as he had arrived in Britain, a terrified eleven-year-old child. I could not help but picture him sitting in the car outside Nans' house with nowhere else to go.

Nans returned from Wales a day or two later to hear that she had missed his visit. What agony I brought her when I called a couple of days later, delivering not just news of Robert's death, but the knowledge that perhaps, if she had been at home, she might just have managed to talk him out of his plan, putting his troubles into perspective and mooring him once more in the idea of endurance and survival.

'She was so upset when she realised that she might have helped and that there were things, who knows what, he wanted to tell her,' Doris said.

They could have recalled his early days in Caernarfon between the Irish Sea and the mountains, the wonders of a new life, the relief and joy of survival. Who knows whether it would have made a difference. What is clear was that at his lowest point, the black hour at the very end, his instinct was to reawaken that connection to the one person left alive who knew him as Bobby, the Jewish boy from Vienna.

Epilogue

THE ZENTRALFRIEDHOF, VIENNA'S central cemetery, covers a huge expanse in the south-east of the city and is a truly magnificent place to be buried. The tombs of Beethoven, Brahms and Schubert are clustered around its centre, which is marked by one of the most elegant Art Nouveau churches in all of Vienna, the green-domed St Karl Borromäus.

The two Jewish cemeteries are at either end of this sprawling necropolis, and stand out for being unkempt, hardly surprising as the ratio of living to dead Jews is so unfavourable. There are not many descendants left to tend the tombs of their parents, grandparents and loved ones. Long grass and wildlife have stamped their authority on the place.

In the oldest section, through the first of the cemetery's four gates, many of the gravestones have become illegible, having fallen face-down into the earth or been robbed of their inscriptions by the elements.

On the Jewish Cultural Community website I found the coordinates of my would-be great-uncles and great-aunt, Emil, Eugen and Marianne Borger, who never made it to adulthood. Their gravestones had long been scrubbed clean by time.

Their parents, my great-grandparents, Johann and Hermine, were in the new Jewish section established in 1917, behind the fourth and last cemetery gate. Their shared grave was easier to find, its headstone still intact and marked with the Hebrew letters, Pe Nun, short for *po nikbar*, 'here lies', and then 'our beloved' in German, above their names and dates. At the bottom was carved the single word *unvergessen*, 'unforgotten', a bold promise we had failed to keep.

I scraped the moss off the tombstone, put a round pebble on it and silently apologised, suggesting we would do better as a family.

My final stop was Mordechaj Sorger's grave. In the short walk to get there, I passed a fawn, which stopped foraging long enough to watch me go past. A few steps further, a cock pheasant fluttered between two stones and disappeared.

On his headstone, he was plain Motti Sorger. My great-aunt Malci had been a mother to him since he had been a one-year-old infant and so Mordechaj would always be Motti for her. He had no more need for the other names he had taken as camouflage, Martin and André Vandroux.

There was a thin layer of pine needles on his white stone slab and a black clump of what I took for soil and twigs. When I began to clear it away, I saw it was made up of bits of metal and small plates of glass, the remains of a lantern, which Malci lit when she visited him. What must it have been like to grieve a son who was tortured for months so his death finally came as a blessing? It looked as if no one had been there since Malci died in 1994.

There was no Hebrew on Motti's grave. Malci would have had none of that. Beneath his name there were the dates bracketing his twenty-four-year lifespan, and the single phrase: *Dein Opfer Bleibt Unvergessen*, 'Your sacrifice will not be forgotten'. It had been forgotten of course, but now remembered once more. Better late than never, I hoped.

Walking between the graves, the wide tree-lined promenade felt curiously familiar, considering this was my first visit. I stood there looking up its history on my phone, and found out why. It was the setting for the final scene of *The Third Man*. Harry Lime had just been buried in the Zentralfriedhof, and Holly is leaning on a cart on the side of the promenade, waiting for Anna to reach him, in the hope he might be forgiven for betraying Harry. The camera does not move for ninety seconds as she approaches him slowly along the long leaf-strewn path lined by pollarded trees. We are counting on a happy ending, some kind of reconciliation, but Anna walks right past him and out of shot without a backward glance.

I had watched that scene countless times and thought about it often, but it had never occurred to me that my ancestors were buried on either side of that lonely road, a cinematic metaphor for solitude. It made me wonder about the unconscious pull of all that buried, unacknowledged history.

I grew up somehow thinking my family had miraculously survived the Holocaust without loss. That was not true at all. It was just that those who had perished, like Motti, were never talked about. Their lives were never recounted and their pictures did not hang on our walls.

Omi, our grandmother, had lost her father and sister, Markus and Marianne, our great-grandfather and great-aunt. They were deported from Vienna in the same train, in late April 1942, which took them to Włodawa, where Poland, Belarus and Ukraine meet. From there, they were taken to the camp at Sobibór, where they were among a quarter of a million people killed in its gas chambers.

Our step-grandmother, Vally, lost her first husband, Rudolf Klinger, who was killed in Buchenwald, and Malci's husband, the mysterious Elias Schickler, simply disappeared, probably killed either by the Nazis or his own comrades in the Communist Party.

As children, we had been among people who daily supported the weight of unmentionable loss. Our family discovered something that any Viennese psychotherapist could have told us: those burdens grow heavier and darker the more you try to ignore them.

I once saw a James Baldwin quote inscribed, somewhat randomly, on the window of a New York supermarket: 'Not everything that is faced can be changed. But nothing can be changed until it is faced.' I wondered at the time how that was supposed to inspire you to buy groceries, though perhaps that was not the point. It also made me think of my father, and how marooned he had felt at the end of his life.

In all my sifting through archives and personal records, I discovered nothing that could explain or excuse his decision to leave us, but I did come to understand something of the suffering and fear he had lived with, which I had failed to acknowledge for all those years before I set out to follow his elusive footprints. I could see that once he had made the decision to bury it all, erasing his childhood from his personal history, he would have been left unmoored and lonely. I thought of all the conversations we might have had.

I was nonetheless glad to have gone looking for him, going as far as any son reasonably could. It led me to scratch under

Robert Borger on arrival in Britain, 1938.

the surface of his and all the other adverts and see what lay beneath the three or four lines of text. Inevitably there was tragedy and horror, but almost every story involved the joy of survival and the lives it made possible, like mine, my brothers' and sister's.

Our collective memory of the Holocaust and the war, no matter how dark it may seem, is still rose-tinted. The stories we hear are told by survivors, so they have a happy ending of sorts clasped like a pearl inside each one. The dead cannot tell their stories, so the recounting of history skews towards the hopeful. Perhaps it would be unbearable if it did not.

Certainly, the tales of Bobby and George, the two Gertrudes, Alice, Siegfried and Paula, Manfred and Lisbeth were all shot through with the wonder of escape and all its possibilities. I came to think of their fate and the different paths they took from Vienna like strands of yarn, twined together through the tiny coincidence of a newspaper ad and then diverging in all directions as a bloom of dazzling colours.

Acknowledgements

I owe my thanks to Ruth Hargove. If we had not been chatting online and she had not mentioned her family background, I would never have gone looking, and this book would not have been written. The same goes for Richard Nelsson, who found the advertisement and gave me the tools to find the rest.

Mark Rice-Oxley edited the original *Guardian* article, which was the seed for this book, and made it far better. Kate Hewson at Two Roads sent a lovely note about it which I failed to spot when it first came. When I wrote back more than four months later, she was gracious enough to overlook my tardiness and discuss the idea of a book. James Pullen at The Wylie Agency adeptly steered me through the formalities.

I am grateful to Richard Pollard and Gadis Arivia Effendi for having me to stay in the most beautiful surroundings on the shore of Chesapeake Bay so that I could write the book proposal. Eric Schlosser gave me early encouragement that solidified my resolve. Philippe Sands made a key introduction and encouraged me in the early stages.

Many people were kind to me in Vienna, foremost among them Nick van Praag and Nadja Zerunian, who gave me wonderful food, good ideas and introduced me to friends who had even more ideas. Bethany Bell was generous with her time, even helping me to find a Gugelhupf pan for my mum and introducing me to Michael Heislbetz, who helped early on with translation.

Wolf-Erich Epstein and his daughter, Theresa, gave me the benefit of their profound knowledge of Jewish Vienna. Thanks also to Clemens Coudenhove Kalergi for a really insightful tour of the 2nd District, Leopoldstadt, which was profoundly helpful.

Martin Weiss, the former Austrian ambassador to Washington, was encouraging, helpful and particularly welcoming when I became a fellow countryman. Oliver Rathkolb gave me an erudite tour of modern Austrian history, and found records of Mordechaj's time at the Linz steelworks.

I was lucky to find Ulrike Wiesner who is not only a skilful and sensitive translator, but also lived near me outside Washington and in Vienna. She billed me for much less than I really owed her because she believed these were stories worth telling. I am in her debt.

Thanks too to Bernd Rest and Stephanie Kirchgaessner, who supplied incidental but vital translations at short notice.

I was repeatedly taken by surprise by people who offered help simply because they had read the *Guardian* article and had expertise and experience to offer. Robert Wiener was extremely helpful with advice on archive sleuthing. Matt Stein guided me through the Austrian online databases and gave some tips that led to important discoveries. Shulamit Druckman was extraordinarily generous with her investigative skills and time and was instrumental in finding the Neumann family, and Jona Cummings pointed me in the right direction with early advice. Yossi Melman helped me track down a couple of people with his knowhow.

I would not have found Fred Schwarz if it were not for Angelina Sutalo, who called on her tracker friends at the Hague war crimes tribunal and her own keen instincts. Iva Vukusic, another war crimes expert, also gave me hints about finding people in the Netherlands.

In researching the story of the Hakoah Wien football team and my great-uncle Fritz, I relied on the selfless help of Jonny

Gould, David Bolchover, Rony Dror and Katharina Lischka. John Sipher pointed me in the direction of the Ritchie Boys legend, which helped tell the story of George Mandler at war. Angel Cossigny at the University of Manchester Library truly lived up to her name when I was looking for traces of the *Guardian*'s correspondent in Vienna in the 1930s, Mike Fodor.

When it came to researching the Shrewsbury era, Ric Graebner, Virginia Greasley and Peter Lobbenberg took time to give me some wonderful anecdotes and descriptions of my grandparents.

Sean Smith gave a lot of his time kneeling over heavy bound copies of the *Manchester Guardian*, taking pictures of the adverts, an act of generosity and friendship.

Three good friends looked at an early draft. Ed Pilkington was very encouraging, as was Hooman Majd, who placed a discreet M in the text wherever I became unduly mawkish. All remaining mawkishness is my responsibility. Paul Hamilos brought the skills of one of the best long-form editors around. He helped me reshape and rethink the book, and I am deeply grateful.

Doris Bingley, Claire Donaldson and Chris Robertson gave me invaluable help when it came to portraying Nans and Reg Bingley, two of the central heroes of the book. So did Norah Davies, who grew up across the road from the Bingleys and showed me around Caernarfon, only strengthening my impression that it is truly the home town of kindness.

Sian Marian talked me through the life of her mother, Megan Stumbles, who had lived with the Bingleys at the same time as my dad, and I really appreciate Mark Hainge putting me in touch with his father Meurig, who was a schoolboy with my dad in Caernarfon, so that I had the chance to talk to him about his recollections.

Lauren Howard and Joe Zigmond ensured the process of editing the book was relaxed and enjoyable. They have improved on the original draft immeasurably.

This book would simply not exist if the sons and daughters of the other children in the *Manchester Guardian* ads had not opened the doors of their family histories to me. I owe special thanks to Peter Mandler, Danny Segal and Ruthie Elkana, Rolf and Madelon Schwarz, Rabbi Leslie Alexander, Dennis and Ronald Schoen, Gila Maroz Toth, and Tom Ruderman. I am especially grateful that I had the privilege and pleasure to talk to Lis Ruderman, who to the best of my knowledge is the last remaining survivor among the *Guardian* children, a genuinely inspirational human being.

Peter Mandler was also kind enough to look through the first proof and suggest corrections, as did Mary Lynch and Jonathan Freedland. They saved me from some embarrassing mistakes.

Finally, I am very lucky that my sister Charlotte, and brothers, Bias and Hugo, were supportive throughout and allowed me to write the book in the first place. And most of all, I owe thanks to our mum, Wyn, who was ready to sit down again and again to go over painful memories of difficult times. Her sole concern was that I write the truth. That is what I have tried to do in this book, and why it is dedicated to her.

Picture Credits

Family photographs courtesy of Leslie Alexander: page 131; Julian Borger: pages xvii, 28, 41, 94, 119, 192, 268; The Mandler family: page 218; The Ruderman family: page 252; The Schoen family: page 71; Rolf and Madelon Schwarz: pages 157 and 183; Danny Segal and Ruthie Elkana: page 57; Gila Maroz Toth: pages 99 and 102.

Additional sources: Alamy Stock Photos pages 68/Austrian National Library, 139/Chronicle; Popperfoto/Getty Images: page 38.

Notes

Introduction

11 **'FERVENT prayer in great distress', the top ad declared.**
The 'FBW' who placed this ad was one of the most elusive
protagonists to find. A search of rental documents eventually
confirmed that Juda Leib Bajer and his wife Cyrel placed the
ad for their son, Siegfried. Ultimately, in order to escape the
Reich, the family split up. Siegfried was given a place at a
boarding school in Haifa, Palestine, and his father followed him
there. Cyrel and their daughter, Henna, found their way to the
UK and then, in 1940, made the transatlantic crossing to New
York. The 'Two very modest Sisters' advertised below were Alice
Daisy and Sylvia Ellinor Manheim, who escaped and made lives
in Britain and Canada respectively.

14 **Hilary Mantel once said that history is 'what's left in the
sieve when the centuries have run through it'**: Hilary Mantel,
'Why I Became a Historical Novelist', *Guardian*, 3 June 2017.

Chapter 1: The Untold Stories of
Leo, Erna and Bobby Borger

19 **Harry Zohn, described the story of Vienna and its Jews
as 'the most tragically unrequited love in world history'**:
George Berkley, *Vienna and its Jews: The Tragedy of Success,
1880s–1980s* (Madison Books 1988), p. xvi.

19 **In 966, less than ninety years later, a town document refers to 'Jews and other legitimate merchants'**: Berkley, *Vienna and its Jews*, p. 29.

21 **'In this vast empire, everything stood firmly and immovably in its appointed place'**: Stefan Zweig, *The World of Yesterday* (Cassel and Company, 1943).

23 **On 28 June, in the centre of Sarajevo, another student from the Austro-Hungarian empire, nineteen-year-old Bosnian Serb, Gavrilo Princip.** The best book on Princip is Tim Butcher's *The Trigger: Hunting the Assassin Who Brought the World to War* (Chatto and Windus, 2014).

27 **The team's name was Hebrew for 'The Strength', a purposeful attempt to embody the spirit of *Muskeljudentum*, 'muscular Judaism'.** I drew on David Bolchover's superb book, *The Greatest Comeback: From Genocide to Footballing Glory*, which tells the incredible tale of Hakoah Vienna and its most famous player, Béla Guttmann (Biteback Publishing, 2018).

31 **Members greeted each other with the word *Freundschaft!* (Friendship).** From Naomi Mitchison's first-hand account of the Civil War, *Vienna Diary 1934* (Victor Gollancz, 1934).

Chapter 2: George and the Unbearable Longing for Vienna

36 **George had written a memoir about it all, first published in 2001**: George Mandler, *Interesting Times: An Encounter With the 20th Century* (Lawrence Erlbaum Associates, 2002).

44 **Only 1,739 Jews emigrated in the years leading up to the Anschluss**: Ilana Fritz Offenberger, *The Jews of Nazi Vienna, 1938–1945: Rescue and Destruction* (Palgrave Studies in the History of Genocide, 2017), p. 2.

46 **On 13 March 1938, he was nine years old and bedridden**: Mandler, *Interesting Times*, pp. 39–40.

Chapter 3: Gertrude and Eichmann's Pianos

50 **The city was home to the biggest UK Jewish community outside London.** Bill Williams *'Jews and other foreigners': Manchester and the Rescue of the Victims of European Fascism, 1933-1940* (Manchester University Press, 2011) provides a comprehensive account of the city's important role in rescuing refugees from Nazism.

52 **'Though the writer has seen repeated Terrors in his two decades covering Central Europe':** *Manchester Guardian*, 17 March 1938.

60 **Five hundred suicides were reported in the Jewish community in the first two months alone:** Offenberger, *Jews of Nazi Vienna*, p. 50.

60 **Viennese Jews came to see it as 'a perfectly normal and natural incident':** George Gedye, *Fallen Bastions: The Central European Tragedy* (Victor Gollancz, 1939), p. 305.

63 **Eichmann's success in ushering out at least 100,000 Jews from Vienna later won him a job in Berlin.** Doron Rabinovici, *Eichmann's Jews: The Jewish Administration of Holocaust Vienna, 1938–1945* (Polity, 2011) is a comprehensive account of Eichmann's time in Vienna.

64 **'Comrades, we cannot allow this attack by World Jewry to go unchallenged':** Nuremberg Document 3063-PS (Walter Buch, Nazi Party Supreme Court chief, to Hermann Göring, 13 February 1939).

65 **All but one of the city's twenty-two synagogues were burned down:** Offenberger, *Jews of Nazi Vienna*, p. 176.

Chapter 4: Means of Escape:
Alice and the Westbahnhof

72 *Housewife* **magazine ran an article declaring: 'Your opportunity! The Case for the Foreign Maid':** Tony Kushner, *Journeys from the Abyss: The Holocaust and Forced Migration from the 1880s to the Present* (Liverpool University Press, 2017), p. 71.

72 **The *Guardian* ran an article in July 1938 titled 'Refugee Housekeeper'**: *Manchester Guardian*, 13 July 1938, p. 6.

80 **The 'J' stamp was an innovation introduced in early October.** For a full account of Rothmund's role, read Alfred Hasler's *The Lifeboat is Full: Switzerland and the Refugees, 1933–1945* (Funk & Wagnalls, 1969).

Chapter 5: Bobby and George in Exile

88 **A few years before my father's advert in the newspaper, the Bingleys had offered to host a child during the summer holidays.** For the complete story of Bunce Court, read Deborah Cadbury's *The School That Escaped the Nazis: The True Story of the Schoolteacher Who Defied Hitler* (Two Roads, 2022).

97 **'Sometimes I forget that in these reminiscences I am talking about a thirteen- to sixteen-year-old boy'**: Mandler, *Interesting Times*, p. 58.

Chapter 7: Salvation and Captivity: Internment in Britain

118 **'Every German or Austrian servant, however superficially charming and devoted, is a real and grave menace'**: Simon Parkin, *The Island of Extraordinary Captives: A True Story of an Artist, a Spy, and a Wartime Scandal* (Sceptre, 2022), p. 73.

120 **Two thousand internees were held at Warth Mills, a disused cotton factory on the northern outskirts of Manchester**: Parkin, *Island of Extraordinary Captives*, p. 90. Parkin's book is a brilliant, definitive account of UK internment policy in the 1940's, with vivid descriptions of the Hutchinson Camp. I draw on his work extensively in this chapter.

Chapter 8: Shanghai

135 **Word went around Vienna that Chinese consugeneral Ho Feng-Shan was issuing them freely**: Ho Feng-Shan, *My Forty Years as a Diplomat* (Dorrance Publishing, 2010).

135 **'The situation now is like a fire in a paper bag and it is going to burn through'**: Jonathan Kaufman, *The Last Kings of Shanghai: The Rival Jewish Dynasties that Helped Create Modern China* (Penguin, 2020), p. 147. Kaufman's superb account of the Jewish history of Shanghai and the stories of the Sassoon and Kadoorie dynasties in particular, was a primary source for me when it came to providing the context for Gertrude Langer's wartime experiences.

140 **He railed against his extended family's 'monstrous wealth' acquired from the 'dirty trading' in narcotics**. Kaufman, p. 41.

142 **On arrival . . . she turned to her son and told him: 'This is one of the capitals of sin in the world'**: Oral history interview with Rabbi Theodore Alexander, May 2022 (United States Holocaust Memorial Museum Collection).

145 **'He was a frightening individual, a large, coarse-faced man with a bald head and an incredibly ugly face'**: Walter Schellenberg, *The Labyrinth: Memoirs of Walter Schellenberg, Hitler's Chief of Counterintelligence* (Da Capo Press, 1956).

146 **In February 1943, a 'Designated Area for Stateless Refugees' was declared.** Rena Krasno, *Strangers Always: A Jewish Family in Wartime Shanghai* (Pacific View Press, 1992) provides a vivid eyewitness account of the ghetto.

Chapter 9: Fred and the Trail to Auschwitz

151 **Twain wrote to a curious journalist: 'The report of my death was an exaggeration'**: Elisabeth Boeckl-Klamper, Thomas Mang and Wolfgang Neugebauer, *The Vienna Gestapo 1938–1945: Crimes, Perpetrators, Victims* (Berghahn, 2022), p. 95.

152 **Their fifty-year-old mother, Helene, wasa beautiful woman**: Fred Schwarz, *Trains on a Dead Track*, unpublished English translation of *Treinen op Dood Spoor* (De Bataafsche Leeuw, 1994), p. 3.

153 **Fred stood for hours in the crowds outside the Palais Rothschild which Adolf Eichmann had commandeered**: Doron Rabinovici, *Eichmann's Jews*.

170 **'In front I see people getting out and getting into line. I see people getting into trucks'**: Schwarz, *Trains on a Dead Track*, p. 76.

173 **Terezin, at the northern tip of Bohemia, was turned into a fortified town at the end of the eighteenth century.** Anna Hájková, *The Last Ghetto: An Everyday History of Theresienstadt* (Oxford University Press, 2020) is the best recent account.

174 **The charade was repeated for a propaganda film shot in August and September.** The United States Holocaust Memorial Museum website has a clip of this completely chilling film, which portrayed Theresienstadt as a 'spa town' where elderly Jews could 'retire in safety'.

178 **On 7 October 1944, after Frits and Fred had been in Birkenau for a week, the *Sonderkommando* in Crematorium IV revolted**: Zalman Gradowski, *The Last Consolation Vanished: The Testimony of a Sonderkommando in Auschwitz* (University of Chicago Press, 2022). Gradowski was in the *Sonderkommando* at Birkenau. He took part in the revolt and was executed, but his account of life and death in the camp, written in Yiddish, was found buried in the ashes near Crematorium III.

Chapter 10: Defiance and Aunt Malci

185 **'The Jews here are no longer a nation, but a nomination. You nominate as a Jew anyone you dislike'**: 'Holocaust Memories Stir Polish Prejudice', *Guardian,* 12 April 1993.

185 **'.. a white city sparkling in the bright summer sun ..'** Ludwig Hevesi, art critic, in 1907, quoted by Leslie Topp *in Otto Wagner and the Steinhof Psychiatric Hospital: Architecture as Misunderstanding* (The Art Bulletin, 87:1, 2005).

188 **In the 1940s the Nazis would turn this architectural attempt to humanise mental care into a crime scene.** Am Spiegelgrund was a children's clinic which was part of the Steinhof complex: 789 patients were murdered under Nazi child euthanasia policies.

190 **In his telling, Elias was 'one of Moscow's most important agents'.** *La Lanterne*, 17 February 1928, p. 2.

190 **'In a bitter tone, he criticised the softness of the party leadership . . .',** *Le Matin*, 17 February 1928, p. 2.

191 **The Austrian-French novelist and psychologist, Manès Sperber, was born a few miles from Elias**: Manès Sperber, *Like a Tear in the Ocean, Qu'une larme dans l'océan* (Calmann-Lévy, 1952).

194 **Tilly Marek, who was part of the Grossmann–Kessler group, described the stress involved in remembering your *légende*.** Marek was born Ottilie Spiegel, a communist activist who married a fellow TA resistance leader, Franz Marek. After the war she helped found the Archive of the Austrian Resistance.

195 **Mordechaj was detained alongside Dolly Steindling, a fellow member of the Grossmann–Kessler group**: Dolly Steindling, *Hitting Back: An Austrian Jew in the French Resistance* (University Press of Maryland, 2000).

195 **'The lice, in astronomical numbers, were the worst'**: Steindling, *Hitting Back*, p. 60.

197 **Malci went to her death convinced that her stepson had been betrayed.** As described in a report, written on a postcard, to the Resistance Archive by historian Willi Kroupa after he had visited Malci towards the end of her life.

198 **As they emerged a French resistance unit threw grenades and opened fire with machine guns**: Steindling, *Hitting Back*, p. 182.

202 **Tucek, the man who tracked down, tortured and killed Mordechaj and his comrades, was sentenced to five years' imprisonment**: Boeckl-Klamper, Mang and Neugebauer, *Vienna Gestapo 1938–1945*, p. 528.

205 **I was based in Poland fifty years later and I was hoping Kurt would come for an anniversary reunion of survivors**: 'Survivors of Sobibor Remember Great Escape', *Guardian*, 14 October 1993.

207 **Another prisoner urged him to run, but he said: 'I don't run any more. I am a free man'** Interview with Kurt Ticho Thomas (USC Shoah Foundation Institute).

Chapter 11: George and the Return to Vienna

211 **Under his new orders he was not to board the waiting troopship with his fellow draftees**: Mandler, *Interesting Times*, p. 93.

212 **He ran from one half-dead inmate to another giving his parents' name:** Leah Garrett, *X Troop: The Secret Jewish Commandos of World War II* (Mariner Books, 2021), p. 247.

213 **'The major tactic we used derived from the very strict German discipline'**: Mandler, *Interesting Times*, p. 103.

214 **The closest George said he came to real danger was when a German rocket attack hit a street he was in**: Mandler, *Interesting Times*, p. 104.

214 **Another officer in the unit, Frank Manuel, stepped in to save George from a possible court-martial**: Frank Manuel, *Scenes from the End: The Last Days of World War II in Europe* (Steerforth Press, 2000).

215 **'We had a fine time,' George recalled fondly**: Mandler, *Interesting Times*, p. 104.

216 **In the summer of 1945, George's unit in the 221st CIC was sent on a mission**: Mandler, *Interesting Times*, p. 111.

221 **'The shock of those immediate post-war years, when I learned about the death in the camps of my relatives'**: Mandler, *Interesting Times*, p. 66.

224 **Their stories 'formed a layer of remembrance that all but stifled the memory of the victims and the survivors of the Holocaust'**: Oliver Rathkolb, *The Paradoxical Republic: Austria 1945–2020* (Berghahn Books, 2010), p. 258.

230 **'The allies in world war two gave Austrians the umbrella of the myth of Austrian liberation'**: Mandler, *Interesting Times*, p. 68.

Chapter 12: Lisbeth and the Will to Live

235 **In July 2015, my mum, youngest brother Bias and I took the train to Caernarfon for Nancy Bingley's burial**:

'Refugees Bring Hope, Not Trouble – My Father's Story is Proof of That', *Guardian*, 7 September 2015.

236 **'I kept meticulous and repetitive notes on the names and addresses of anybody who I met'**: Mandler, *Interesting Times*, p. 59.

238 **'After 14 years of being an Austrian – a patriot with a feeling of belonging'**: Mandler, *Interesting Times*, p. 45.

248 **'Hitler took the stage away from me'**: interview with Lisbeth Weiss-Ruderman (USC Shoah Foundation Institute).

249 **'There was a sense of doom, of fear, of not knowing'**: Weiss-Ruderman interview (USC Shoah Foundation).

250 **'The swastikas, the Nazi flags appeared in windows and rooftops all over the city, instantaneously'**: WeissRuderman interview (USC Shoah Foundation).

250 **'But, as I got to realise later, nobody wanted us'**: Weiss-Ruderman interview (USC Shoah Foundation).

258 **'I think I was torn by loyalties,' she said later**: Weiss-Ruderman interview (USC Shoah Foundation).

About the Author

Julian Borger is the *Guardian*'s World Affairs Editor, based in Washington. He covered the Bosnian war for the BBC and the *Guardian* and returned to the Balkans to report on the Kosovo conflict in 1999. He has also served as the *Guardian*'s Middle East correspondent and its Washington Bureau Chief. Borger was part of the *Guardian* team that won the 2014 Pulitzer Prize for public service journalism, for its coverage of the Snowden files on mass surveillance. He was also in the team awarded the 2013 Investigative Reporters and Editors (IRE) medal and the Paul Foot Special Investigation Award in the UK. He won the One World Media Press Award in 2016 for a feature story on the investigation of war crimes in Syria.